VAN NOSTRAND REINHOLD MANUALS
GENERAL EDITOR: W.S. TAYLOR

Mosaic

J. Mellentin Haswell

Van Nostrand Reinhold
Manual of **Mosaic**

VAN NOSTRAND REINHOLD COMPANY
New York   Cincinnati   Toronto   London   Melbourne

Acknowledgments are made to the following for permission to reproduce the illustrations on the pages shown:

Amigos de Gaudí, Barcelona, 156; British Museum, 41, 183; Crown copyright, reproduced with the permission of the Controller of Her Majesty's Stationery Office, 199; Gabinetto Fotografico Nazionale, Rome, 203; German Archaeological Institute, Rome, 43; Hirmer Fotoarchiv, Munich, 13 (top), 15 (bottom), 34, 144, 212; Antony Hollaway, 169; Kungliga Livrustkammaren, Stockholm, 143; Alfred Lammer, 70; Emily Lane, 161; Mansell-Alinari, 11, 204, 213, 216 (top), 222, 224 (bottom), 229; Mansell-Anderson, 16, 33, 187, 189, 202, 207, 209, 215, 216 (bottom), 219, 221, 224 (top), 225 (bottom), 227 (top); the Mansell Collection, 47, 217; Mexican National Tourist Council, London, 167; The National Tourist Organization of Greece, Athens, 134; Scala, 35, 36, 191, 192; Eileen Tweedy, 133; Warburg Institute, London, 200

Van Nostrand Reinhold Company
Regional Offices: New York
Cincinnati Chicago Millbrae Dallas

Van Nostrand Reinhold Company
International Offices: London
Toronto Melbourne

Copyright © 1973 by Thames and
Hudson Ltd, London
Library of Congress Catalog Card
Number 73-14117
ISBN 0-442-23197-0 (cloth)

Printed in Great Britain by
Jarrold and Sons Ltd, Norwich

Published in the U.S.A. in 1974 by
Van Nostrand Reinhold Company
A Division of Litton Educational
Publishing, Inc. 450 West 33rd
Street, New York N.Y. 10001

16 15 14 13 12 11 10 9 8 7 6 5 4 3 2 1

Contents

1 Historical techniques

During its most expressive phase, mosaic was an illustrative medium of an almost exclusively religious nature. Yet, no matter how functional or illusionistic his intention, the craftsman rarely overlooked the essential nature of the materials of his craft. Apart from economic considerations, the decline of mosaic as a viable art form was due to the imposition of notions of plasticity, which more properly belonged to the sphere of painting. After the Renaissance, if the medium was introduced for a specifically religious purpose craftsmen were normally employed to translate paintings into mosaic.

Consequently, failure to understand the fundamental basis of ancient mosaic has led to the establishment of a tradition of ecclesiastical work which, being assembled from diverse and often misunderstood elements, is sometimes little more than rather drab pastiche. An admirable way in which to broaden one's technical resources is to investigate the problems which the ancient craftsmen were called upon to solve, which has little to do with the utilization of style and technique culled from ancient works because of a superficial visual appeal. If maximum benefit is to be derived from research into ancient methods, a thorough understanding of the basic procedures will be necessary.

The total impact of the great mosaic cycles of the past was achieved by the evolution of a style of design which attempted complete accord with both the materials and the architectural setting. Obviously, methods of application have varied slightly during the various periods of development, and precise details as to how large mosaic schemes were organized cannot be established with absolute certainty. Documentary evidence exists which suggests that after AD 300 most major schemes were undertaken by teams of men to whom were allotted specific tasks which carried an established rate of remuneration.

A number of pictorial schemes were fairly well established by the time of Justinian. Artists inherited pictorial vocabularies derived from those prototypes which had gained reputations for special sanctity and efficacy. These, in their essential form, had weathered considerable changes of style. For instance, the Roman churches of Sta Prassede and Sta Cecilia in Trastevere contain themes derived from the apsidal mosaic of SS. Cosma e Damiano. Occasionally the subject-matter was directly related to current theological

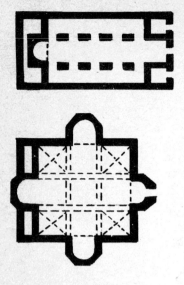

(*Top*) Basilica; (*above*) cross-in-square church.

decisions, for instance the decoration of the triumphal arch of Sta Maria Maggiore, which was commenced after the great Council of Ephesus which took place in 431. The dogma which established the Virgin as the Mother of God was pronounced at the Council, and in all probability the mosaic narrative, which depicts the childhood of Christ, is a direct reference to this event. Of great significance is the dress of the Virgin, akin to the ceremonial costume of an Empress of Byzantium, which suggests that she is being honoured in a special manner. Often the order of a scheme was directly related to the style of architecture, the pictures being 'read' in a specific sequence. Consequently the basilican structure required a somewhat different scheme from that of the cross-in-square church with its domes, apses and squinches. Frequently schemes were instituted by great ecclesiastics, who not only commissioned and gave instructions as to the nature of the decoration, but were sometimes responsible for the actual foundation of the churches which contained them.

Some evidence exists which suggests that the preliminary design for a mosaic was painted either on to the bare wall or on to the first layer of plaster. The church of Hagios Georgios in Salonica contains an instance of this practice; the design was found to have been painted directly on to the brick wall of the dome. Sometimes the underpainting (known as the *sinopia*) was applied to an upper layer of mortar, which suggests that such paintings were used as rough guides and not necessarily strictly adhered to in detail. It is thought that the designer painted on the wall while evolving his designs, and the appearance of *sinopie* in such positions may be accounted for by such a practice. The term 'design' must not be construed in the modern sense, however, as designs were not free inventions but were based on traditional schemes sometimes derived from manuscript illustrations or written matter.

The mortar was applied to the wall in several stages. A foundation coat – which was fairly coarse and included aggregates such as sand or crushed brick – was applied and followed by a second coat of a finer consistency, which may have contained a little aggregate. Finally a third coat, which usually contained lime putty, was applied in sections of suitable size for a day's work. A number of examples show that these work areas (*giornate*) were joined by means of bevelled edges, although in spite of this practice it is often possible to detect the divisions. Sometimes the final layer of mortar was coloured in order to avoid compromising the final colour effect if mortar should appear in the interstices. Generally the first layer of mortar was thicker than the subsequent coats, and was sometimes worked over with a pick which roughened the surface to provide a 'key' for the next layer. There is evidence that a waterproofing agent – such as bitumen, tar or resin – was applied to the wall surface before the first layer of mortar was laid. Clamps or coarse flat-headed nails were sometimes driven into the first coat of mortar, and allowed to project slightly, although this form of reinforcement was more commonly used on overhanging areas such as domes. The total thickness of the coats varied, but as a rule did not exceed a maximum thickness of 3 in.

If a painting was to be used as a setting guide, it was carried out directly into the still damp mortar and frequently in full colour, with red substituted for gold. Traces of underpainting have been detected in a number of mural mosaics. Gold is represented by red underpainting in a mosaic in the Dome of the Rock in Jerusalem. Fresco painting can also be clearly seen in a number of areas in the vault mosaic depicting Christ as Helios, situated under St Peter's in Rome. Owing to the loss of a number of tesserae, the top coat of mortar has been revealed in a number of places. The tesserae have left their imprint in what can be clearly seen as a painted design. The principle of the emblema (see p. 186) – set in a separate bed and then transported to the site – which was a feature of classical practice, was occasionally employed for details during the Christian period. The head of Christ in the crown of the apse of S. Giovanni Laterano in Rome was known as the 'miraculous head' because owing to the fact that it was independently bedded it was believed to have arrived by a miraculous agency. This was of the emblema type, although the present version is a replacement made in 1884. A similar example has been detected in Hagios Georgios in Salonica.

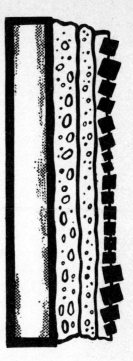

Profile diagram of setting beds, wall mosaic.

A method of laying mortar so as to produce an undulating surface is an interesting feature of Byzantine or Byzantine-inspired work. Some authorities have suggested that there was a degree of calculation in these surface irregularities to enable the mosaicist to obtain intended effects. By this means maximum visual impact when seen from a specific viewpoint was ensured. When laid in an irregular bed a remarkable vitality was transmitted by the medium. This was particularly true of gold tesserae, which gained richness from an undulating surface; this helped to subdue the hard metallic effect that occurs when gold tesserae are closely laid on a flat surface. Another disadvantage is that the glare tends to reduce figures to silhouettes, to the detriment of their plastic qualities.

The lovely gold background of the apsidal mosaic of S. Clemente in Rome is a perfect demonstration of the principle of the undulating surface. The figure and background appear completely homogeneous. The tiny chapel of S. Zenone in the church of Sta Prassede in Rome is an equally felicitous example of the technique. The surface undulations are very pronounced and give an appearance of depth to the gold layer, almost as if the surface were padded. The device of setting tesserae at different angles was frequently employed in mural mosaics. This was opposed to the extreme flatness of setting which was the rule in pavimental mosaics – due

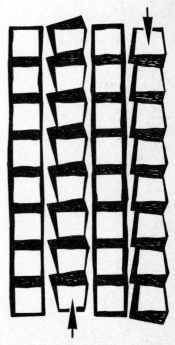

Angled setting of mosaic to produce an undulating surface.

no doubt to utilitarian considerations – but ceased to be of consequence when mosaic was applied to wall surfaces. By means of this deliberately induced irregularity, light was transmitted from one plane to another with mercurial effect. An early example of irregular setting can be seen in the fifth-century work on the triumphal arch in Sta Maria Maggiore. The deliberately contrived flat surface of classical Roman emblemata, coupled with the use of small and closely set tesserae, enabled the artist to reproduce the tonal effects of painting. The principle was not lost on the Byzantine mosaicists, who employed very small pieces to produce subtle modelling, especially on such details as faces and hands in their mural decoration. These details, worked in marble or natural stone, are deliberately contrasted with more broadly worked areas in which glass smalti were employed. Another important aspect of the use of very small and regular tesserae is the manner in which they were employed to make articulate both form and line, when used on the curved surfaces of domes, apses and vaults.

It is impossible to determine to what extent the use of grout was a regular procedure. Antique floor mosaics may have been grouted in order to produce a reasonably impervious surface. There are examples of Byzantine wall mosaics in which definite traces of grout have been detected but this may be due to restoration. Although glass was insufficiently durable to be used extensively in floor mosaics, examples do occur in which glass was incorporated either as a special feature, or in order to produce passages of colour unattainable in natural stone. The advent of mural mosaic diminished these functional requirements, thereby extending the range of effects which could be obtained. Ultimately, glass became commonly used although, oddly enough, marble and natural materials were retained for special effects. The vault decoration of Sta Costanza in Rome, still influenced by pagan floor decoration, has a background of marble against which figurative and decorative motifs were worked in glass smalti.

The mosaic depicting the procession of Holy Virgins in the nave of S. Apollinare Nuovo in Ravenna is an excellent example of mixed media showing Byzantine influence. The saints are clad in elaborate Byzantine-influenced court dress. The tunics and dalmatics are set in fairly closely worked coloured glass smalti, in contrast with the soft 'woollen' veils covering the heads of the saints, which are made up from large units of white marble. The non-reflective surface of the marble, when seen in contrast with the highly reflective surface of the glass, perfectly conveys the soft texture of woollen material, an effect which could not have been obtained by the use of white smalti.

Another interesting practice was the incorporation of imitation or semi-precious stones, which were used to suggest the elaborate jewelled court dress of Byzantium. A well-known example of this type of elaboration is the

Procession of the Holy Virgins,
S. Apollinare Nuovo, Ravenna:
detail.

mother-of-pearl decoration on the costume of the Empress
Theodora, the wife of Justinian, who appears in a mosaic in
S. Vitale in Ravenna (see p. 13). Natural stone and marble
were used in Byzantine mosaics for those areas which had a
'stony' character, as for example architecture or rocks and
rocky ground, which were often emphasized by highlights
of glass smalti.

Gold

Gold first made an appearance during the early Christian
period, when it was used to highlight certain details in the
vault mosaic of Sta Costanza in Rome. An example from
Antioch (of the fourth century and therefore roughly contemporary with the work in Sta Costanza) in which gold is

used depicts Chresis (a personification of productive labour) offering her gifts. Areas of gold appear in the costume and are used to represent jewelry. The development of the over-all use of gold in backgrounds, which became so distinctive a feature of the Byzantine mosaic technique, was almost certainly an eastern innovation. The small fifth-century mosaic panels which occupy a position high in the nave of Sta Maria Maggiore in Rome show gold smalti inextricably mixed within representations of naturalistic landscape. Gold did not, however, replace blue as an over-all background until a century later, although a landscape background with a gold sky occurs in a mosaic in S. Apollinare Nuovo in Ravenna, which is of the sixth century. The scene represents the walk to Emmaus and is of further interest as Christ is depicted with a silver nimbus. Gold has been used to represent nimbi since early Christian times, although its use was reserved for the Divinity and His attendant angels. The use of gold in this context conveyed a specific meaning – the representation of heavenly light, as opposed to the suggestion of natural light as in Sta Costanza in Rome.

The indication of the presence of divine light remained the chief function of metallic smalti, although in a more general sense, as the gold or silver nimbus came into use to designate holy persons other than Christ and his angels. Silver was probably introduced to solve the problem which arose when a gold nimbus was set against a gold background; however, this introduced a note of ambiguity which tended to diminish the idea of gold as the emanation of divine light. A less contradictory solution was introduced by the use of a red or blue contour line around the nimbus, which sufficiently distinguished it from the background without lessening the symbolic value of the gold. Another interesting solution to both the visual and the iconographical problem was the differentiation of the setting lines of the nimbus from those of the background. Further emphasis was often given by tilting the gold smalti of the nimbus, and so varying the light value. Occasionally the device of tilting tesserae was used in areas which received insufficient light; the units were set so that they inclined towards the light source, which ensured maximum light reflection.

THE RAVENNA MOSAICS

The mosaics of S. Vitale are among the best-known examples of the mosaic technique, and certainly rank among the finest examples of technical expertise. Although the city of Ravenna was still in the hands of the alien Goths when the building was begun in 526, the chancel mosaics demonstrate the continuation of the eastern Hellenistic tradition. This tradition, when merged with a local style, exhibits a naturalism quite foreign to the impressive series of the apse. However, it is the lower wall of the apse which houses two

memorable panels depicting the 'Oblatio Augusti et Augustae', the ritual bringing of gifts to the consecration ceremony by the Emperor and Empress of Byzantium. These panels are notably different in style from the mosaics of the chancel, and show a strong Byzantine influence. The luxurious figures, which are frontally placed against the full glory of the background of Byzantine gold, are hierarchical and at first sight abstracted and static. However, the first impression, of stiffly aloof figures, strongly lacking in naturalism, is misleading.

To the left of the apse is depicted a processional group which includes the Emperor Justinian and to the right a similar group which includes the Empress Theodora. The head of Theodora, which is surrounded by a gold nimbus, differentiated from the gold of the background by means of a red contour, is subtle and essentially feminine. Of particular merit is the beautiful way in which the smalti have been cut, which gives cohesion to the surface without attempting to deny the fragmented nature of the technique. The colour range is extremely beautiful and used with great subtlety. The flesh tints are sufficiently varied to add warmth and form without detracting from the whiteness of the skin with its suggestion of patrician delicacy and fineness. By such means, and in a manner typical of propaganda art, the 'plebeian' origins of Theodora are belied. Unlike the fully developed Byzantine style, the lines of setting are not strongly emphasized, although a hint of later developments can be detected, as for instance the directional lines beneath the left eye which emphasize the form. The eyes are large and luminous, and show a markedly eastern influence. Their

(*Above*) Procession of the Empress Theodora and her attendants, S. Vitale, Ravenna; (*below*) detail of Theodora's left eye.

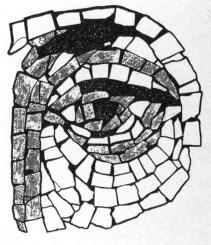

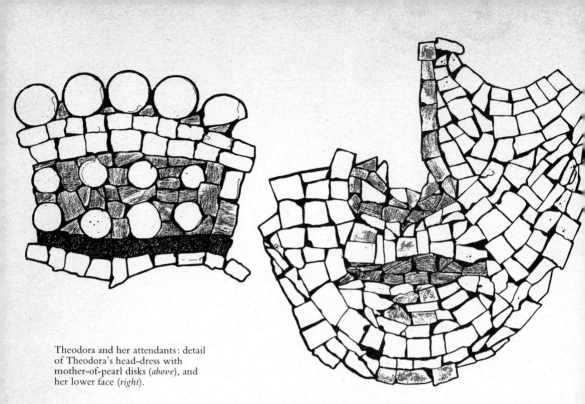

Theodora and her attendants: detail
of Theodora's head-dress with
mother-of-pearl disks (*above*), and
her lower face (*right*).

softness and luminosity are achieved very skilfully: the
large, linear Egyptian eye has a hardness and lacklustre
quality, unlike the eyes of Theodora in which the impact of
the delineation is lessened by a dramatic change of colour.
The change from black to red on the upper part of the top
lid, and the use of red and soft brown on the lid itself, allows
a return to black and soft browns for the emphatic eyebrows.
The shadows under the eyes are skilfully suggested, that
under the right eye being rather stronger in tone, in contrast
with the softer shadow under the left eye. One realizes that
the existence of a light source has been subtly suggested,
although it is by no means constant.

The liquid quality of the eyes is expressed by means of a
subtle softening of the relationship between the dark pupil
and the lighter iris. The dull purplish colour touching the
pupil and extending into the iris is soft enough to allow the
pupil to retain its identity, yet strong enough to suggest an
area of shadow in the iris. A play of light is suggested to the
right of the mouth and chin, and the point of the chin is
emphasized by means of three cubes which are fractionally
extended into the shadowed area beneath the chin, leading
on to the delicate yet firm neck. The neck modelling is
simple but extremely subtle, contained by two precise flesh-
tinted contour lines which are set in a vertical direction, and
are in turn emphasized by an outer line of black. The
remainder of the neck area is filled by a series of curved rows
which run in a horizontal direction in fairly correct perspective relationship with some emphatic orange lines on the
head-dress, and the line of the necklace and neck line of the

robe. On close inspection the mouth appears to be a red gash. However, from an appropriate viewing distance the beautifully cut units of the top lip, which are laid in a some-what irregular contour, prove to be complementary to the softer, rather vague delineation of the lower lip and the shadow beneath it.

The modelling of the thin nose is a *tour de force*. The bridge of the nose is suggested by small rectangular smalti, fairly light in tone, with the emphasis on the horizontal in the setting lines. A warm area of colour, made up of three larger pieces, square in shape, which have been placed to the right of this area, strikes the right tonal balance between the bony prominence of the nose and the soft flesh of the cheek. The warm shadow which forms a line to the left of the nose, and the red line beneath, help to express prominence without disturbing the tonal balance of the face as a whole.

The heavy, elaborate head-dress is distinguished from the head and neck by means of a strong dark line, which helps to emphasize the apparent weight of the head-dress. The treatment of costume throughout these panels is of great interest. The rich ceremonial costume of the Empress con-veys a sense of exotic splendour and authority. Extensive use is made of disks of mother-of-pearl around the area of the head and shoulders. The crown with its perpendula of pearls conveys a feeling of arrested movement. This impression is so strong that one can believe that the pearls have just ceased to swing after a slight movement of the Empress's head. Two female attendants to the left of Theodora are depicted with a considerable degree of portraiture, in contrast with the group of five females to the far left who are represented in a much more stereotyped manner: possibly the immediate companions of the Empress were persons of some distinc-tion or were held in particular regard. The figure immedi-ately to the left of Theodora wears a mantle woven with a geometric pattern. The pattern is carried out in a greyish-fawn colour on a white background; small tesserae have been used, to suggest the folds of the drapery. The artist has used fairly large units of the same greyish-fawn to lay in the main lines of the drapery. As a result, the emphasis on the folds appears to be tonal rather than linear.

Numerous subtleties of setting appear throughout the panel, as for instance in the treatment of the classical foun-tain; the sparkling movement of the water is in contrast with the fabric of the fountain. Great vitality is suggested by the play of light over various forms, yet the actual source of light remains undetected. This is a technical device where light is used to reveal and emphasize forms in space without the need to show light and shade in a regular manner, so preserving the tonal integrity of the whole. This brilliance of treatment may be contrasted with the portrait of the Empress Irene, *c.* AD 1118, in Hagia Sophia at Istanbul. In spite of superficial similarities between the portraits of Irene and Theodora, there are fundamental differences of

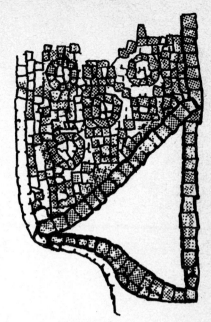

Theodora and her attendants: detail of pattern on the robe of the attendant on Theodora's left.

Empress Irene: detail from mosaic in Hagia Sophia, Istanbul.

15

Emperor Justinian: detail from mosaic in S. Vitale, Ravenna. Compare the small, regular tesserae of the face with the irregular materials surrounding it – a typical Byzantine feature.

(*Opposite, above*) Detail from 'Paradise' pattern, vault mosaic in Sta Costanza, Rome (see also p. 212). (*Opposite, below*) Apsidal mosaic in basilica of S. Clemente, Rome.

approach. The portrait of Irene has been carried out with a high degree of decorative stylization, the emphasis being on linear qualities which appear trivial in comparison with the Ravenna portraits.

The panel which depicts the Emperor Justinian and his entourage contains some notable examples of portraiture. The features of the Emperor express the ruddy joviality which was attributed to him. He, too, is distinguished by means of a halo of gold, which symbolizes the power invested in earthly rulers by God and, like his Empress, he is sumptuously robed and crowned. His crown is considerably less elaborate than that worn by Theodora; and his heavy, fleshy features are powerfully modelled, with strongly marked eyebrows. A dark contour line is carried right round the face, including the area underneath the chin. This line is further emphasized by an inner line of a brownish colour. Unlike the mouth of Theodora, the lower lip of the Emperor is full and rather heavy, and is set in tesserae of a strong red colour. Again, in contrast with the softness of Theodora's eyes, those of the Emperor are hard and staring. The pupils are clearly distinguished and a very positive line of white runs between the iris and the lower lid. The neck is short and fleshy, modelled in stronger tones than those used on the slender neck of the Empress. The dark hair is short and wiry, expressed by means of an almost staccato setting technique.

The tesserae used for all the heads are considerably smaller than those used to depict garments, backgrounds and other

details. Contrary to later Byzantine practice, they are exclusively of glass. The impressive figure of Bishop Maximian, who precedes the Emperor, has strong elements of portraiture. The church of S. Vitale had been inaugurated by Bishop Ecclesius, but completed and consecrated by Maximian about 547. Maximian is robed as a bishop, and carries a gold and jewelled cross as a symbol of authority; his name is inscribed above his head. He was described as being tall and thin, bald, lean of face and with grey eyes. The mosaic portrait presents an impressive image of such a man. The high, bald forehead is splendidly handled, without using the over-emphasis of regularly set directional lines. When such lines are used in the Maximian portrait they establish the structure without the use of overstated whorls such as can be seen on the head of St John Chrysostom, *c.* 1150, in the mosaic depicting the fathers of the Church in the Cappella Palatina, Palermo. The great orator, whose name means John the golden-mouthed, was described as thin and spidery with a high, wrinkled forehead and receding hair. A similar portrait exists which, although much later (probably mid-fourteenth century), maintains the same tradition of the portrait of the saint. This portrait in the form of a small mosaic icon, 7 in. × 5 in., is now in the Dumbarton Oaks Collection, Washington.

The short, sparse hair of Maximian is treated in a similar fashion to that of the Emperor, and in marked contrast with the thick, smooth hair of the young soldiers who form part of the retinue. The Bishop has a rather Semitic nose, which is rendered in a linear fashion. A dark line encloses most of the face and beard except for the top of the noble domed head, a device which suggests the continuation of the skull. The ears are outlined in brownish tesserae, which makes them appear to be set back from the black outline of the head, although the colour is strong enough visually to support the brown hair. The grey-blue eyes are intelligent and piercing, without the staring hardness of those of Justinian. The difference is due to the retention of the identity of the pupil, while the iris is softened by a slight admixture of colour; the stark white area between the iris and the lower lid, which occurs in the portrait of the Emperor, has been omitted in that of the Bishop. The thick, spiky eyebrows are composed of a group of sharp lines, similar in treatment to the hair. Perhaps the most memorable touch is the way in which the artist has placed two gashes of vivid red which, when viewed from a distance, express the leanness of the face in a convincing manner. These lines, when seen in conjunction with the strong brown lines to left and right of the nostrils, remove all traces of blandness. We are confronted by the face of a man of integrity striving to fulfil his mission on earth, not an idealized saint in heaven.

The Archiepiscopal Chapel, dedicated to St Andrew, is situated close to the baptistery of the Orthodox, which lies

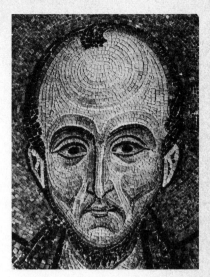

St John Chrysostom: detail from mosaic in Cappella Palatina, Palermo. Notice the convex effect of the exaggerated whorls on his head.

Head of 'Christus Militans', Archiepiscopal Chapel, Ravenna: detail.

(*Opposite*) Head of Empress Theodora in S. Vitale, Ravenna.

Head of the Good Shepherd,
Mausoleum of Galla Placidia,
Ravenna.

Hair treatment:
Heads of Abel (*above*) and Moses.

near the city gates of Ravenna. It was the private chapel of the bishops of Ravenna, and was used to administer the sacrament of penance. An interesting mosaic, which depicts Christ in the garb of a warrior – 'Christus Militans' – can be seen in a lunette above the vestibule door, though the panel has suffered serious damage and only the top section of the figure survives. The head and the halo are of considerable technical interest however. A strong classical influence can be detected, but the gold background represents a very early departure from the traditional blue, due to the intervention of new influences. The face is youthful and beardless, obviously in stylistic descent from the Christ in the Mausoleum of Galla Placidia but, as befits his militant aspect, is of sterner countenance than the gentle shepherd of the Mausoleum. The features are linear and strongly marked, and the flesh tones are arranged in a naturalistic manner. The tesserae which are used for the features are considerably smaller than those used elsewhere on the figure. The pieces are irregular in shape, closely set, and arranged in lines which reveal the structure of the face. The hair is set in lines of light and dark tesserae: these give a smooth, thick quality, especially to the fringe, which falls low on the brow. The halo, which is oval rather than round, is distinguished from the background by a strong, dark contour line, and, in addition, the smalti are set in a different direction. The outer edge of the halo is set in white, which gives way to an apparently random admixture of colours interspersed with gold, lending an exciting sparkle to the area behind the head. The device of separating gold from gold by means of a contrasting contour line is used here to distinguish the gold of the military cuirass from that of the background. The figure holds a book in one hand which is inscribed with the words *Ego sum via, veritas et vita* ('I am the way, the truth and the life'), in the other a cross resting against his right shoulder.

Insight into technique and colour handling can undoubtedly be gained from the Ravenna cycles. Innumerable visual experiences have been expressed in what is a difficult, almost intractable medium. The four elements are represented, also fur, feather and foliage; men and women of all ages, the inhabitants of both heaven and earth; rich materials and simple wool; architecture, furniture, portraits and abstract forms. To take simple contrasts in setting technique – the rough, dark hair of Abel in 'The Sacrifice of Abel', which is to be seen in S. Vitale, is so different from the strange flame-like hair of the young Moses who stoops to unfasten his sandal on Mount Horeb, or, in the same church, the short, tonsured hair of S. Ecclesius with the new growth already showing on the shaven area. In complete contrast, a beautiful rendering of the fine white hair of an old man can be seen on the figure of S. Apollinare in the church of S. Apollinare in Classe, and the thick, curling blond hair of a young man which occurs on the splendid figure of St Michael in the same church.

Innumerable winged creatures are to be seen in mosaics of all periods. The small 'amoretti' of ancient Rome, the winged Pegasus and other fabulous beasts, gradually gave way to winged beings from heavenly regions. The Mausoleum of Galla Placidia at Ravenna contains a series of mosaics which are considered to be the oldest in Ravenna. Included in the decoration of the dome are the winged symbols of the four Evangelists. The dome symbolizes the dome of Heaven in which, set against a background of deep and sparkling blue, gold stars appear to swirl. The stars diminish in size towards the apex, and the kinetic effect is extraordinary; real space appears to be dramatically increased by this simple perspective device.

The symbols of the Evangelists are set against this glorious blue background. The symbol of St Mark – a winged lion – is specially fine. The head and shoulders of the beast appear as if rising from a cluster of small clouds. The figure is largely composed of gold smalti which flash and shimmer, and give emphasis to the curiously spear-like quality of the winged form. The darting shape is emphasized by means of a flashing line of white smalti which extends almost the full length of the upper edge of the nearer wing. This line is itself emphasized by a broad strip of grey set across the lion's chest in the same direction. Flashes of white are used, too, on the expressive head. The individual pinions of the wings are set in a perfunctory fashion: the lines which are used to describe them are set in smalti of various shades of grey, again with sharp flashes of white here and there. Although the wings are readily recognized as such, the emphasis remains on the forceful quality of the over-all form rather than on the detail.

An angel from S. Vitale shows a considerably different approach to the problem. The outspread wings are set in purplish tesserae ranging from light to dark. Here, however, the emphasis seems to be on weight. The forms are more fully modelled, so much so that the great forearm, humerus, and hand sections of the wings, especially that on his right, have

Different treatments of hair in the Ravenna cycles. (*Top*) S. Ecclesius, (*above, centre*) S. Apollinare and (*above*) Michael.

(*Left*) Lion of St Mark from dome of Mausoleum of Galla Placidia, Ravenna.

21

Right wing of an angel in S. Vitale, Ravenna, compared with medieval treatment of wings by Toriti.

an almost reptilian appearance. The left wing is treated in a flatter manner, which allows it to fall behind the outstretched arm of the figure immediately to the angel's left. Although the groups of feathers are not represented in great detail, the wings are related to those of a great bird, both in form and colour.

ROMAN MOSAICS

The Roman cycles are a treasure ground for those wishing to investigate technique. A number of these works exhibit transitional styles, so enabling one to observe the way in which the craftsmen of the period drew their inspiration from established sources while adapting their style to meet changing requirements. The continuation of the classical style in mural form can be seen in three groups in Sta Maria Maggiore in Rome, which are discussed in their historical context in Chapter 10. These mosaics are considerably earlier than the Justinian mosaics at Ravenna. The fifth-century panels of the nave represent the first group, the mosaics of the triumphal arch the second group, and the main mosaic of the apse, by Toriti, almost certainly contains elements from its antique predecessor.

The nave mosaics were made on independent beds, in the manner of the antique emblemata, and authorities have disputed the question of whether the nave series were actually made for the present church. It has been held by some that the panels were incorporated in the present fabric, and are, in consequence, of an earlier date than the mosaics of the triumphal arch. A number of obvious stylistic differences between the two groups have been cited to support the attribution of an earlier date to the nave panels. Other authorities have stressed the equally obvious stylistic affinity between the two, and regard them as being roughly contemporary. Close examination reveals a number of elements associated with the classical tradition which can be seen in both groups. Common ground can be detected in the classical solidity of certain forms and the notable individuality, which amounts almost to portraiture, of a number of heads, also the realism of stance and gesture. And yet there are differences; of particular interest is the link with classical technique which can be detected in the nave series. The regular square tesserae, closely set to form an even surface, are directly in line with the classical pavimental technique. The mosaic of the triumphal arch is composed of more irregular units and achieves a looser surface texture – both factors which give credence to the theory that the arch mosaic is later than the work in the nave. A common factor can be detected in the 'impressionism' of the technique, which can be related to a stylistic device adopted in a number of Roman paintings, yet seldom found in Roman mosaics.

The conclusion that both groups are roughly contemporary is probably a fair one; the interest lies in the fact that the nave series derives from the past, whereas the decoration of the triumphal arch contains a strong foretaste of the future. The head of the Virgin from the presentation scene of the triumphal arch (c. 435) is largely original work. The tesserae are of glass, and a remarkably loose setting technique is exhibited. There is no regularity of structure, and the volume of the head is conveyed by the exploitation of the effects of light on form rather than by linear devices. Such a

Head of Virgin: detail from presentation scene on triumphal arch, Sta Maria Maggiore, Rome.

Head of Sta Agnese: detail from apsidal mosaic, Sta Agnese fuori le Mura, near Rome.

technique expresses the true nature of the fragmented medium, although several passages of the mosaic of the triumphal arch presage the use of setting lines to describe the structure of forms.

Technical evidence of the influence of the Byzantine style on the mosaics of Rome must be sought in the decisive development of lines of setting as a means of expressing form; in the use of smaller tesserae for certain areas of detail; and in the use of natural stone (as opposed to glass) in the representation of flesh. A typical example can be seen in the representation of the head (which is substantially original) of Sta Agnese in the mosaic of the apse of Sta Agnese fuori le Mura. The setting lines clearly explain the structure of the face, and the strange theatrical patches of colour on the cheeks of the otherwise bloodless face are in the true Byzantine tradition. Another significant factor suggesting Byzantine influence is that the tesserae are considerably smaller than those used elsewhere, especially on the neck. The whole figure is elongated, with a strongly marked linear emphasis, which expresses the other-worldly quality of the saint, in contrast with the much more robust portraits of the two Popes, Honorius and Symmachus, who are also depicted. Again, this is very much in keeping with the transcendentalism exhibited in Byzantine work, although in this case the treatment is reserved for the saint, and forms a contrast between the depiction of living beings, and the young saint believed to be dwelling in Paradise.

A useful comparison can be made with the picture of the face of St John Chrysostom (see p. 19), which shows the typical setting lines of the fully developed Byzantine technique. The figure of Sta Agnese is physically detached from the figures of the popes to left and right, a characteristic Byzantine frieze effect. However, the real triumph of the work lies in the expression of spiritual detachment, which is achieved in a remarkably economical manner. The gaze of the young saint, intense and contemplative, is focused above and far away, and is expressed in simple linear drawing.

Other heads represented in a number of mosaics in Rome which are of the same period, substantiate the theory of the influence of Byzantine craftsmen, or, at the very least, the participation of craftsmen trained in Byzantine traditions.

Examples from the next Roman group are products of a very interesting period of development which took place roughly between the late eighth and early ninth centuries. The court of the Emperor Charlemagne was the centre of a revival of the arts in which interest in the works of antiquity played a considerable part. Indeed it has been argued that a close study of the works of the Carolingian Renaissance is directly relevant to the study of classical antiquity. The most complete scheme to remain from this period in Rome is to be seen in the tiny chapel of S. Zenone, *c.* 820, in the church of Sta Prassede. A considerable part of the mosaic decoration is original and unrestored, and can be studied in detail owing to the intimate scale of the architecture.

The style is linear, sometimes perfunctory, and occasionally naïve – far removed from the sophistication and organization of Byzantine work. At its worst the work of this period lacks clarity and form, as if the artists were groping to recapture a lost idiom; at its best it displays a subtlety of technique in line with some of the finest coloristic achievements of late antiquity. One has a feeling of being isolated within a jewelled box, vivid with gold and the sparkle of coloured glass, a feeling which is often a reality as the church is not well known to tourists. The total scheme is breathtaking; each tiny brilliant patch of colour can be appreciated independently yet gives an impression of its relevance to the whole. Another strong factor in the appeal of this tiny chapel is the tactility of the glistening surface. The diagram shows the head of a female saint, which forms one of a number situated above the entrance to the chapel. The material is largely opaque glass, but certain areas are set in natural materials, in the manner of the mother-of-pearl roundels which are so predominant a feature of the Theodora mosaic at Ravenna. It has been suggested that some of the blue material which can be seen in the crown may actually be amethyst quartz, although, without chemical analysis, it is impossible to be certain. The gold smalti consist of gold leaf sandwiched between transparent glass which is of a distinct greenish hue. Another feature is the loose, random setting of the tesserae, which are angled – a technique which allowed the artist considerable play in his control of the effect of light and reflection. The importance of the colour may be appreciated by reference to the diagram, which shows the arrangement of the tesserae. It will be observed that without colour the head is completely formless.

The mosaics in the main church, which can be seen on the apsidal arch, the triumphal arch and in the apse itself, are of the same period as the S. Zenone cycle. They have all been subjected to considerable restoration, especially the mosaic of the apse. Again, a strong linear emphasis can be detected, the colour distribution is most striking, the gold background contrasted with blue, and great chromatic variety is displayed in the setting of the tesserae. The arch of the apse contains an Apocalyptic scene in which the twenty-four elders are depicted offering their crowns of glory to the Holy Lamb. The abstraction of the group is especially interesting, again with strongly emphasized linear rhythms. A similar feeling for graphic analysis can be seen in the apsidal mosaic of Sta Maria Domnica, c. 818, which was also founded by Pope Paschal, although a little earlier than the mosaic decoration of Sta Prassede. The colour is extremely fresh and beautiful as the result of thorough cleaning and restoration. The marvellously suggested groups of angels appear to the left and right of the central group, which depicts the Virgin and Child.

Head of female saint, crowned: detail from mosaic in chapel of S. Zenone, church of Sta Prassede, Rome (see also p. 35).

Another Paschalian work can be seen in the church of Sta Cecilia in Trastevere, although this is a later work than Sta Maria Domnica. The heads are of great gentleness and the gestures much less decisive than in other works of the period. Even the right hand of Christ, blessing in the Greek manner, has a curiously tentative quality. One receives a strong impression that all the figures are tenuous, and are about to dissolve into the atmosphere. The head of Sta Cecilia retains some of the characteristics of the Roman manner, the setting technique being loose, with a noticeable lack of directional lines, although the tesserae which are used in the face are smaller than those in the surrounding area. The young saint is splendidly garbed in gold, but the heavy garment does not alter the extreme elongation of the figures. This unnatural attenuation is common to all the figures, and is given emphasis by the fact that the treatment is largely two-dimensional and linear.

ROMANESQUE MOSAICS

The works within the next group, which can be classified as Romanesque and are completely unrelated to the work of the previous chronological group, would appear to represent an attempted re-establishment of a lost technique. This may indeed be the case, as the earliest example from the period, the apsidal mosaic of S. Clemente of approximately 1125, is at least three hundred years later than the last surviving example from the previous group. I should like to consider the scheme of S. Clemente in more detail, as some very interesting comparisons can be made. The work, although not particularly elegant, exhibits a number of curious features which, while divorcing it from the style of its immediate predecessors, establish a link with the tradition derived from classical antiquity. On the other hand, certain details place the work within the orbit of the approaching medieval style. This can be seen especially in the humanization of the holy personages. They display their vulnerability in the face of human suffering, which is a remarkable departure in a work of such an early date. The classicizing elements can be explained by the fact that the present mosaic was designed to replace a much older work, of which, no doubt, stylistic elements were retained. The great classically inspired scroll, which extends over the area of the apse, is inhabited, and includes a number of popular classical motifs juxtaposed with Christian symbols. For instance, amoretti with grapes and dolphins can be seen, as well as the Christian symbol of the caged bird, infinitely touching in its reference to Christ imprisoned for our sins.

To begin with, I should like to consider the figures of the prophets, Isaiah and Jeremiah. These figures are present as witnesses of the crucifixion and the fulfilment of the prophecy, and are to be found to the left and right of the triumphal arch. At first sight they seem almost identical, although this may be partly accounted for by the similarity of the shape of the area in which they appear. It may also be a device to emphasize their role as supporting figures. A marked resemblance of feature and height can be seen, although the eyes of Isaiah (on the spectator's left) are larger than those of Jeremiah. Of particular interest is the use of linear abstraction as a method of expressing plasticity. The colour and border of the under-tunics are markedly different, and differences can be detected in the areas of ground at the feet of the prophets. Isaiah's patch is strongly rectangular, whereas that of Jeremiah has a broken outline on the inside edge. The feet are outlined in black and red, and it will be noticed that a gold line appears outside the black outline, but is confined to the heel and the sole of the foot. It has little bearing on the modelling, but introduces vitality and sparkle into the area, and helps to balance the distribution of the gold. Although the form is expressed in linear terms, there are marked dissimilarities in the way the fullness of the outer garments is suggested. Visually, the linear convolutions are quite acceptable as drapery, but they have little bearing on the anatomical structure beneath. The small amount of tonal modelling is perfunctory, and in illusionistic terms adds little to the volume of the figures; yet it emphasizes and contains certain areas, and gives even more emphasis to the abstract patterns which are formed.

A very subtle compositional device can be seen in the way in which the left hand of Isaiah appears to support the scroll, which exhibits an upward thrust. In contrast, the right hand of Jeremiah appears to be drawing the scroll downwards. It will be noticed that the upward and downward movements emphasize the direction of the inscription. That on the left of the spectator is read from left to right following the ascending form, whereas that on his right is to be read from left to right following the descending form. The upward-downward movement is further emphasized by two subtle touches. The termination of the scroll which is held by Isaiah is drawn as if it were in the act of unrolling, whereas the scroll held by Jeremiah appears to be in the process of rolling up.

Another point which adds emphasis to the ascending or descending thrust is the way in which the drapery, which falls from the arms of the prophets, has been manipulated. The fall of the drapery is actually divorced from the figure of Isaiah, and is drawn in such a way as to suggest a swinging motion, which would normally follow an upward thrust of the arm. In the case of Jeremiah, the drapery swings backwards into the main form. A number of small details appear to indicate the principal direction of interest, for instance, the downward spiral of Jeremiah's hair, and the lack of linear emphasis on the draperies of the left shoulder (as opposed to the animated lines in a similar position on the right shoulder of Isaiah). The sinuous folds of the drapery which falls across the body of Jeremiah, directly above the scroll, appear to be retracting rather than thrusting. The small group of fast-moving lines which are attached to the lower corner of the scroll (like the tail of a comet) give the impression of moving downwards rather than upwards, in contrast to the slower lines, in a similar position on the figure of Isaiah, which contrive to suggest that the soft draperies are being sucked upwards. The folds on the right shoulder of Isaiah are almost skittish, and appear to be blown away by the movement of the scroll. Of particular interest is the firmness of the base upon which Isaiah stands, which seems to serve as an anchorage to counter the upward movement of the figure.

The emphatic symmetry of the great cross of the apsidal mosaic dominates, both by its size and its colour. The body of the cross is set in rich purple-blue smalti, given liveliness and emphasis by an outer line of red and an inner line of white. Both these colours are distributed within the form of the cross by the agency of twelve doves, which symbolize the apostles, significantly sharing the cross of Christ. The gold background which covers the remainder of the apse supports a magnificent curvilinear arrangement in the form of a great inhabited scroll. The subtlety of detail within the scroll does nothing to destroy the dominance of the cross yet contrives to dispel the monotony which can result from strict symmetry.

The most symmetrical area of the scroll is to be seen at the point where the great branches reassemble at the base of the cross in the form of an acanthus root. The elegant plasticity of the two birds which flank the acanthus root is in marked contrast to the flat stylization of the symbolic doves within the members of the cross.

A rich assortment of motifs appears within the great scroll. New themes, such as scenes from everyday life, appear in contrast with motifs from the old classical repertoire, for instance the playful amoretti. The doctors of the Church, Ambrose, Jerome, Augustine and Gregory, solemnly debate amid beautiful representations of deer and birds of many species, including peacocks, enfolded by the fresh colour of the great scroll. In spite of the classical genesis of a great number of the figures and motifs, they have a vigour which places them firmly within the sphere of medieval art. Examination of style and technique will reveal, however, that a remarkable similarity exists between a number of representations which appear in the S. Clemente mosaic and some of the fifth-century nave mosaics of Sta Maria Maggiore. The retention of certain aspects of the Roman style can also be seen in the technique of the superb head of Christ which appears in a central roundel on the triumphal arch. The facial characteristics are derived from the eastern Byzantine prototype but have undergone a process of humanization to become what we recognize as the typical medieval representation of Christ. Yet the loose, random

Head of Christ: detail of mosaic in roundel, triumphal arch, S. Clemente, Rome (see also p. 36, top).

setting of the tesserae maintains a close link with the past. The stags and the peacocks are among the most beautiful details of the apsidal mosaic. Considerable technical skill is displayed in the manner of expressing the form while retaining the essential softness of hide and feathers. One should notice especially the way in which a line of fawn smalti extends from the light area of the belly of the stag, to describe the form of the cheek.

Although the figures of the Virgin Orans and St John, who flank the great central cross of the apse to left and right, are symmetrically located, the contours of the figures are asymmetrical and introduce variety into the group. Perhaps the most daring feature of the central group is the brilliant red of St John's tunic. In spite of its dominance it is held in place by innumerable touches of red which are distributed throughout the composition. The theanthropical aspect of the crucifixion has been emphasized: the figure of St John seems to have been cast in a role halfway between mourner and comforter and on the other hand the anguish of the Virgin as the mother of the crucified Christ is intense and concentrated. The figure of Christ, although static and represented with a cruciform nimbus, displays the bleeding wounds on the flesh of a man. Although the figures lack the majestic aloofness of the great Byzantine images, nevertheless they convey with dignity their isolation within a circle of silent grief. There is great poignancy in the dolorous contour of the Virgin in contrast to the nervous agitation of St John which is expressed by the helpless gesture of the right hand and the agitated clutching gesture of the left. One finds oneself obeying the injunction in the Byzantine ekphrasis when contemplating the group – 'Admire the art silently lest you disturb with noise the figures.'

2 Restorations and revivals

Ideally, mosaic should be regularly maintained in order to preserve it from falling into an advanced state of disrepair which may require wholesale restoration. A comprehensive programme of restoration which includes a thorough examination, the production of a full photographic record, as well as the necessary repairs by expert craftsmen, is an extremely costly process. Expert examination usually reveals a considerably larger number of defects than originally envisaged, as the most serious damage usually occurs behind the mosaic surface, and can unfortunately remain undetected for a considerable time. Examples have been found in which the mosaic 'skin' has actually separated from its supporting wall.

Inevitably, when serious damage has taken place, it is often found necessary to reset the work completely, which gives rise to innumerable problems. During the course of resetting, the original form of the work will generally be retained, although the essential character may be irretrievably lost. A number of mosaic schemes remain to us as little more than copies of the originals. But a more enlightened policy of conservation prevails today, and whenever possible, serious attempts are made to preserve the essential character of the original work. Particular attention is paid to the original colour schemes, and where feasible, old material is reused, and missing parts replaced from a 'bank' of old material, as far as possible of the same period. The setting technique of the original is very carefully studied; in fact new repairs often re-establish the original setting technique which has been obscured by earlier restorations. On balance, patching and the use of insertions are more desirable than complete resetting, and the best modern repair work allows the scholar to distinguish the old work from the new, without destroying the homogeneity of the whole.

Repairs and replacements have been carried out during various periods, and, fortunately, specific reference was often made to the event, either by means of an inscription incorporated into the work, or in documentary form. One document, the *Liber Pontificalis*, contains an account of such an undertaking – '*Hic renovavit absidem beati Petri apostuli ex musibo, quod dirutum erat*' ('This [Pope] restored the apse in the basilica of the Apostle St Peter in mosaic. It had been in ruins'). The reference was to Pope Innocent III (1198–1216). It is not possible always to establish the precise meaning of

(*Opposite*) Hull museum staff performing a delicate rolling-up operation for the removal of a Romano-British mosaic pavement from its site at Brantingham, Yorkshire, to the museum (see p. 39).

such a passage, as clear distinction may not be made between restoration and complete replacement. In this instance the work is thought to have been a genuine restoration. Painstaking research has established the precise location of many ancient repairs on most of the major monuments and others have been established with a fair degree of certainty.

Sta Maria Maggiore

The panels in the nave of Sta Maria Maggiore in Rome show evidence of very early restoration, and the oldest surviving fragment from the first basilica of St Peter, which portrays St Paul, appears to have been restored at a date little later than the original work.

Ambitious architectural schemes which brought about the enlargement, or sometimes the complete rebuilding, of ancient churches, frequently caused the destruction or truncation of ancient mosaic decoration. The basilica of S. Clemente – one of the most interesting churches in Rome – was enlarged in this manner during the eleventh century. It seems fairly certain that the existing apsidal mosaic decoration was adapted from a similar work in the original church, founded by Pope Syricius (384–99), and some of the ancient material may have been incorporated in the scheme.

A similar replacement can be seen in the apse of Sta Maria Maggiore in Rome, one of the four patriarchal basilicas with the privilege of extra-territoriality. The foundation of the church is traditionally assigned to the reign of Pope Liberius of Rome (352–66), rebuilt during the pontificate of Sixtus III (432–40), enlarged by Pope Eugenius III (1145–53) and further enlarged by Nicholas IV (1288–92). The apsidal mosaic is the work of a Franciscan, Jacopo Toriti or Turriti, who had been employed by Nicholas on the mosaic decoration of the apse of S. Giovanni Laterano. As seen today, the body of the church is largely a Renaissance restoration; the medieval choir was removed, and reinforcements, in the form of pillars, were added to the medieval columns. The fifth-century mosaics of the nave were altered, and the main apsidal mosaics of Toriti have retained very little of the original work, although the lower frieze, which contains the classical theme of a river god, appears to be of ancient workmanship reused by Toriti in 1294.

The Tribune of Benedict XIV

A sixteenth-century replacement can be seen on the so-called Tribune of Benedict XIV, near S. Giovanni Laterano in Rome. The original mosaic formed part of the decoration of the Triclinium of Leo III. The Triclinium, which was built about the year 800, formed part of the Pontifical Palace which was destroyed in the sixteenth century to make way for the town planning programme of Sixtus V. The Triclinium was the scene of the banquet which was traditionally

given in honour of the Holy Roman Emperor, after his coronation by the Pope. The mosaic depicted the relevant theme of the division of spiritual and temporal power. The inscription which can be seen on the present version asserts that the mosaic is a copy of an ancient work of the early ninth century, and no doubt represents a genuine attempt to re-create the iconography of the original. Unfortunately, in comparison with a fragment of the original scheme which is exhibited in the Vatican, neither the spirit nor the technique of the original has been retained.

Tribune of Benedict XIV near
S. Giovanni Laterano, Rome.

Hagia Sophia

Replacement mosaics are, however, of supreme icono-graphical importance when they are known to have pre-served the original *schema*, however much one may regret the loss of the original. The question of authenticity is a complex one, especially when restorations are themselves of an early date. Problems of this nature occur in most of the great mosaic cycles, particularly in view of the fact that those which were especially revered would naturally be sub-jected to constant repair. The *Deesis* panel in Hagia Sophia was obviously damaged before the fall of Constantinople in 1453. The *Deesis*, or 'Supplication', an iconographical *schema* which depicts Christ between the Virgin and St

Deesis panel from Hagia Sophia, Istanbul.

John the Baptist, has suffered serious losses. The inscription remains more or less intact, although less than half the figure of Christ has survived, including the right hand and fragments of the book of the Gospels and of the throne. Little more than the head and right shoulder of the Virgin remains and only half the figure of St John.

The panel was covered with plaster by the Turks after their occupation of the city in the fifteenth century. Between 1847 and 1849 renovation of the church, now a mosque, was carried out by Giuseppe and Gaspare Fossati. During the course of the work they discovered the *Deesis* panel in a damaged condition, and sensing the artistic value of the panel, they effected repairs using a mixture of plaster and brick dust. They discovered a rupture between the wall and the setting bed, and to prevent further damage, the Fossati drove nails across the panel in order to secure it. The work was then sized and completely coated with a layer of plaster and rubble. Further coats were applied, and then a finishing coat of fine white plaster, painted to simulate marble. This method of securing mosaics to the wall by means of nails or metal ties had been quite commonly practised during the fifteenth and sixteenth centuries, and often missing or damaged areas were made good with plaster, which was then painted and scored to represent individual cubes.

A much more recent investigation of the *Deesis* which was the subject of a report by T. Whittemore, revealed several curious facts. When the marble slabs were removed from beneath the area occupied by the existing panel, the imprint

(*Right*) Detail of crowned female saint in chapel of S. Zenone in Sta Prassede, Rome.

(*Below*) The prophets Isaiah (*left*) and Jeremiah: detail of mosaic of apse, basilica of S. Clemente, Rome (see pp. 26–8).

(*Above*) S. Clemente, Rome: detail of mosaic on triumphal arch (see pp. 28–9).

(*Below*) River god – classical fragment used by Toriti, apsidal mosaic, Sta Maria Maggiore, Rome (see p. 32).

of mosaic cubes was discovered. Traces of yellow paint were also revealed, probably remnants of the *sinopia*, and a number of gold smalti were discovered – embedded in the wall. Apparently the glass was of a different chemical composition from that used on the existing panel, and it is thought that the original work was about 2 ft. larger than the existing replacement panel, itself of ancient origin.

The Dome of the Rock

In Jerusalem the Dome of the Rock was found to have been subjected to a number of earlier restorations. The mosaic decorations had remained surprisingly intact, although other decorative features had suffered considerably at the hands of restorers. The reign of Sultan 'Abd-al-Aziz saw the instigation of an extensive restoration programme, which was carried out between 1873 and 1874, though very little work was done on the mosaics, apart from a few minor repairs which were carried out in plaster. It was subsequently established that a great deal of damage had been caused, particularly by the infiltration of water, always a serious matter where mosaic is concerned. During the period 1923–27 minor repairs were undertaken, and attempts were made to deal with the problem of water seepage. Between 1927 and 1928 Marguerite Gautier-van Berchem was allowed to make a thorough examination of the mosaic decoration. Her survey was published and brought up to date in 1969. During the interim, in the 1960's, extensive restorations had been carried out by Italian craftsmen, and Marguerite van Berchem was in a unique position to make comparisons between the appearance of the mosaic decoration before and after restoration. Although recognizing the genuine dilemma of those in charge of the restoration she is firmly of the opinion that the repairs have been too radical, especially in the replacement of old material, which has seriously affected the colour relationships of the interior. It would appear, however, that the original design has been scrupulously respected. In 1946, the Director of Antiquities in Cyprus, A. H. S. Megaw, submitted an important report accompanied by a comprehensive photographic record, which stressed the urgency of a programme of restoration. The report was brought up to date in 1952, although it was never published.

FLOOR MOSAICS

Pavimental mosaic fulfilled quite a different function from that of mural mosaic, although they had in common a markedly decorative aspect. Floor mosaics were originally conceived for purposes of utility, consequently the material used was almost invariably hard-wearing natural stone rather than glass, and the surface was polished to a smooth, flat finish, in order to withstand the exigencies of everyday use. As discussed in Chapter 9, examples of practical and, at the same time, decorative pavimental mosaics have been found in all parts of what was once the Roman Empire, varying between large-scale elaborate ones to those of a more domestic nature, as, for instance, the black-and-white floors of the guest rooms (*hospitalia*) of Hadrian's Villa. Pavimental mosaics were never used in the fully expressive manner of mural schemes, although it is true to say that the function of a particular floor area was often made clear by means of the decorations.

The restoration of floor mosaics poses a different problem from that of mural mosaic. Generally they are only revealed by excavation, and although they frequently appear to be intact and in good order, on further examination it is usually discovered that the mosaics have become completely detached from their bed. When this sort of condition is apparent there is no alternative but to lift the floor completely and supply a new backing. Three Roman pavements were discovered at Rudstone in Yorkshire and remained *in situ* for a number of years. When they began to deteriorate it was decided to remove them to Hull Museum. The actual removal proved to be a difficult operation. One mosaic, containing a figure of Venus as a centre piece, measures 10 ft. × 14 ft., another is decorated with a geometric pattern and another, depicting marine life, is a very large panel which measures 108 ft. × 5 ft. A new backing of steel-reinforced concrete ensured the stability of the panels, but tremendous problems were raised, as the geometric pavement alone weighed four and a half tons. The work was successfully completed by the museum staff in 1962, but the decision to display the geometric mosaic on the wall in the museum involved the use of temporary scaffolding, which added considerably to the cost of the project.

Another pavement was unearthed at Brantingham near Hull in 1962 and when it was decided to lift it for removal to Hull Museum a different method of preservation was evolved, utilizing Araldite epoxy resin. This pavement, the largest to be found in Yorkshire, formed part of the decoration of a Romano-British villa of some importance. The mosaic formed the floor of the largest room in the villa, measuring about 36 ft. × 268 ft. Part of the floor had collapsed into the flues of the underlying hypocaust though a number of large panels were sufficiently well preserved to make removal possible; it was decided to remove the two largest by means of a rolling-up operation and smaller sections were to be taken away flat. The subsoil was sandy and the pavement appeared to be fairly dry; however it was decided to ensure that the mosaic was completely dry before the rolling-up process was attempted. A frame of metal scaffolding was erected over the pavement, and polythene sheets were stretched over the frame to form a tent. Butane gas heaters were then directed on to the pavement for about three days. When the mosaic was judged to be absolutely dry, two coats of PVC solution were applied to the surface of the panel, after which a bandage material was laid with a further coat of PVC although on one part of the pavement a PVA solution was used as an alternative.

The next step was an extremely difficult one; the mosaic had to be carefully wound over a large cardboard roller which was strengthened internally and fitted with a suitable axle. The tesserae were then cut away from the old mortar (which had perished) by means of a long iron blade. Several people were engaged in turning the roller in order to ensure that the pavement was evenly wound. Each layer was inter-leaved with two sheets of corrugated paper as the rolling-up progressed and finally, when the process was completed, a strong dust-sheet was stretched tightly over the tesserae to keep them in place (p. 30). The smaller sections of the pave-ment which were to be removed were undercut, and then eased on to flat sheets of hardboard. The mosaics were trans-ported to the museum at Hull and the major sections rolled face downwards on to a sloping surface and surrounded by a wooden frame, which was to serve as a container for the backing material. The panel was carefully cleared of all loose mortar, and a coat of Araldite was applied, together with chopped glass fibre, and then a backing of vermiculite and iron reinforcing bars, bonded with Araldite. This pro-duced a light but very rigid structure. Very little further work was required on the front of the panels. They were stable, and protected from subsequent attack from chemicals and moisture by virtue of the special qualities of the Araldite, which greatly added to the advantages of the method.

RELATED TECHNIQUES

A number of techniques exist of a similar nature to mosaic but with certain basic differences which are not always readily discernible. 'Mosaic inlay' is a type of work which is usually carried out in hard stones, glass and various kinds of marble. 'Intarsia', sometimes referred to as 'tarsia' or 'intarsiatura', which may derive its name from the Arabic *tarsi*, is a form of inlay in which the basic material is visible and forms part of the design, the whole being polished to give a uniform surface. One of the essential differences between mosaic and inlay is that mosaic is an encrustation and stands clear from its bed, although there are examples in which mosaic material has been inlaid into marble which makes definition difficult. Well-known examples, such as the Standard of Ur, in the British Museum, have been variously described, being sometimes referred to as mosaic and sometimes as inlay. Perhaps the greatest difference lies in the fact that chromatic range, chiaroscuro, rhythmic and

Commesso work.

linear effects, so much a part of the mosaic technique, lie
outside the scope of intarsia. Rigidity of design is a
characteristic feature of inlay.

Commesso work (from the Latin word *commissus* meaning
'put together') is usually composed of hard stones. The
pieces are cut to shape and attached to a support with mastic;
after assembly, the surface is highly polished. The close
setting of the pieces almost eliminates the lines between the
joins; this work, often referred to as 'Florentine mosaic', had
its origin in *opus sectile*. *'Cosmati' work* is more closely
related to mosaic, and again involves the use of hard stones
alongside other materials. It is believed to be of Arabic
inspiration, and is confined to geometric designs made up
from a large number of pieces in a variety of shapes, carefully
cut by hand. There are other forms of inlay which, because
of the materials used, lie outside the scope of this book, for
example 'niello', a method of inlaying gold and silver with
various metals, and 'Damascene' work in which iron or steel
is inlaid with gold wire. In fact, any material which can be
satisfactorily engraved may serve as a bed for inlay.

Intarsia, like mosaic, has a long history and a fairly extensive application, including the embellishment of architecture. Many beautiful examples have survived from
antiquity. A number of objects from Egypt demonstrate the
extensive use of inlaid decoration, and include such items as
furniture and musical instruments. The coffins of the young
King Tutankhamun are excellent examples of the technique,
being inlaid with glass and semi-precious stones. In the Near
East intarsia work was used on friezes, gaming boards and
musical instruments, a most splendid example being a
lyre from a royal tomb which was discovered at Ur. The
lyre, which is of wood, is inlaid with shell, lapis lazuli and
red jasper. The Standard of Ur, a panel of very fine workmanship, depicts a number of scenes of complex design. A
similar technique can be seen in a frieze from al-'Ubaid, in

which white and coloured stones are used to portray a scene of cows being milked.

Vitreous pastes were frequently employed to give colour and contrast; typical examples of the technique may be seen on cosmetic boxes in which ivory panels are inlaid with glass pastes of various colours, as well as gold and precious stones. The tomb of Tutankhamun contained a number of objects with intarsia decoration, including furniture and small coffers, and a number of materials including gold, ivory, glass paste and various woods were used. The technique remained popular in Egypt until the first century B C, but the quality gradually declined. Inlaid figurines were discovered in Crete, made of steatite and inlaid with rock crystal, wood, mother of pearl and precious metals. A number of objects made of glazed terracotta were also discovered there. These may have been used as insertions in other materials which are now lost. A quantity of sculptural stone vases, enriched by intarsia of various materials, have been found in Crete. Beautifully figured stones such as granites, grained marbles, alabaster, rock crystal and occasionally stones of exceptional hardness such as basalt and obsidian were used for the purpose. Related to these hardstone vessels are the sculptured rhytons which were used for libations. Some were of clay, but one of the finest examples is a rhyton of steatite, a soft stone, dated to a period between 1600 and 1500 B C, fashioned to represent a sacred bull. The rhyton was discovered at Knossos, and is now in the Heraklion museum. Although it is only 12 in. high the features are inlaid with a variety of contrasting materials, such as mother-of-pearl, red jasper and rock crystal.

Alabaster decorations on a large scale were used on the façades and interior walls of Cretan palaces. The classical architecture of Rome exhibits a similar style of encrustation which utilized marbles and various types of coloured stone, applied both to interior and exterior surfaces. The technique, which appeared in Rome during the middle of the first century B C, was an inheritance from the Near East. Pliny the Elder makes reference to the practice, but, as is usual, his

Detail from Standard of Ur, now in British Museum, London.

Divinized Sun: detail of *opus sectile*
panel, found in Sta Prisca, Rome.

description is imprecise. The fashion for this type of decoration persisted, and examples can be seen at Ostia Antica,
Herculaneum and on the Palatine at Rome, in a form which
later developed into the style known as *opus sectile*, or sometimes as *opus interrasile*. In the latter a slightly different method
is used, the sections of material being cut from thinner pieces
and inserted into slabs of greater thickness.

Genuine *opus sectile* is, in reality, a form of marquetry in
which marble slabs of equal thickness are fitted together in
jigsaw fashion. A number of representational figurative
works remain, for instance the Divinized Sun which was
discovered in the Mithraeum under Sta Prisca in Rome. The
head is depicted in a somewhat theatrical manner, and is
reminiscent of the Hellenistic heads derived from portraits
of Alexander the Great. Another group of *opus sectile* panels
from the Basilica of Junius Bassus are of particular interest.
They have been assigned to the fourth century AD and
appear to be the work of different hands. It is probable that
the panel depicting Hylas and the Nymphs and the 'Egyptian'
subjects are the work of an artist of Hellenistic origin, whereas
the panel depicting the Consular Triumph strongly suggests
a Syrian craftsman, or at least a craftsman trained in the
Syrian school. The manner in which the faces and garments
are represented is similar to the style of the mosaics of
Dura Europos. Perhaps the most striking feature of the
group is the symmetry of the composition, the figure of the
consul being accorded the central position and represented
on a much larger scale than the remainder of the figures.

Calf attacked by tiger: *opus sectile* panel from tomb of Junius Bassus, now in Capitoline Museum, Rome.

Although one assumes that the mounted horsemen are intended to occupy a position in the background, it is interesting to notice that the rump of the horse immediately to the right of the chariot actually overlaps in such a manner as to suggest that it occupies a position in front of the vehicle. The figures appear to be abstracted, although this is probably a condition imposed by the technique. The pieces are cut from a variety of coloured marbles, many of which are beautiful, but they are rarely capable of inducing a convincing sense of plasticity in the forms.

The African influence may also be detected in the panels depicting calves being attacked by tigers (also from the tomb of Junius Bassus), which was a popular subject during this period. The striation of the marble is strongly marked in these examples which, in a curious way, exhibit greater expressiveness than those panels in which a more rigorous definition of form has been attempted, in keeping with the Hellenistic tradition. Perhaps the very naïvety of the forms in the tiger panels is responsible for the more successful exploitation of this particular technique.

The eastern tradition of intarsia continued to expand within the western Empire, the inlay technique becoming a predominantly architectural feature. The intarsia in the baptistery of the Orthodox, in Ravenna, for instance, denotes the continuation of the late antique tradition, the work consisting of an admixture of geometric and foliated patterns, intricately laid. This form predominated in the later development of the technique in northern Italy,

43

The eastern silk design (*top*) shows a striking similarity to the pattern on the floors of S. Miniato al Monte (*above, centre*) and of the Baptistery in Florence.

(*Below*) Cosmati work: detail.

examples of which can be seen in Lucca, Pistoia and Pisa. A more typically western style can be detected in the form of inlay which was used to decorate different surfaces in the architecture of the Tuscan Romanesque style, a refined form usually referred to as *opus Alexandrinum*.

A typical example of this development can be seen in the baptistery of S. Giovanni in Florence. The Piazza del Duomo (the name derived from *Domus Dei*, House of God) forms the setting for the cathedral, the campanile or bell-tower, and the baptistery. The baptistery – a Romanesque re-modelling of a much earlier foundation – contains pavements carried out in *opus Alexandrinum* which contain areas of figural decoration, some from the twelfth century, in addition to the celebrated 'Zodiac' pavement of the thirteenth century.

Another splendid floor decoration of this type is to be seen in the church of S. Miniato al Monte near Florence, which was built in 1018 on the site of a much earlier foundation. The church was originally Benedictine, although taken over by Olivetans in 1375. The façade has a marble inlay, and the floor of the nave is intricately and richly paved. A great variety of pattern has been introduced – animals contrarampant, lions, doves and other motifs which are obviously derived from eastern textiles, translated into a western idiom. The pavement also contains a superb square insert decorated with the signs of the zodiac. All these decorations are carried out in a compound of pitch, which contrasts with the white marble. The figural sections of the floor are enclosed within meandering bands of geometric *opus Alexandrinum*.

Later developments in the field of intarsia displayed an increasing concern with figural elements. Vasari in his *Lives of the Artists* writes of this new development, which he describes as 'another kind of mosaic made of marble fragments so joined together that they imitate subjects depicted in chiaroscuro'. The technical aspect of this attempt to achieve figural expression by means of inlay is of particular interest. Slabs of white marble were prepared to receive the inlay – which was composed of a black substance made from pitch. The recesses in the marble were created by means of drilling and routing, the hollows then being filled with a compound of pitch. These storiated pavements achieved great intricacy, and displayed a considerable degree of skill in graphic expression. But the technique lacks resistance to wear, a disadvantage when used as a form of flooring. An example of the *graffito* technique of the late fourteenth century can be seen in the Cathedral of Siena. Almost the entire floor area is covered with carefully cut sections of white marble fitted together to form a silhouette against a background of black marble. The details are incised and filled with a compound of pitch, resin and clay. Polychrome marble was later introduced into the borders which surrounded the storiated panels, and later into the pictorial areas.

The type of work known as *opus Romanum* or 'Cosmati' work is so named because of the stylistic characteristics common to groups of marble workers active in Rome during the twelfth and thirteenth centuries. The incidence of the name Cosma has led to the inference that work typical of this style was produced by a family named Cosmato. Undoubtedly the craft of marble working was a family affair, the expertise passing from father to son, in common with many other crafts. It is possible, however, to make specific identification of some of the individuals working in the Cosmatesque manner in the medieval period by reference to a number of inscriptions which remain *in situ*. Where this occurs it is possible to gain some impression of individual techniques, but many of these works are anonymous, and it seems unlikely that further information will be forthcoming. Work in the Cosmatesque style was essentially decorative and usually non-figural. Composed principally of geometric designs, these works, especially those which comprise large floor areas, are monuments to patience and skill. Tiny geometric elements were hand-cut from hard stone and incorporated in an over-all design, or sometimes included as a partial decoration on a variety of architectural surfaces.

The oldest recorded family group descends from a Roman craftsman named Paolo who was active about 1108. He was

Cosmatesque floor in Basilica of S. Lorenzo al Verano, Rome: detail.

responsible for certain works in the Cathedral of Ferentino, about fifty miles south of Rome. Paolo left his name on the chancel barrier which is richly decorated with marble inlay. A stylistic affinity between the work of Paolo at Ferentino and a number of panels on the reverse of the chancel barrier in the church of Sta Maria in Cosmedin at Rome can be detected, but this cannot be verified either by documentary evidence or inscription. Paolo had four sons working in Rome, Giovanni, Pietro, Angelo and Sasso, all of whom have left signed work there, in the churches of S. Marco and S. Lorenzo fuori le Mura. Another branch of Cosmati workers was descended from Angelo and documented work can be seen in Rome and as far south as Gaeta. The existence of another group descended from a craftsman named Tebaldo has been established by the evidence of signed work. He and his son Lorenzo collaborated, and Lorenzo and his son Jacopo were responsible for important work in the Duomo of Civita Castellani. The portico and façade of the cathedral still retain the Cosmatesque decoration dated to 1210. A richly ornamented doorway of 1205 forming a decorative entrance to the church of Sta Saba and an iconostasis in another Roman church, S. Allesio, appear to have been the work of Jacopo alone. According to the inscription on the portal of the former hospice of S. Tommaso in Formis, dated 1218, Jacopo worked with his son Cosma. It appears that Cosma worked alone for some time, to be joined by his sons Luca and Jacopo at a later date.

Pietro Mellini and his son Cosmato were also notable craftsmen in the Cosmatesque style. Cosmato is mentioned in a number of documents between 1264 and 1279, although his only known signed work (dated 1278) is within the Sancta Sanctorum which was originally part of the old Lateran Palace. Cosmato's son was responsible for three important signed funerary monuments in Rome. These are the Durante tomb in Sta Maria sopra Minerva, an attractive and graceful work, the De Surdis tomb in Sta Balbina, and the Rodriguez tomb in Sta Maria Maggiore. Another family, the Vassalletti, were descended from a craftsman named Basiletto. The cloister of S. Giovanni Laterano in Rome contains one of the most important examples of Cosmatesque decoration, the work of Pietro Vassalletto and his son Vassalletto the Younger. The decoration is carried out in polychrome in which fragments of gold add life and sparkle to the columns. The garden in the centre of the cloister walk contains a ninth-century well, the whole forming an attractive setting for the vibrant decoration.

Innumerable works remain in and around Rome which, although they cannot be attributed to specific craftsmen, are excellent examples of the style. Of particular interest is the group of S. Clemente, which has been carefully reassembled. Apart from the pavement, the group includes the *ciborium*, the altar, the *schola cantorum* with its double pulpits, and the candelabrum for the Paschal candle, used during the Easter celebration. The typical Cosmati style can also be seen in the small chapel of the Presepio, at Sta Maria Maggiore. The chapel, which originally stood outside the basilica, was built to represent the grotto of the Nativity at Bethlehem. It was restored by Arnolfo di Cambio (c. 1232–1302) but was damaged during its removal, when Pope Sixtus V (1585–90) commissioned the building of the Sistine Chapel in the basilica. Examples of Cosmati work are also to be found in the church of S. Cesareo in Rome, a very ancient foundation which was restored during the reign of the Aldobrandini Pope, Clement VIII (1592–1605). The Cosmatesque group is one of the finest things to be seen in the church. The 11 ft. wide altar is most unusual in that it is decorated with representations of various animals derived from early Christian symbolism.

A craftsman named Odoricus was employed as far afield as England: he laid the floor of the sanctuary of Westminster Abbey in 1228. The decoration was typical and formed from sections of green porphyry and glass inlaid into Purbeck marble. The inscription reads '. . . the year of Christ 1268, King Henry the third, the city [Rome], Odoricus and the Abbot [Richard de Ware] assembled these porphyry stones together'. A similar decoration, of which little remains, was carried out in the Confessor's chapel. The style lingered on in a remarkable way; the mid-fifteenth-century chapel of James of Lusitania, Cardinal of Portugal, who died in Florence in 1459 and was buried in S. Miniato al Monte, contains a floor decoration in the Cosmatine style with semi-precious stones such as porphyry and serpentine set in granite.

Certain Byzantine work, which may be seen in Hagia Sophia and the church of the Pantocrator in Istanbul, offers the closest analogy to Roman Cosmati work, although the art of Islam has obviously exerted a considerable stylistic influence. The ornamental style lends itself to surface decoration, and examples can be seen on a wide variety of objects, including doors and floors. Like Cosmati work, the Byzantine style involves the use of small geometric elements, cut by hand from materials such as red porphyry, green serpentine and fine white marble, and at a later date, glass fragments and gold smalti. Sometimes panels of what can be described as mosaic were framed with bands of marble or, conversely, tesserae were used to surround disks or rectangles of porphyry.

In Italy a later development of the intarsia technique, which included the use of units of fired terracotta, can be seen in the Hall of Justice in the Castello di S. Angelo in Rome, and in the Laurentian library which adjoins the church of S. Lorenzo in Florence, the latter being a superb example of the style.

The use of intarsia as a medium for wall and pavement decoration began to decline during the seventeenth century and further development was confined to the application of the technique as a form of furniture decoration. This was

Commesso work in Medici chapel, S. Lorenzo, Florence.

known as 'commesso' work, and it was immensely popular in sixteenth-century Florence during the reign of Francesco I, Grand Duke of Tuscany, the founder of the Galeria degli Uffizi. He was succeeded by his brother Ferdinando I, a man of more stable character, who, in 1588, organized the commesso workers (who had been attracted to his brother's court) into what is known as the *Opificio delle Pietre Dure*, that is, an atelier for craftsmen working in hard stones. The *Opificio* was originally housed in the Casino di S. Marco, and later in the Uffizi. It is now established in a former monastery in the Via degli Affani in Florence, and run by the state as a craft training school. Numbered among the early directors of the workshop were Bernardo Buontalenti (1536–1608) and Pietro Tacca, the sculptor and architect (1577–1640). It is said that the stockpile of hard stones and rare marbles still includes a quantity of the original collection which was accumulated by the Medici. A decree was published by Duke Ferdinando, which afforded protection to polishable hard stones such as agates, jaspers, chalcedonies and amethysts, reminiscent of the way in which attempts are made to preserve wild life today. Anyone found removing or damaging hard stones became liable to severe punishment. The quality of all branches of jewelry was rigidly controlled, and artisans were not permitted to work at night, nor in any place hidden from public view. Commesso work became universally popular, and craftsmen in hard stones were greatly sought after. The style developed in accordance with the tendency towards naturalism which predominated during the seventeenth century. The Medici chapel, adjacent to the church of S. Lorenzo in Florence, exhibits the full range of commesso and intarsia work. However, the intimate connection which the city of Florence had with commesso work is not yet dead; a number of workshops carry on the craft today and restoration work is in the hands of expert craftsmen.

3 Tools and structural materials

It is possible to begin working in mosaic with very little equipment: a pair of tile nippers, a level table, and boxes in which to store mosaic materials. As work progresses, however, demands will inevitably be made on certain household utensils, so even at the outset some equipment should be bought for the exclusive use of the mosaicist. Kitchen utensils which are useful include rolling-pins, for rolling clay, plastic buckets with lids, plastic spatulas, scrapers, measuring spoons, scales and rubber gloves. In addition, scissors of various sizes are necessary, also scalpels and 'Stanley' knives, hammers and common woodworking tools such as saws, chisels and a vice. Ordinary pliers of various sizes will be needed, as well as the type with a wire-cutter attachment, and, more specialized but absolutely indispensable if working with glass or tiles, a pair of square-jawed pliers for snapping away narrow strips and ragged edges. Metal-cutting shears and tin-snips, capable of cutting curved and straight sections from thin sheets of tin and copper, are useful. Trowels, plasterer's small tools and palette knives are necessary; and a tool for cutting lead strips (*calmes*) can be made by cutting down and sharpening a paint scraper. Torches and soldering irons allow an extension of the work; small inexpensive torches are available which run off a butane gas cylinder. They have an adjustable flame and certain types can be obtained with a special tip for soldering. If a torch is needed for melting and forming glass, it will be found that a range of propane torches are available to choose from. In addition a cradle will be required for holding the torch in position, and a number of asbestos sheets of various sizes. Special tools, which will be required if the mosaicist wishes to extend the range of material used in his work, should include a pottery kiln, a jewelry kiln, a lapidary tumbler for polishing pebbles, and power tools suitable for woodworking and metalworking. There are a number of highly specialized crafts which would provide excellent material for mosaic, as for instance metal-casting. Where facilities exist, it is to be hoped that experiment will extend into these fields, although they will remain outside the scope of most people.

CUTTING

Cutting mosaic material requires skill, a sense of rhythm, and persistence. In common with most crafts, skill comes with practice, although the cutting principle is a simple one.

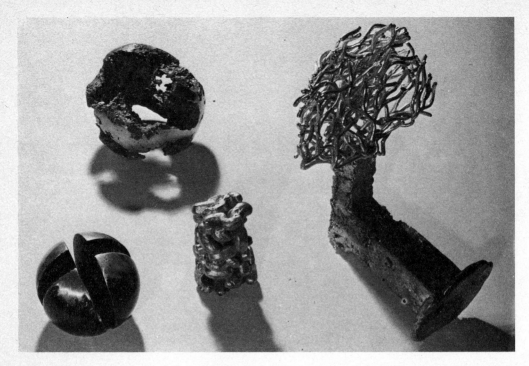

Metal castings for use as mosaic material.

Pressure is applied to both sides of the tessera at the same time, causing a line of weakness which eventually fractures, although the pressure is applied only to the extreme edge of the material. This simple but important principle must be adhered to; an attempt to cut through the tile entirely will cause it to shatter rather than fracture. The beginner would be well advised to wear some form of eye shield until he can undertake to cut considerable quantities of material into various shapes with speed and accuracy. In principle, some form of eye protection is desirable at all times, but in practice most people prefer to work without. It is wise to remember that flying glass particles are dangerous, and even the most experienced operative can make a mistake. If one is responsible for the instruction of other people, one should insist that some form of eye protection be worn.

It will be found that the most economical procedure is to cut a large quantity of such shapes as will be most commonly used in a particular project, leaving special shapes to be cut as required. If a number of people are involved in the cutting process, ensure that the cut tesserae are well mixed before use, as personal characteristics can be detected even in this simple process. Fragmented material, which may be left over after cutting, should be sorted and stored, especially if the mosaicist intends to produce his own material by some of the methods suggested in Chapter 4. Protracted cutting sessions can be tedious, especially when the work in hand is well advanced. However, it is better to persist with regular sessions during which a quantity of material is prepared than to run short at a crucial point during the setting process.

It is wise to prepare material before commencing work for the day in order to avoid undue fatigue later. If possible, avoid cutting and sorting mosaic units in artificial light, which can considerably alter the appearance of many colours; indeed, subtle or closely related colours can become practically indistinguishable. Whenever possible, major decisions concerning colour arrangement should be taken in daylight, and if working in artificial light remove all boxes containing extraneous material rather than run the risk of picking out the wrong colour which may then have to be chipped away the next day.

The most satisfactory tools for accurate cutting are a mosaic hammer and a 'hardie'. The hardie is like a large chisel, with a cutting edge of tungsten carbide, embedded in a block of wood with the cutting edge uppermost. A log is usually employed for this purpose and should be cut to a suitable height to enable the operative to sit comfortably with the log between his knees. The mosaic hammer is curved along the upper edge, rather like a bow, and has two tungsten carbide cutting edges. Mosaic hammers can be made to order, or stonemason's hammers may be substituted. The weight and balance of the tool remains a matter of individual choice. These are factors which must be carefully considered, as an unsuitable tool can cause the operative to experience acute muscle fatigue. The mosaic material should be firmly held between thumb and forefinger, with its lower face placed on the cutting edge of the hardie and at right angles to it. The material is held at the extreme edge and as near the base as possible. A light, firm blow with the hammer should be directed on to the material at a point directly above the blade of the hardie, which should cause the tessera to fracture cleanly. The hammer should be held firmly but lightly, and receptacles for the cut material should be placed within easy reach of the operative in order to facilitate the rhythm of the work.

Mosaic hammer and (*right*) using it with a hardie.

(*Below*) Shapes which may be cut from vitreous mosaics.

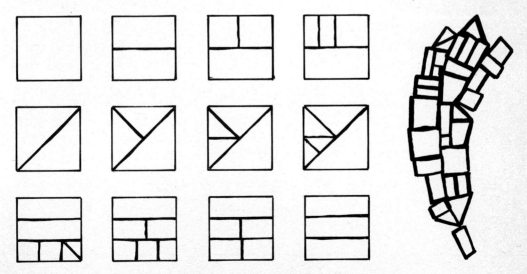

(*Right*) Cutting tesserae.

(*Below*) Japanese spring-type mosaic nippers and the ordinary long-handled variety.

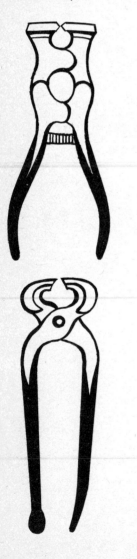

Special clippers are available which will, with practice, enable one to cut tesserae rapidly and accurately. The most satisfactory type (also the most expensive) is spring-loaded with toggle joints and adjustable jaws, controlled by a setting screw, which is most useful when working with material of different thicknesses. The cutting principle is simple; the tessera should be held at the extreme edge with the thumb in position at centre top, and the first and second fingers directly underneath. The opposite edge should be presented to the jaws of the nippers at a point near the edge and in the direction of the proposed fracture. The handles of the nippers should be squeezed gently but firmly, causing the tessera to fracture accurately. If triangular pieces are required, the tessera should be held with the fingers in the same position as described, but at the extreme tip of one corner, and the jaws of the nippers applied to the opposite corner. The fracture should occur cleanly across the diagonal (see diagram). Ordinary long-handled tile-nippers can be used, although the jaws tend to become blunt rather quickly, and they are apt to tire the hands. The cutting process is such an important aspect of the craft that cheaper and less efficient tools are a false economy. A very efficient spring-type tool with carbide-tipped jaws is being imported from Japan by a number of firms. The tool is $7\frac{1}{2}$ in. long, is remarkably cheap, and with care should give long service. It is preferable to own even the simplest tool rather than depend on a communal source, since familiarity with the weight and balance of the nippers is such an important factor in the cutting process.

The method employed for cutting glazed tiles is very different from that for cutting tesserae. A line in the direction of the fracture must first be scored along the glazed surface of the tile. An ordinary glass-cutter can be used, although a special tile-cutter with a tungsten carbide tip is more satisfactory. These tools may be held in several ways; held in one hand they can be steadied by allowing the free fingers of the cutting hand to rest lightly on the surface of the tile; held in two hands, they can be guided in an upright position along the line of the proposed fracture. The cutting edge of the tool must be held at right angles to the surface and a firm and constant pressure maintained. The cutter can also be guided along a metal straight-edge, in which case the tool is generally drawn along the edge towards the user. The best method is the one most suited to the individual. After scoring, the tile should be laid, scored side uppermost, over a strip of wood with the line corresponding to the edge of the strip and firm pressure applied to each side, using both hands, whereupon the tile should break cleanly. Tiles are easy to handle with a little practice and they are also cheap and readily available; small pieces can be nipped in the same manner as tesserae. They are especially useful for filling large areas, or forming a contrast with other materials. Natural materials such as marble and stone often prove difficult to split, although marble cubes can be fractured on a hardie; sometimes other natural stone may be similarly split if the surface is previously scored with a chisel or a saw.

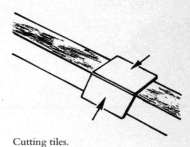

Cutting tiles.

THE WORKSHOP

The amount of capital to be expended on setting up a work-shop cannot be specified as this is a matter for the individual to decide. Mosaics of great aesthetic value can be produced with a minimum of equipment, and very few tools are required if the craftsman is to work exclusively with smalti, although this can be countered by a considerable expenditure on materials. Found and scrap material, and a number of materials which can be manufactured in the studio, do require processing, and fairly large sums of money may have to be spent on special equipment. If the mosaicist is working in a professional capacity, the initial cost of items of equipment may be recouped over a period of time, but recurring expenditure should not be overlooked. For instance, if an electric kiln is to be used, the running costs may be quite high. Before any large investment is made, one should consider whether special items will earn their keep within a reasonable period of time. Many lightweight power tools are available which are of general use about the house and garden as well as the workshop, and which may prove to be a sound investment. If the purchase of a power tool is to be considered, it would be wise to obtain a model with a variable speed and for which a wide range of drill bits and attachments are available.

SUPPORT MATERIALS

In theory, almost any permanent material can be used as a support or base for mosaic, provided changes do not occur either in its physical nature or in its rigidity. In practice, the choice of support is governed by other factors. The location of the work must be considered carefully when making a choice, as a suitable base for indoor work may be unreliable out of doors. The actual setting technique which is to be used may play a large part in the decision, and consideration of the size and shape of the work, and the type of adhesive to be used, are also important.

Cement mortar is one of the most suitable support materials as it is weatherproof and cheap, although if the work is to be transported there is the disadvantage of weight to be considered. It is one of the oldest materials to have been used as a base for mosaic decoration. The precise date and place of origin of mortar are unknown, although the Middle East seems the most probable location. The word 'cement' is derived from the Latin verb *caedere*, to cut, and was used in reference to the aggregate, which consisted of stone cuttings, although in modern terms the word cement refers to the chemical binder.

Gypsum plaster was used in Egypt at a very early period in a somewhat impure form in common with many ancient materials; the place of origin of quicklime has not been established although slaked lime is known to have been used by the Greeks. Calcium carbonate, a fairly pure type of limestone, is burnt to a temperature of 900 °C., considerably in excess of the temperature required for burning gypsum, which is about 170 °C. Carbon dioxide is driven off, and by this action, limestone is converted to quicklime. In order to produce hydrated lime (calcium hydroxide), quicklime is slaked in water; during this process, expansion occurs and considerable heat is generated. When slaked lime was used for building purposes, sand was added to produce a more workable mortar. The old rule-of-thumb method for the production of slaked lime had a notable disadvantage: excess water was added to the lime and allowed to evaporate, leaving behind what is termed 'lime putty', but this procedure often failed to break down all the lumps which were present. These lumps had a tendency to slake after the application of the lime and the consequent expansion caused damage to the surface finish. High-calcium limes are known as 'fat', that is workable, limes, and 'fatness' improves when lime putty is allowed to age. They are classified as non-hydraulic because they will only harden when air is present. Magnesium limes are also non-hydraulic although of greater strength than high-calcium limes. They are obtained from limestone which contains magnesium oxide, in a quantity varying between fifteen and forty per cent, and are more difficult to slake than the high-calcium limes. Hydraulic lime is of a cementitious nature and will harden under water; it comes from impure limestone, which contains large quantities of silica and alumina and which, when calcined, forms a sufficient quantity of calcium silicates and aluminates to give the characteristic hydraulic properties. These limes harden by chemical reaction, but can present some difficulty, as excessive water used during the slaking causes an acceleration of the setting process.

Non-hydraulic or semi-hydraulic limes can be converted into hydraulic limes by the addition of suitable materials. The Romans originated hydraulic lime, prepared by mixing lime putty with volcanic ash, which gave the lime its hydraulic property. These limes are termed 'pozzolanas', a name derived from the town of Pozzuoli near Naples from which the volcanic ash was obtained. Pozzolanic materials contain silica, alumina and some iron oxide, and although they are not necessarily of a cementitious nature in themselves, will combine with non-hydraulic limes to produce a cement with hydraulic properties. Apart from the volcanic ash of Pozzuoli, other natural pozzolanas were found to be present in areas around Rome and Civita Vecchia. Trass, another additive, which is composed of fragments of pumice, originated in regions of the upper Rhine and Bavaria; another form called 'Santorin' or 'Santorin earth' came from the Greek island of Santorin in the Aegean (known to the ancient Greeks as Thera). A number of artificial pozzolanas have also been utilized including certain types of slag from blast furnaces, burnt pumicite, and burnt and crushed clay. The Romans successfully exploited hydraulic limes, including those made from artificial pozzolanas, which, because of their greater strength and waterproofing properties, made possible the developments associated with Roman building construction, especially vaults and marine structures such as baths, drains and aqueducts. The most common artificial pozzolana used by the Romans in Britain was produced by the addition of crushed burnt clay, although it is surprising that they failed to discover a natural source of hydraulic cement which was to be found in the form of the so-called 'cement stones'. These were nodules of argillaceous (clayey) limestone which were deposited along the coast of the Isle of Sheppey, Leigh, Southend, Harwich and a number of other places on the Thames estuary. A form of hydraulic cement made from cement stones was developed by a man named James Parker in 1796, and was known, oddly enough, as 'Roman cement', until well into the nineteenth century.

Portland cement

Today the most widely used product is a hydraulic cement known as 'Portland', a name derived from a product patented in 1824 by a man named Joseph Aspdin, a bricklayer of Leeds. The name Portland was adopted because of a fancied resemblance to Portland stone – a limestone which was quarried in Portland, England. The development of Portland cement could hardly be termed an invention, for others had been working on similar lines, notably a Frenchman, Vicat, and another Englishman named Frost. Aspdin's product was of great importance, in that he carried the calcination of the raw material to a much higher temperature than hitherto, although not sufficiently high to ensure complete reliability. The first person fully to appreciate the importance of high-temperature calcination was a man named Johnson (1811–1911) who understood that the purpose of calcination was to ensure the complete vitrification of the ingredients, and he produced the first truly reliable Portland. The raw material is ground to a considerable fineness which, in order to decompose the calcium carbide and recombine the calcium oxide, is subjected to a temperature of 1500 °C. This high calcination produces a partly fused clinker. The clinker then undergoes a grinding process, and this is one of the stages when special properties may be imparted to the product by the introduction of various agents. In fact, the name Portland is a generic term for a wide range of products, some of them with special qualities. For example, there is a rapid-hardening type, specially designed for use in very cold weather (although it has a setting time similar to that of ordinary Portland). Another type is designed to attain strength more rapidly during the early part of the hardening process. Other varieties include waterproof and water-repellent properties. A white Portland is available, but it is considerably more expensive than the ordinary grey variety.

The chemical reaction which causes cements of this type to hydrate is stimulated by the action of water, which continues until complete evaporation has taken place. The quantity of water to be added to the cement is critical; the qualities of strength and durability are related to the density of the mix, and density is related to low water content, which also reduces shrinkage. The addition of water in excess of the amount required to hydrate the mixture causes weakness, for the excessive water evaporates, leaving voids in the concrete mass. On the other hand, the addition of too little water, which produces an excessively stiff mix, can cause air to be trapped during the mixing process, and prevents the mass from becoming sufficiently compact. In general, drinking water is quite suitable for mixing concrete; even seawater can be used, provided the cement is not to be used in proximity to metal, and it should never be used with high-alumina cement because the salt has a corrosive effect on the alumina content.

Basic raw materials fall into four groups. Those which supply the alumina component comprise a group known as argillaceous; included in this group are clay, shale, slag, kaolin and aluminium-ore refuse. The iron component is obtained from a group of ferriferous materials which includes iron ore in the form of dust, pyrite, oxide and sinters, among others. The silica component is obtained from the siliceous group which includes sand, quartzite, Fuller's earth and calcium silicate, and the calcareous group supplies the lime component which includes cement rock, limestone, chalk, marble and marl.

The distinction between mortar and concrete is somewhat arbitrary. The term 'concrete' is applied to a mixture of cement, aggregate and water in a mass which may be formed or moulded and when properly made, it is strong and durable. Hardness is a term of some importance when applied to the setting process of concrete, and it is essential that it be thoroughly understood. Hardness in concrete has to do with the strength of the mix when it reaches maturity. The term 'setting' means that the mixture has stiffened sufficiently to enable a mould or form to be removed. This process can be governed to a certain extent by the addition of other components, as, for instance, retarders which may be based on starches, sugars, and zinc and boric oxides. In fact, gypsum is nearly always combined with Portland cement at the clinker-grinding stage in order to retard the set, which would otherwise be too rapid. Concrete must never be allowed to dry out completely until it has developed its full strength.

Modification of the properties of cement concrete by the addition of other components has certain dangers. The strength of the material may be considerably reduced, and it may become prone to shrinkage, which will cause the concrete to crack. Mineral powders such as chalk, kaolin and lime, ground very finely, may be added to increase the workability of the material, provided they are used in moderate quantities. The action of concrete may be accelerated by the addition of proprietary products, based on calcium chloride, which must be used in accordance with the manufacturer's instructions. These additives cause an increase in the temperature of concrete and are essential in excessively cold weather. As a general rule concrete must never be allowed to fall below a temperature of 10 °C. It ceases to develop strength below freezing point, and must at all times be protected from the effects of excessive cold and frost. If work must be carried out under these conditions, steps should be taken to protect the concrete. Artificial heat may be introduced, but wet concrete must never be artificially dried. Moulds, forms and aggregates should be kept as warm as possible, and the mixing water may be warmed, although not in excess of 82 °C., and it is advisable to cover the work with insulating material during the hardening process. Formed concrete should be protected during excessively hot weather. One of the simplest measures is to cover work with sand which should be sprayed with water for a period of at least seven days.

Aggregates

It would be something of a loss not to have some experience in the use of cement, although successful mosaics can be produced by other means. Today even cement has entered the realm of convenience packaging and small quantities of ready-mixed sand and cement may be readily obtained, although purchase of such material is more expensive in the long run. Packaged mixtures are subject to the same conditions of use as the regular material and cannot be stored for an unlimited period. Consequently, by avoiding the relatively simple operation of mixing carefully measured amounts of cement, aggregate and water, one is liable to incur more expense. Both the expensive white and the more commonly used grey Portland may be obtained in 94-lb. packs, and the packaging material is damp-resistant, which reduces the problem of storage. To obtain coloured cement, fast colour in powdered form is available, which should be thoroughly mixed with the dry cement powder.

The type of concrete to be used is governed by the purpose for which it is required. A variety of aggregates may be used, of which sand, gravel and crushed stone are the most common. All aggregate material must be clean and free from extraneous matter. Aggregates are obtainable for special-purpose concrete: some reduce the weight of the mass per cubic foot, and some increase it. Normal concrete weighs approximately 150 lb. per cu. ft. but it is possible to increase the weight to more than 250 lb. per cu. ft. by the introduction of heavy stone aggregates, or decrease it to as little as 30 lb. per cu. ft. A good rule by which to decide the size of an aggregate is that it should not exceed one-fifth of the narrowest dimension of the formed or moulded mass. If the aggregate is wet, less water should be used in the mix. A good average mix will be in the ratio of one 94-lb. bag of Portland cement to five imperial gallons (or six USA gallons) of water. It is possible to obtain ready-mixed concrete which may be delivered to the site, although only in such quantities as make it more suitable for industrial application.

Plaster of Paris, stucco, gesso

Plaster of Paris is widely known, and is in common use, being an indispensable material in sculpture or pottery. It is substantially the same as the gypsum plaster of the Egyptians, examples of which have endured for 4,000 years. The Greeks developed a variety known as 'stucco', which was of great refinement and of sufficient durability to be used externally. Plaster of Paris is made by calcinating gypsum rock at a suitable temperature in order to drive off seventy-five per cent of the chemically combined water, which forms a hemihydrate of calcium sulphate; if all the water is driven off, anhydrous calcium sulphate is formed. A number of proprietary brands have been developed, which are more workable owing to a number of additives, for example, Parian cement, made from calcinated gypsum which has been steeped in a solution of borax, dried, recalcinated and reground; and Keene cement, which is similar but with alum substituted for borax. Stucco, a slow-setting plaster of great fineness, is formed from a mixture of gypsum, washed sand and lime. It lends itself well to the technique of modelling, although it is more generally considered as a rendering material; indeed the word is thought to be derived from the

Old High German *stucchi*, which means 'crust'. The term is often used rather loosely to denote any form of rendering material, including Portland cement and sand.

The Greeks made extensive use of a form of stucco to which they added marble dust. This was frequently used to coat the external stonework of temples, usually limestone, which had been used when marble was not available. The Romans used lime stucco extensively to decorate architecture with great beauty and delicacy. The art was further developed by the Persians and Arabs after the decline of the Roman Empire, and gradually spread throughout the Near East, Turkey and North Africa. The craft reached Spain by the agency of the Moorish conquerors, and exquisite decoration in the medium, dated to the thirteenth and fourteenth centuries, is still to be seen in the Alhambra, the Moorish palace at Granada.

The craft of stucco-working was revived in Italy during the sixteenth century, and became extremely popular. Existing examples of ancient Roman stucco were carefully studied, although Roman enthusiasm for the work of their predecessors did not prevent them from obtaining marble, which was used as one of the ingredients of *stucco duro* (hard stucco) in a barbarous fashion by looting antique statues from the ruins.

> Take three parts of pounded Parian marble – easily got from among the ruins in Rome, and from broken statues
>
> Pirro Ligorio

Another form of stucco which is based on gypsum is gesso, composed of plaster of Paris and glue. It is of a marvellous whiteness and can be modelled in intricate relief; the word 'gesso' actually means gypsum. Another type of gesso made from plaster of Paris, glue and powdered resin can be modelled or moulded in sprig moulds. The material is mixed and formed into small slabs, which may be stored until required. The slabs may be softened by being immersed in warm water, then removed and worked with the hands after they have been 'floured' with plaster of Paris. A typical recipe consists of:

    1 part brick dust (brick ground to a very fine powder)
    1 part marble dust
    1 part lime putty (aged for several months)
    3 parts boiled linseed oil

All the ingredients are thoroughly mixed to a smooth, dough-like consistency and then flattened until a slab approximately 1 in. thick is formed, which may be cut into squares of a convenient size, and allowed to dry before being stored until required (the drying time will vary with the climate).

When stucco is required, some of the small squares are pulverized (with a rolling-pin) until a very fine powder is obtained to which is added a mixture of one part of raw to four parts of boiled linseed oil. The oil must be mixed into the powder with a small trowel until the mixture is smooth and fine-textured like putty. A mixture of four parts of resin to one part of beeswax which is incorporated with a suitable filler, such as plaster or whiting, was once used as a cement to fix the blades of knives into handles. Another type, based on whiting, linseed oil and gold-size, was, and is, used as a cement for stained glass, the mixture being brushed into the cavities between the glass and the lead *calmes* which hold the sections of glass together. It serves as a form of weatherproofing and gives sufficient rigidity to the glass panel without making it completely inflexible. Common putty is a mixture of whiting and linseed oil. Faraday's cement, which is used to fix brass to glass, is made from five parts of resin to one part of red ochre and one part of beeswax. Apart from their historical interest, many of these old recipes can be of use to the mosaicist. For instance, a number of them may be used as setting beds for small-scale work, and especially for miniature work, and areas of mosaic may be included in modelled stucco. The mosaicist with an urge to experiment could find this field of research very rewarding.

Wood

Provided it has been waterproofed, wood makes an ideal base for portable mosaics which are to be used indoors. Wood bases should never be used out of doors or in a damp situation indoors, however efficient the waterproofing. Products of a porous nature should be avoided; plywood and composition boards are very suitable. Plywood is assembled from layers of wood which have been 'peeled' from logs. The layers are not necessarily of equal thickness, or even of equal strength. Each layer is crossed so that the grain of one lies at right angles to those immediately above and below, and in consequence, plywood is potentially stronger than natural wood, provided it is satisfactorily bonded. The material is graded, but only in reference to the surface finish, and different indications are used. For interior use the bonding material is casein, soya or animal glue, or, if synthetic glues are used, they are extended with other glues which have a limited resistance to damp conditions. Plywood which is considered suitable for exterior use is bonded with synthetic resins, not all of which have the same degree of water resistance. All products described as marine ply must be composed of wood which has an inherent resistance to water, or which is capable of being treated to make it so.

Plywood can be obtained in a wide range of sizes, with a maximum of 10 ft. × 5 ft. and a thickness range of between 3 and 25 mm. One should remember that thickness is not classified according to the number of plies (that is, layers) and that the greater the number of plies the more expensive the product. A number of decorative finishes can be applied to the surface of plywood, including decorative wood veneers, and etched and moulded surfaces. These can be useful if sections of the base of a mosaic are required to be exposed in order to form part of the composition. Another useful product is plywood with tongue-and-grooved edges, which is of great benefit if a panel is to be made in regular sections.

Various types of laminated board make satisfactory bases, provided they are of suitable thickness, are non-porous, and do not warp. Good grades of blockboard make excellent base material, although, like plywood, blockboard must never be used outside, or in a damp position inside. It has the advantage of being readily obtainable in a wide range of size and thickness, and is sufficiently rigid to make it suitable (although rather heavy) for fairly large panels. If the edges of the panels are to remain in view, they should be filled or framed, as the laminate is exposed on cut edges. 'Laminboard' is a similar product, but is of superior quality and more expensive than blockboard. Particle boards are useful and cheaper than blockboard, although heavier, and in the larger sizes much less rigid. These boards are made from wood or flax particles, and are bonded with synthetic resin. Unlike blockboard, the surface of this type of board is rather rough. This is not necessarily a disadvantage when mosaic is to be applied with adhesive, as the irregularity of the surface forms a 'key' between the board and the bonding agent. Particle board may be obtained with wood- or plastic-veneered surfaces which give added strength.

Standard hardboard, which is made from wood fibre, has a smooth face but is textured on the reverse, and can be obtained in a variety of finishes. It can be used for panels of less than 1 ft. square, although if larger sizes are required, the material must be battened, for it is extremely flexible. Tempered hardboard has superior qualities of strength and resistance to water, but it is more expensive than the standard type. Other types of composition board are available, including products which are manufactured from cement, asbestos and a variety of pulped material, but only rigid, non-porous types are suitable for use with tesserae or other heavy materials. These products are available in standard sizes and, for a small charge, most stockists will supply material cut to specification, and usually have available offcuts and reject material at reduced prices.

ADHESIVES

All materials used for bases, other than concrete, require some means of securing the mosaic material to them in permanent bond. Natural adhesives have been in use since ancient times but today a wide range of manufactured materials is available. These include products with special qualities such as fast bonding and weather resistance which, if correctly used, are extremely durable.

When selecting bonding agents, choice should be governed by the type of base and mosaic material which are to be used. Another important consideration is whether the work is to be functional or non-functional, as certain restrictions may apply. The setting process of bonding agents can take place in a number of ways: through loss of moisture by cooling; through loss of moisture or solvent by evaporation, or by absorption; and certain adhesives harden by chemical reaction. Most products have what is known as a 'shelf life', that is, the length of time for which they may be stored without deterioration, and within the specified period must be included time which has elapsed before the material was purchased. 'Pot life' refers to the period of time in which a material may be used after it has been prepared according to the manufacturer's instructions. The length of time during which a material remains workable has a bearing on the amount of work that can be done with it.

Natural adhesives include animal glues, starch, casein and bituminous glues. Animal glues which are made from the skins, bones and hides of animals are less frequently employed today, although starch glues and solutions of gum arabic and gum tragacanth are used in various craft fields. Bituminous adhesives, based on bitumen and coal-tar, include varieties which are suitable for use with mosaic, although they are more widely used for bonding floor tiles. Casein-based glues, known as 'white glues', are based on a powder made from soured milk curds, and are satisfactory only with fairly small mosaic units. They are totally unsuitable for exterior locations, and even when used indoors, must never be exposed to damp conditions such as those which occur in bathroom and kitchen.

4 Glass and its applications

Where and in what manner the craft of glass-making originated can only be conjectured. Pliny the Elder (AD 23–79) relates in his *Historia Naturalis* that crude glass was discovered by shipwrecked Phoenician sailors who noted the presence of nuggets (smalti) in the dead embers of a fire which they had lit upon the shore. According to Pliny the site of this discovery was the shore of the sacred river Belus, and Tacitus (*c.* AD 55–120) writes: 'the sacred river Belus, though it has a beach of only five hundred paces, has always been an inexhaustible mine for glass workers; between Ptolemais and Tyre the beach is covered with particles of sand from which they make white glass'. Pliny rarely discriminated between the true and the false; however, the discovery may well have occurred in the manner to which he refers as it amounts to little more than an observation of the action of heat on silica. Similarly it is probably true that Syria was the country in which the industry was developed, as the earliest known examples of glassware originated there. The rather sudden appearance of a well-developed glass technology in Egypt has been accounted for by the possibility that skilled Syrian craftsmen were included among the spoils of war.

Before the time of the Roman conquests, glass from the ancient world could more properly be described as vitreous paste and transparent glass was exceptional. This paste may have originated from the accidental vitrification of pottery which in some way became mixed with metallic oxides, probably in ancient copper foundries. Glass, probably of Egyptian manufacture, has been discovered in Abu Ghalib and ascribed to a date prior to 2000 BC. Glass technology in ancient Egypt seems to have been primarily concerned with the exploitation of colour rather than the development of transparency. The immense attraction which coloured glass held for ancient peoples may have been due to their regard for precious stones. Gems were considered to be the emanation of benign influence. It was believed that their cordial nature awakened a similar response in the beholder, and that they connoted celestial qualities, probably because of their radiance and indestructibility. In consequence, the earliest use of glass seems to have been confined to the imitation or simulation of gem stones. Judging from examples taken from various sites, ancient colour technology appears to have been reasonably efficient. For instance a quantity of opaque glass from Tell el Amarna exhibits a considerable range of colour including light and dark green, light and dark blue, a vivid violet, black, and brilliant red and yellow.

Inevitably, the production of glassware with a greater degree of transparency became possible although there would seem to have been a transitional period during which glassware was translucent. The small free-standing objects of Egyptian and Mesopotamian origin, which have been given an approximate date of 2500 BC, are more of the nature of 'frit' than true glass. Although these objects have been exposed to the action of the fire, it is obvious that the temperature was insufficient for complete vitrification to take place although true glass, that is, glass which has been fully vitrified, has been discovered in the form of blue and green beads with a probable date of 2200 BC.

The history of glass technology is a classic example of the type of technical evolution which does not show a regular progression. Often the most brilliant technical innovation was followed by what appeared to be a static period, although upon examination it may be found that a process of consolidation had taken place. In consequence, the extension of the acquired experience often resulted in a further period of innovation. Occasionally periods of regression occurred, sometimes due to events of a calamitous nature or to radical philosophical changes, as for example iconoclasm. Conversely technological development, inspired by the incidence of an all-pervading ideology, can occur, as for instance the acceptance of a theory of 'grace through works' as an aspect of Christian ethics.

Generally most ancient techniques included two major phases not necessarily isolated one from the other nor necessarily in sequence; in fact they were sometimes interrelated. The first phase can usually be seen as a form of 'palace art', the work being of a high standard – the product of skilled craftsmen. During such periods luxury articles were in short supply, a fact which tended to increase their desirability. Naturally the output from such a limited field was reserved for royal or religious use. The second phase is usually instituted by the intrusion of certain pressures, often economic ones, into the old supply and demand system. For example, a shift in the distribution of wealth can force demand to outstrip supply, thus radically altering the balance of the situation. Impetus may also be given to technical development by sudden alteration in the availability of raw materials, which may happen as a result of disagreement between trading nations. Consequently the continuance and development of a craft depends not only on the availability of skilled craftsmen but also on their adaptability.

The progress of glass manufacture is typical of the progression from qualitative to quantitative design which can be detected in most ancient crafts. Glass and glazes are identical in their chemical components, therefore it is true to say that glass in the form of glaze was in use as early as 4000 BC. In essence it also occurred in the form of faience – a composition of quartz which was kneaded and then baked. Green glass vessels cut from solid glass slabs have been found in Mesopotamia and are most probably representative of an established tradition. An example of this type bears a cartouche of King Sargon (722–705 BC). However, from the sixth century BC glass appears in greater quantity in Greece and the islands of the Aegean, in Italy and Sicily, and during the Ptolemaic period in Egypt.

A number of glass-finishing processes were developed in the ancient world, for instance a process known as fire-finishing which necessitated the return of the article to the furnace. Another method bearing a resemblance to lathe-turning was employed, the glass being turned against abrasive material which remained in a stationary position. Alternatively, a rotary polish was applied by the use of a spinning wheel which was fed with abrasives, the glassware remaining stationary. The development of glass-blowing may be accredited to the Syrians and no doubt the rewards of an expanding market induced Syrian craftsmen to establish themselves in Rome, which thereafter became the centre of a thriving industry in the West.

The regions of northern Gaul and the valleys of the Rhône and Rhine were the major glass-producing areas of the Roman Empire. England, in common with other provinces of Rome, certainly produced glassware, although the bulk of the raw material would be imported from one or two central areas of manufacture. The glass would be distributed in the form of lumps (*massae*); consequently the chemical composition of the material would remain fairly constant, the provincial craftsmen being concerned only with the processes of remelting the raw material, colouring and reworking. In spite of the dissolution of the Roman Empire the glass industry did not undergo a complete recession, although there was a considerable decline both in quality and in production. Ultimately glass-making in the northern provinces was restricted to a few isolated workshops producing objects of inferior quality and restricted design.

During the initial stages of glass technology the major problems were concerned with the establishment of fool-proof methods of procedure, by which clear glass could be produced. The opacity of early glass was due to the inadequacy of technical resources, for instance the inability to attain a furnace temperature in excess of $1100 °C$. At such a comparatively low temperature it would be impossible to expel the bubbles of gas which would form in the molten mass. The inability to control the rate of cooling posed another problem. When cooling can be fully controlled a slowing down of the process enables the mixture to become more viscous, and depending on the purity of the chemical composition, it will remain clear after hardening. On the other hand rapid cooling induces a process known as devitrification during which the silica content crystallizes and the mixture remains opaque.

Once the difficulties were resolved, the methods of manufacture changed very little until the middle of the nineteenth century. Two basic processes are involved in glass-making: the calcination (or fritting) of the raw material in a furnace which induces the initial stages of fusion and eliminates some of the gases, and the vitrification of the frit. There is no established melting point for glass in general terms. Soda glass achieves viscosity at the comparatively low temperature of 1100 °C., although the temperatures achieved in ancient glass foundries would inevitably be much lower than those attained today. The simplest and oldest method of manufacture consisted of a fusion of an acidic silica with two basic oxides such as sodium or potassium, and an oxide of calcium, barium, lead or zinc, heated in a furnace fuelled by wood. In his report on the finds at Tell el Amarna Sir Flinders Petrie drew attention to the fact that the Egyptians manufactured glass which was sufficiently free from impurities to accept coloration. He noted that the composition of the glass did not include lead or borates, but consisted of pure silica, obtained from crushed quartz pebbles, combined with an alkali (probably wood-ash). It seems probable that colour was obtained by the inclusion of partly fired frit. The mixture, including the frit, would be fused in earthenware pans. After the mixture had cooled the earthenware would be laboriously chipped away from the glass and the frothy top of the glass chipped away likewise. The earthenware pans were approximately $4\frac{1}{2}$ in. in diameter and the glass would be poured to a depth of $\frac{1}{2}$ in. to 1 in.

Development of colour

The Romans employed a method of casting glass which enabled them to produce sheets suitable for glazing window openings, the largest so far discovered being a sheet measuring 112 cm. × 81 cm., from the baths at Pompeii. Between the first and second centuries A D cast glass was rather impure, with a pronounced discoloration, bluish, greenish or brownish. A much improved variety was manufactured between the third and fourth centuries, the glass being of a greenish hue much nearer the type which is manufactured today. A typical chemical composition consisted of 69 parts of silica, 17 parts of soda, 11 parts of lime and magnesia and 3 parts of alumina, iron oxide and manganese oxide.

The quality of sand which was used in the manufacturing process had a crucial effect on the colour of the finished product. The clear colourless glass of Alexandrian manufacture was the product of a fine, pure silver sand completely lacking in iron content. The addition of manganese dioxide oxidized the iron content and helped to neutralize the colour. Conversely, the deliberate addition of metallic oxides in small controlled quantities enabled coloration to be effected. Blue was obtained by the addition of cupric oxide, an increased percentage of the additive producing a deeper blue. Bottle green was obtained from ferrous iron, clear amber from ferric iron; manganese oxide was the colouring agent for glass of purple amethyst colour; a brilliant sealing-wax red was achieved by a suspension of cuprous oxide, and white by a suspension of tin oxide. Antimony compound was used to produce opaque yellow, and black was obtained by the addition of a fairly large percentage of iron, or a mixture of copper and manganese.

The colour technology of the ancient world was the basis for the wide colour range of glass mosaic. The excavation of the site of Hagia Sophia at Kiev, founded in AD 1037 by Prince Yaroslav, has produced evidence of a colour range of at least 170 tints. Included was a green range of thirty-four tints and a red range of nineteen. The Christianity of Kievan Rus was of Byzantine inspiration, the religion being adopted after the marriage of Prince Vladimir to the sister of the Byzantine Emperor Basil II. Not unnaturally, the new religion drew upon the resources of Byzantium for its image-making, including the craftsmen, techniques, forms and materials, at least until such a time as local labour could be trained. Similarly Muslim art was exposed to the influence of late classical culture by the transfer of the capital from Medina to Damascus. In the minute examination made of the Dome of the Rock (the Qubbat as-Sakhra of the Umayyads) by Marguerite Gautier-van Berchem between 1927 and 1928 (see p. 37), she notes a considerable range of colour, including eight shades of green and six shades of blue, brick-red, reddish-violet, brown and black. Gold and silver smalti were present and cubes of rose, yellow and white stone were noted, the latter being somewhat smaller than the glass cubes. A similar investigation into the colour range of the tesserae which had been used in the decoration of the Great Mosque of Damascus revealed a range of thirteen shades of green and nine shades of blue, brick-red, brown, red and black. Grey-white and rose cubes of stone were included as well as a range of gold and silver. Silver leaf was used on bases of brown, green-tinted and colourless glass, and gold leaf on dark brown, light green, light brown and colourless glass.

Making glass

Different forms of manufacture have been evolved to produce four basic types of glass: slab, 'muff' or cylinder, crown and plate. To produce *slab glass* a hollow metal rod with a flared end, known as a blowing iron, is inserted into a crucible of molten glass, referred to as 'metal', and the glass is 'gathered'. When a sufficient quantity of molten 'metal' has been gathered it is inserted into a square or rectangular wooden mould. Blowing is continued until the glass takes the form of the mould. When cool the four sides of the glass bottle are cut along the corner edges to give four panes of glass and a bottom, the latter being less expensive. After separation the sheets are transferred to an annealing oven, reheated and then allowed to cool very slowly, so softening the edges. Before the invention of the cutting wheel, glass of this type would be cut by tracing a line with a hot iron rod and then wetting or spitting on the glass.

The manufacture of *muff*, or cylinder glass, has changed very little over the years. The blowing iron is dipped into the molten 'metal' and the 'gather' blown into a pear-shaped bulb. More glass is gathered and regathered by dipping the iron into the molten glass until sufficient material is acquired to produce a sheet of the desired size. The glass is blown and shaped by wooden tools and then manipulated and flattened on a smooth block of stone, referred to as a 'marver'. The bulb is reheated and blown, swung and rotated on the end of the blowing iron until a large cylindrical bulb is formed. Both the base and the top of the bulb are removed, leaving an open-ended cylinder or muff. In order to transform the muff into a sheet of glass it must be softened in an annealing chamber. The muff is cut lengthwise and placed on its side with the cut side uppermost, heated very slowly and allowed to flatten under its own weight, aided by a smoothing block; it is then allowed to cool very slowly to prevent the sheet from becoming too brittle.

Crown glass is blown from a gathering of 'metal' of sufficient size, the bulb being rotated during the operation. After being worked and flattened on the marver the bulb is reheated and a solid metal rod known as a 'punty' is attached to the opposite end and the blowing iron is detached. The bulb, now held on the punty, is alternately heated and rapidly rotated with sufficient velocity to enlarge the hole left by the removal of the blowing iron. When a disk of the required size has been produced, the punty is removed, leaving the characteristic thick centre known as the 'bullion' or 'bull's eye', the remainder of the disk being of a more or less uniform thickness. Sheets are obtained by cutting the flat areas of glass away from the bullion, although they are rarely in excess of 18 in. square.

Cast plate was introduced into England in the late seventeenth century. It was manufactured by pouring molten glass on to a heavy table and spreading it evenly by means of a moving roller running on metal bearers. By this method was produced sheet glass of a more even thickness than hitherto and of greater size. The modern method of production is to pass a broad ribbon of molten glass through water-cooled rollers, rapidly chilling the material, which is then passed slowly through an annealing oven, known as a 'lehr'.

The second book of the treatise *De Diversis Artibus* by the monk Theophilus is devoted to glass-working, how to make sheet glass, the coloration of glass, kiln construction, cutting, painting and installing coloured glass windows. Of particular interest to the mosaicist are the sections on 'The Various

Colours of Opaque glass' and 'The Greek Glass Which Decorates Mosaic Work', the latter being concerned with the manufacture of 'metallic' smalti. He writes: 'In the ancient buildings of the pagans, various kinds of glass are found in the mosaic work – white, black, green, yellow, blue, red, and purple. They are not transparent but opaque like marble, and are like little square stones.' He makes particular reference to sheets of clear white glass being used as a backing for gold smalti. He describes how sheets of clear white glass are made to 'the thickness of a finger' and cut into squares. He goes on to say: 'They cover them on one side with gold leaf, coating it with very clear glass ground as above' (a reference to a previous chapter of his book). He also describes the method of firing the cubes on an iron tray from which the glass is protected by a layer of lime or ashes. The relevance of the work lies not only in the fact that so many of the techniques he describes are carried out in exactly the same way today, but also because of his concern with all the processes involved in a particular craft.

The properties of glass

Glass has some unique qualities which contribute to the effect of 'glassiness' – a word which has passed into the language and is frequently used metaphorically. Among its properties are a number of utilitarian factors, for instance its durability (under reasonable conditions), ease of maintenance and cleanliness. The structure of glass is unusual; it is a solid, but when examined microscopically it does not reveal a crystalline structure. By the definition of the American Society for Testing Materials, glass is recognized as a product of inorganic origin. Plastics or high-polymer organic substances – for example polystyrene – though possessing uniformity of properties and transparency, which are characteristics of glass, cannot be so described.

The colour of glass is integral and, as already explained, can be achieved by the addition of dissolved material or by the introduction of crystalline or non-crystalline substances in suspension. Responsiveness to light, shade and reflection are unique features, and a number of other physical properties can be induced, such as resistance to heat as well as heat transmission. Optical properties and a number of other features can be embodied in glass by the introduction of a number of chemical elements. For instance, the density of glass can be varied, as can its thermal expansion and electrical resistance. Another distinct advantage is that, being compact and without texture, glass can be exposed to a considerable variety of surface treatments. Indeed, the process of glass-making is unique by virtue of the fact that it is concerned with both the production of the material and its direct conversion into the finished article.

Glass is liable to deteriorate when exposed to the corrosive action of the atmosphere and, broadly speaking, its chemical

Fragment of fourteenth-century stained-glass window in Marsh Baldon Church, Oxfordshire, showing its pitted surface.

durability is controlled by the alkaline content of its composition. The greater the amount of alkali the poorer the durability of the product. A noticeable feature of severe atmospheric attack is a loss of transparency and, once started, little can be done to reverse the process. Glass appears to be impermeable but even unpolluted water can exert a solvent action, and once corrosion has begun, deterioration can take place rapidly. The underlying cause is the decomposition of the soluble silicate in the surface layer of the glass; acids are thereby liberated, more water is absorbed into the the surface film, and the corrosive action progresses. The dissolution of the soluble salts has the effect of roughening the exposed surface of the glass, resulting in a substantial loss of transparency. Surface deterioration is often revealed when ancient stained glass and painted windows are closely examined. Many of them, owing to the inaccessibility of their location, have rarely been cleaned and as a result have become extremely fragile with a tendency to craze. A similar effect may be noticed on old glass vessels, which often appear opalescent owing to the roughness of the surface; hence the care which must be exercised if ancient glass and glass mosaics are to be preserved. Alkaline solutions attack glass readily, and even soap can have a deleterious effect on ancient pieces. If the attack has proceeded beyond the

siliceous surface of the glass, a further danger threatens:
fungus growth may develop in the pitted and engrained
surface.

SMALTI

Vitreous glass smalti, inseparable from the concept of
Byzantine mosaic, are still manufactured in Italy today. The
advantages of smalti have been examined in previous
chapters and remain relevant to the needs of the contemporary craftsman. The virtual indestructibility of the
material, under normal conditions, and the extensive colour
range, coupled with the intrinsic beauty of the opaque
glass from which the smalti are made, combine to produce
a material unlike any other. The only disadvantages are
economic ones – the initial expense of the material and the
high cost of labour for work to be carried out in smalti by
skilled mosaicists. These factors help to explain the lack of
patronage for the execution of large-scale works in this
beautiful material. The Church, for so long the major
patron of the craft, is today financially less able to commission major works in what is virtually a luxury material,
and the same difficulty is apparent in the secular field.
Consequently, many works commissioned for churches,
and public or private buildings, are executed in alternative
materials and frequently much larger mosaic units are used
in order to cut down the setting time and the consequent
high cost of labour. In spite of this the mosaicist would be
well rewarded if he were to stock even quite small quantities
of smalti in as wide a colour range as possible. Even small
areas executed in this lovely material can enrich and enliven
the whole.

The centre for the manufacture of smalti, known to the
trade as 'Byzantine' or 'Venetian' smalti, is the island of
Murano in the Venetian Lagoon. The island has been the
major centre for the manufacture of 'Venetian' glass for
centuries and is now almost completely given over to the
trade, many of the factories being housed in decaying
patrician villas. The precise method of manufacture, especially in relation to the colour chemistry, is a jealously
guarded secret. To the basic components – silica and an
alkaline substance such as soda-lime or potash-lead – must
be added oxide of tin for opacity, which is a vital factor if
the colour is to maintain its value when set in mortar. The
colouring agents both for smalti and stained glass manufactured today are the same metal oxides whose properties
have been known for centuries. A full range consists of more
than five thousand shades, infinitely greater than that available to the early craftsmen. (Apart from the manufacturers,
one of the few workshops to hold anything approaching a
full range is the Vatican workshop in Rome.) The following
list is included for general reference, and relates only to
oxides which are in common use.

COLOUR	COLOURING AGENT
Yellow	iron oxide, uranium oxide, titanium oxide, antimoniate of lead
Blue	cobalt oxide
Green	copper oxide, chromium oxide, copper carbonate
Red	gold chloride, selenium dioxide, cadmium sulphide

The process during which the alkaline and the metal oxides are melted down with the silica relies on a series of critical temperatures which are timed according to the precise colour requirement. Many manufacturers advise the purchase of smalti from one batch if identical colour is required for a particular job, but generally the very slight colour variation is desirable. During the cooling process, temperature control is again crucial. The viscous material obtained from melting together the various ingredients is known as 'pot-metal', in which the colour pervades the whole; this material is gathered and dropped into a shallow metal mould and then pressed flat by means of a metal press. After being carefully annealed – that is, toughened by gradually diminishing the heat – the slab is removed from the mould and cut into tesserae by means of a metal chopper. Anyone lucky enough to obtain a slab of smalti may of course cut it in the ancient manner by means of a mosaic hammer and a hardie.

The fractured surface, as opposed to the pressed surface, is the true source of the unique qualities of colour and reflection obtained by the use of smalti, and is usually exposed in the finished work. Gold smalti, the use of which can never be dissociated from the masterpieces of the Byzantine era, are manufactured in a slightly different manner. The rich, glittering effect of metallic smalti is not obtained by the use of colouring agents introduced into the molten mixture, nor are the fractured sides exposed in setting. Metal leaf, gold, silver, aluminium or copper, beaten to an incredible thinness, is applied to the already manufactured 'flat', which is the shallow saucer-like disk of glass made in the mould. Batches of flats are produced ready for the application of metallic leaf, which is applied by hand. The flats are warmed to facilitate the adhesion of the leaf, after which another layer of glass is poured over the leaf and pressed flat, so sandwiching the leaf between two layers of glass, a thin surface layer and a thick backing layer. In this manner the metal is protected from the atmosphere and the consequent danger of oxidation.

Metallic smalti are available in various shades of gold, variety still being achieved by the use of different-coloured glass for the backing layer as in ancient times; more rarely the facing layer is coloured. Typical backing colours are turquoise, red, pale green and amber, as well as clear glass. Silver smalti are useful but lack the rich lustre of the gold and are more prone to discoloration. Apart from the regular size of $\frac{3}{8}$ in. square, metallic smalti are supplied $\frac{7}{8}$ in. square; they are more expensive than the coloured variety but fortunately all types can be bought in fairly small quantities from the importers. The professional working with this material would probably require a range of several hundred shades, but the serious amateur should also stock as wide a range as possible in order to introduce them into his work for special effects. All smalti are sold by weight and approximately 3 lb. are required to cover an area of 1 sq. ft. if used whole ('approximately', because the width between the tesserae can be varied). This is done to produce variety of texture and to provide contrast, although each individual has a natural setting style as personal to him as his handwriting and invariably several people setting a test area of 1 sq. ft. will use different quantities. This is one of the problems inherent in the employment of assistants for large-scale work, and unless they can be regularly supervised the different hands will show up in a startling manner. If smalti are chipped into smaller units or special shapes, more will be required to the square foot as a certain amount of waste is unavoidable, although all fragments large enough to be sorted should be stored for later use.

Prices per pound vary according to the colour range and the colours are grouped under various headings as follows:

GROUP	COLOUR RANGE
Metals	gold, silver, copper, etc.
Imperials	reds, oranges, yellows
Fines	pure white, blues and greens
Flesh	a full range from very light to very dark
Ordinaries	off-whites, black, greys, browns, certain greens and blues, ochre yellow

Price lists may be obtained from the importers and often actual colour samples will be sent on payment of a nominal sum. It is possible to obtain the material direct from the manufacturers in Italy but only in fairly large quantities, and with the attendant difficulties and formalities of importation.

FILATI

Another type of mosaic manufactured in Italy is the 'filato', meaning thread. These filati are used for the manufacture of miniature mosaics and jewelry and are also used in the technique known as 'millefiori', often seen in glass paperweights. Filati are rods of coloured glass and very passable examples may be produced at home or in the studio. It is a simple but

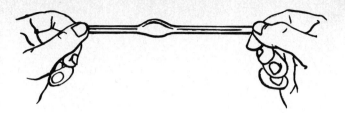

Making filati.

interesting process and the great advantage of home or studio manufacture is the fact that odds and ends of glass and smalti can be utilized.

For home use a small liquid-gas burner is available which will melt small quantities of glass, and for large-scale use in the studio a small welding torch using a combination of gas and oxygen is ideal. The welding torch will of course enable the operative to work faster, and the use of oxygen reduces the risk of a colour change in the glass. Also required are tweezers, duckbill pliers, a wheel glass-cutter and an asbestos pad. The asbestos pad is useful as it does not conduct heat from the hot glass pieces which will be placed on it during the course of the work, so reducing the risk of the glass fracturing. It also protects the working top.

The burner is mounted on the bench with the flame pointing away from the operative. If scrap glass is to be used the strips are cut about $\frac{1}{2}$ in. wide by 4 to 6 in. long. Glass is not a good conductor of heat so the strip can be held in the fingers reasonably close to the flame without the risk of burning. A piece of glass $\frac{1}{2}$ in. long should be cut from the prepared strip and two lengths of soda-glass rod 3 to 6 mm. in diameter should be to hand. This can be bought from a chemical and scientific equipment supplier. One end of the rod should be warmed in the flame while the small piece of coloured glass, held in the other hand, is warmed on one corner. When hot enough the two pieces may be joined together and the process repeated with the other rod so that the small glass square is held between the rods. Secured in this manner the glass square is thoroughly warmed, the cut edges being given attention first. When the coloured glass becomes molten the rods are rotated in order to produce a molten ball of glass. Care must be taken not to cause folds in the glass as air may be trapped, causing bubbles to form. When the glass is rounded and molten it is withdrawn from the flame. The glass rods are pulled gently apart and the molten glass stretched into a rod of the desired thickness. It is important to understand during this process, that when glass is very hot it draws thin and as it cools it draws thick. When completed, the soda-glass rods are severed from the freshly made piece by placing each joint in turn into the flame and drawing it until it is sufficiently thin to snap away.

Various shapes can be made in a similar fashion, the most useful for the mosaicist being leaf or petal shapes and small disks (flats). To make these shapes the glass is first cut into strips of the same size as before (see above). The glass is warmed at the extreme end of the flame then gradually brought to the hottest part, the cut edges being presented first. When the cut edges are molten the glass is rotated until a small ball forms at the ends of the strip. This molten ball is first held to the flame while the tweezers or pliers are warmed, then pressed between the jaws of the pliers, which are pulled slightly to cause restriction. Next the shaped glass, including the restricted part, is warmed and then held by the extreme tip in the pliers. The flame should be allowed to cut through the restricted area and the shaped piece may be pulled away. Metal conducts heat very rapidly so the completed piece should be placed on the asbestos pad as quickly as possible to avoid the risk of shattering.

VITREOUS GLASS

A modern form of vitreous glass mosaic is now available and it has the advantage of cheapness although it cannot compare with smalti for colour, quality or range. These mosaics are manufactured in various shapes although the standard size is approximately $\frac{1}{8}$ in. thick by $\frac{7}{8}$ in. square, other shapes and sizes being supplied to special order. They are now manufactured in several countries although those from Italy and Sweden are among the best. Perhaps a more accurate description of this material would be 'vitreous glass tiles', as they are quite shallow. They are formed by pouring the molten vitreous mixture into grid-like metal moulds which are then pressed. After the slabs are removed from the mould the individual squares, which are marked off by the heavy indentations made by the grid-like mould, are separated by hand. Occasionally a batch of these tiles contains clusters which have not been broken away and it is interesting to see how easily they are separated. The tiles are bevelled, and usually raised lines (straight or criss-crossed) are to be seen on the back. They are obtained, like the bevel, from the mould and the purpose of both the bevel and the raised pattern is to facilitate adhesion as they are so much shallower than smalti. The surface is matt and somewhat granular in appearance, and the lustre and reflective qualities of smalti are absent though some colours, notably reds, oranges, yellows, black and white and one or two others can be supplied with a smooth, shiny finish.

A small range of semi-transparent tiles enlivened with gold flecks is also available; if used with discretion they can be attractive, especially the blues, browns and greens. Compared with smalti the colour range of vitreous tiles is limited, but they can be cut into smaller units quite easily and are comparatively cheap. They are ideal where functional surfaces are required, in kitchens, bathrooms, swimming baths and pools, even table-tops – indeed, anywhere requiring a smooth, impervious surface which is easily maintained.

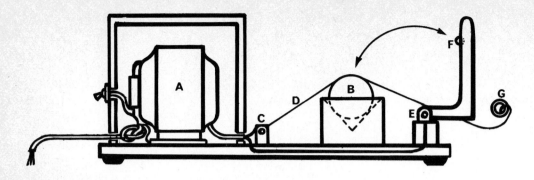

Slices from bottles make useful material for mosaic. The diagram above shows a home-made bottle slicer in which the bottle, previously scored with the glass-cutter, shown in detail opposite, is revolved by hand under an electrically heated wire which acts somewhat after the manner of a grocer's cheese-cutter. A transformer; B base of bottle; C, E brass rails (see opposite); D heated nichrome wire; F scorer; G plastic handle for wire.

These vitreous tiles can also be bought ready-mounted, in plain colours, in panels 1 ft. square. They are pasted on to brown paper or butter-muslin, and are mounted in reverse ready for setting by the reverse method. They are ideal for cladding as they can be applied to a curved surface, which facilitates their use commercially. Alternatively, metal setting trays can be bought, accommodating sufficient tiles to make up 1 sq. ft. Each tile is laid face upwards in a section of the grid-like tray; when the tray is full, a sheet of brown paper of the same area as the tray is pasted over the face of the tiles. A liquid solution of gum arabic in water is suitable for this purpose as it is essential that the gummed paper be easily removed after the panel has been set by this reverse method. It is possible to buy sheets of brown paper measuring 1 ft. square and already gummed, which is convenient if a large area is to be pasted up. When completely dry the small 'parcel' may be lifted out of the tray and stacked until required for use. If pattern is required it can only be rectangular or square, but if the colour range is carefully exploited these panels can be very attractive. As with smalti, prices vary according to the colour range, reds, oranges and yellows being the most expensive. Approximately $1\frac{1}{2}$–2 lb. will be required per square foot. There are price reductions for quantities and some firms offer attractive lots of mixed or misshapen tiles at very low prices. It is well worth the trouble to seek out firms which offer material of this type as the purpose of the mosaicist is often better served by imperfections of colour and shape.

SCRAP GLASS

At the other end of the scale, splendid mosaic material can be obtained from scrap glass, although generally it must be processed in some way to make it usable. Filati have already been described (see pp. 73–5) and details are given here for the assembly of a home-made 'bottle-slicer' which can be run off a domestic electricity supply and is absolutely safe to use. Slices from bottles can be used as mosaic material exactly as they are, or they be given further treatment in a gas or electric kiln; free access to such a kiln greatly facilitates the production of mosaic material from scrap glass. Slices from

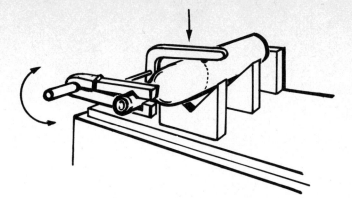

bottles can be softened in a kiln until they assume random shapes or they can be suspended from fireclay rods and allowed to sag. Small fragments of glass can be melted until they assume the appearance of tiny jewels, conveniently flat on the reverse side from contact with the firing bed. Before such material can be produced, however, it is necessary to introduce some system into the workshop. Broken glass fragments should be roughly sorted into size, colour and type and stored in boxes. When fragments are too large it is possible to reduce their size simply by placing the pieces on a thick pad of newspaper on a concrete slab, covering them with another thick pad of newspaper and tapping them firmly with a hammer. As this is literally a hit-or-miss method the ultimate size of the pieces cannot be controlled. The eyes must be protected, and great care must be exercised when gathering up the pieces, as fragments can become embedded in the newspaper and cause cuts.

Cutting glass

It is well worth the trouble to cut the glass – quite a simple process when the basic principles are understood. First, glass is weakened, not cut; the purpose of the incision which is made on the surface of the glass with the cutting wheel is to weaken the glass and establish a line of fracture. When the glass is firmly tapped on the reverse side beneath the scored line a fracture will occur along the whole length of the mark made by the glass-cutter. The reverse end of the cutter is generally used for the purpose of tapping the glass on the underside. It is absolutely essential that a single incision be made along the whole of the line which is to be fractured. A series of halting cuts, even if they appear to form a single incision, will cause the glass to fracture in various directions, producing a jagged cut instead of a clean break. Similarly one must never attempt to rescore a mark already made by the cutter, as recutting along the same path will have the same jagged result. If the cutter does not mark clearly, either the wheel is blunt or the glass is greasy. It is always wise to wash the glass in pure Teepol or a commercial washing-up liquid before use, as grease, which is difficult to detect, can be troublesome. A margin of at least $\frac{1}{2}$ in. must be allowed round any shape which is to be cut from a sheet of glass; it is

(*Above*) Melted glass.

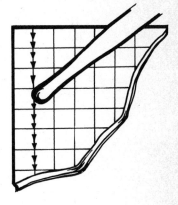

(*Below*) Cutting glass squares by tapping along scored line with metal handle of wheel-type glass-cutter.

Pattern cutting with the aid of a 'cut-line' or drawing underneath the glass.

(*Below*) Sequence of cuts for a curved shape.

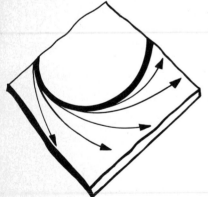

also difficult to cut strips from a piece of glass less than $\frac{1}{2}$ in. wide. A very unorthodox method of cutting glass is to hold it under about 18 in. of cold water, where it may be roughly cut with a pair of kitchen scissors.

The tools required for glass cutting are very simple: a cheap glass-cutter of the wheel type with a metal handle (which can be obtained from a hardware store) and a pair of grooved or duck-billed pliers. The duck-billed pliers are to be preferred although ordinary pliers will do very well if a piece of cloth is placed over the edge of the glass and held between the jaws of the pliers before breaking the piece away. How to hold the cutter? This is a personal matter so long as the cutting wheel is held perpendicular to the glass. The wheel is guided firmly across the glass, which should be placed on as flat a surface as possible, until a white line is scored exactly where the fracture is to occur. For straight lines a metal straight-edge may be used, in which case it is advisable to draw the cutter towards you. For free cutting it is preferable to start at the bottom of the line so as to keep the direction of the cut in view. A small receptacle containing paraffin should be kept near at hand and the wheel dipped in it from time to time; this helps to lubricate it.

When a precise guide for cutting shapes is required, a drawing known as a 'cut-line' is prepared showing the exact

area of the shape or shapes to be cut. The glass is placed over the cut-line and the wheel is firmly drawn over the glass, guided by the pattern beneath. Some coloured glass is too dense to see through unless it is held up to the light, in which case cutting should be done on a light-box. At its simplest a light-box is a piece of plate glass in a deep frame which is placed over an electric light bulb or electric lamp. The cut-line is placed on the sheet of plate glass and the coloured glass which is to be cut is placed in position over the cut-line. When the light is switched on it is easy to follow the guide. If a light-box cannot be rigged up, a piece of brown paper may be cut to the required size and pasted on to the glass with a water glue; when dry the edge of the brown paper will serve as a guide for the cutter. If the scored line is straight it is often possible to fracture the glass by exerting pressure with the thumbs on the line. Curved cuts will require a series of firm taps on the underside of the glass, using the handle of the glass-cutter. Sharp curves have to be treated differently as glass can take a line of its own choice if the curve is particularly acute. In this case the glass must be removed gradually in separate sections until the desired shape is achieved, and circles are cut with radiating lines. The diagram should make the procedure clear. Fortunately most of the waste glass can be utilized in other ways.

Cutting round a paper pattern.

(*Below*) Breaking off at the scored line with pliers and glass-cutter.

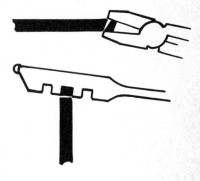

Melting glass

It is possible to melt glass in home-made clay moulds if a kiln is available, and to turn the formed glass out as if from a jelly mould. Before this can be successfully done, however, another basic principle must be understood. Different types of glass will only fuse together if they are chemically compatible. To the layman all glass is glass but it must be remembered that utility products, such as bottles, from which the greatest quantity of scrap glass is obtained, have been processed for a particular purpose, and so much depends upon the degree of hardness or softness which has been introduced to serve this purpose. There is probably no single firing temperature for glass which can be considered the perfect one.

All glass expands upon heating and contracts upon cooling, but the degree of contraction and expansion is variable. Consequently if fragments of glass from varied sources are mixed at random, melted and then cooled, the inner strains will inevitably cause fracturing – although with very small amounts the problem is reduced. It is an interesting fact that even if glass of an incompatible nature were to be ground to a powder, mixed, remelted and carefully annealed, the chemically established nature of each type would be retained. As a general rule most glass which melts at the same temperature will be compatible but the only way to be sure is by experiment. The mosaicist is in an ideal situation to benefit from this type of experiment as even an unpredictable result can yield valuable material. Classification of glass into degrees of softness or hardness is almost impossible without endless experimentation. The best solution is to classify glass which melts at the lowest possible temperature as soft glass and that which melts at the highest possible temperature as hard glass. The establishment of a fairly comprehensive middle range depends on the curiosity and tenacity of the experimenter.

Kilns and equipment suitable for firing glass are considered in more detail in Chapter 5. Those fitted with a pyrometer are more generally useful, particularly if they are to be used for clay as well. When firing glass it is fairly easy to judge the temperature after a little experience, and where particular effects are required or in cases where the probable firing temperature has not been established, it is essential to work from observation. The firing bed may be a metal tray, as used for firing painted glass, or a fireclay 'bat' of the type used for firing pottery. The glass must never come into contact with the firing bed as in its molten state it would become firmly and permanently attached. Suitable separators for metal trays with a retaining edge are whiting (calcium carbonate) or plaster of Paris (gypsum). The powder is poured into the tray to a suitable thickness according to the depth of the tray and then smoothed to a perfectly flat surface with a glazed tile. It is essential to

obtain a smooth, flat surface as glass after it has cooled will
retain the impression of any irregularities it may have encountered in its molten state.

Feldspar sieved on to fireclay bats is a useful separator; it is
desirable to place a number of bats edge to edge on several
sheets of newspaper and sieve the feldspar over all the bats
at one time; the surplus material can be collected from the
newspaper and reused. Kiln-wash, which is used to protect
kilns from accidental splashes of glaze, is an excellent separator
and must be used when glass is being melted in a clay mould.
It is made up from four to five parts of powdered flint and
one part of liquid china-clay. This mixture is painted on to
the bed and must be allowed to become completely dry
before the glass is placed upon it. Almost invariably a white
film will be transferred to the back of the glass but this can
serve as a reflector when used for mosaic.

Individual moulds on the same principle as jelly moulds
can be made from earthenware clay and fired to maturity
according to the temperature recommended by the manufacturer. When making the mould care must be taken to
ensure that there are no undercuts, as they would prevent
the cast from being removed. The inside of the mould must
be coated fairly thickly with kiln-wash and great care must
be taken to ensure complete coverage as the glass will
adhere to any uncoated portion. The wash must be allowed
to dry out completely before the pulverized glass is placed
into the mould. Again, an ideal temperature for sagging
glass into a mould cannot be established when the chemical
composition is unknown, although the following points,
if observed, will prove to be a reliable guide. The glass must

81

be seen to have assumed the shape of the mould completely, the edges must be smoothly rounded and upon cooling the glass should be clear and sparkling. If a mixture of glass is used it must be compatible and the amount of heat required depends upon the nature of the glass, whether hard or soft, and also upon the size of the fragments used. The larger the pieces and the deeper the mould the more intense is the heat required to melt them into a viscous mass.

When individual pieces of glass are to be melted on a tray, great care must be taken to ensure that the pieces do not touch at any point, and they should be arranged at least 1 in. from the edge of the tray. A separator should be applied, suitable to the type of tray, and if kiln-wash is used it must be completely dry before the pieces of glass are laid upon it. The kiln should be fired at a very low temperature for at least an hour, then raised to medium heat for an hour. The heat may then be raised to 600–650 °C., appearing a dull red, at which point the bung holes should be closed, although the bungs may be removed from time to time to allow for observation of the contents of the kiln. When the glass reaches the desired state the kiln should be switched off and the bungs removed, so enabling the heat build-up to be reduced immediately. The glass must be absolutely cold before the trays are removed from the kiln. If the pieces of glass are very thick it may be advisable not to switch the kiln off immediately the desired state has been reached, but to replace the bung and reduce the temperature to medium or low heat and allow it to remain so for half an hour, after which the kiln may be switched off and the bungs removed. It is impossible to anticipate the results from this type of firing but generally a fairly high temperature which reduces the glass to a completely molten state will produce rounder shapes, even turning squares into domed circular shapes, whereas a low temperature may simply round the edges. Overfiring can cause colour changes or even a complete loss of colour but the majority of such pieces can be stored for eventual use.

Attractive and surprising results can be obtained from pieces of 'flashed' glass known as *Antique* or Cathedral glass ('Antique' referring to the type of glass, not to its age). This glass is extremely beautiful and is produced by 'blowing'. The 'backing' glass is blown first; this glass is usually colourless or of a pale colour. The second gather of molten glass forms the surface layer, and gives the eventual colour to the finished sheet, and it is the fact that two layers of glass are present which produces such fascinating pieces when melted in a kiln. When allowed to become completely molten the pieces emerge from the kiln with domed centres formed from the surface colour, surrounded by a rim formed from the backing glass.

A similar effect can be achieved by placing small squares of coloured glass on to slightly larger squares of a different colour and firing to a molten state; the pieces must be compatible, otherwise fractures may occur upon cooling, or, more disappointingly, some considerable time later. Intriguing experiments may be conducted along similar lines by substituting glass marbles, glass buttons or glass beads for the top square of glass. Slices of glass obtained from bottles may also be melted but it is advisable to grade the slices according to size and thickness and to do separate firings for each type.

If the compatibility of certain types of glass has been established it is possible to proceed with the firing as described, but instead of keeping the pieces apart allow them to touch and overlap; this can also be done with fragments cut or broken from the same piece of glass. The small chunks which result from this method have fascinating possibilities when used as mosaic material. If regular shapes are required it is possible to contain the pieces in a loose frame made from four strips of firebrick or fired clay carefully coated with separator and arranged on the firing bed. The glass fragments may then be placed in the central cavity. Other shapes, such as rectangles and triangles, may be similarly arranged and circles made by means of a containing border of fired earthenware coated with separator.

It is possible to achieve interesting effects by combining clear glass, $\frac{1}{4}$-in. plate glass or 32-oz. window glass, with fragments of coloured glass, beads, buttons and even solid glass rods. The clear glass should be cut or broken into suitable pieces and coated with a solution of gum tragacanth mixed with equal parts of water. The pieces of coloured glass should be laid on the gum while it is still wet; when the pieces are completely dry they should be arranged on the firing bed and fired until the coloured glass appears as rounded drops, after which the standard cooling procedure is followed. Decorative pressed glass may be substituted for the base, and the fragments of coloured glass can then be arranged in accordance with the impressed patterns, which can be obtained in considerable variety.

Gum tragacanth solution is quite simple to make and will keep well in an airtight container. Powdered gum tragacanth should be mixed in a clean bowl, one heaped tablespoonful of gum to a quart of distilled water. The gum will dissolve more rapidly if it is first passed through a metal sieve and then mixed to a paste with a small amount of the distilled water before the remainder is added. The mixture should be brought to the boil very slowly and constantly stirred to reduce any lumps of gum which may remain, after which it should be strained through muslin or nylon, and bottled. The concentrated solution should be kept in a very cool place and well stirred before use.

Attractive material can be made by arranging glass fragments on a base of aluminium foil, which should be placed smoothly on a firing tray. The temperature should be such as to melt the edges of the glass and cause the foil to oxidize; when quite cold the surplus foil should be trimmed away. As explained previously (see p. 81), glass in a molten state will pick up surface irregularities from the firing bed, and this can be exploited. If whiting is used it must be made perfectly flat and smooth and then impressed with the fingers, a spoon, a piece of faceted costume jewelry or any other tool which comes to hand; the pieces are then arranged on the bed and fired to a molten state. If kiln-wash is used it must be built up into a texture by successive applications, which may be dropped or dribbled on to the initial coating. If a considerable quantity and variety of pieces is required it is worth while to make slabs from grogged clay (see p. 88) rolled to a thickness of at least $\frac{1}{2}$ in. The pattern or texture should be impressed into the surface of the wet clay. After it has been fired the slab should be thoroughly coated with a smooth layer of kiln-wash and is then ready for use. Great care must be taken to avoid under-cutting as this would prevent the glass pieces from being removed from the slab.

The mosaicist should remember that he is rarely faced with a product which is completely unusable; indeed, unpredictable and unexpected results often produce stimulating material. Almost anything made from glass can be subjected to heat provided the basic rules are observed, and it is well worth the time and trouble to experiment with any material which comes to hand. For instance, mirror glass can often produce beautiful results if fired with the coated side uppermost. Hollow soda-glass rods can be laid in short lengths on the firing bed and fragments of coloured glass, smalti or glass beads inserted at intervals with the aid of a piece of wire. Sometimes the rods will shatter but more often they remain intact and emerge from the kilns as knobbly strips of clear glass with enclosed globules of colour.

In spite of the empirical nature of these experiments, organization of materials and procedure is essential if any future benefit is to be gained. I have emphasized the fact that very little material emerges from the kiln completely unusable but it is important that highly successful experiments should not be regarded as 'one-off' events but should be capable of being repeated. To this end, careful records should be kept for each firing, giving information about the type of glass used and also the position of each type on the firing tray so that the results can be identified; time and temperatures should also be recorded. It is frustrating to lift out a tray of beautiful material and then find it impossible to match the results with the original glass. A small square of the original glass should be glued to the front of a cardboard box alongside the fired piece taken from the test tray, with a label giving details of procedure, time, temperature, etc. Glass of the same variety can be stored in the box until required for use, after which the fired pieces may be replaced and readily identified by the sample on the front. Never glue information or identification samples on the lids of boxes as these can become detached and replaced on the wrong box.

BACKING

Stained glass unfortunately loses its brilliance when laid in cement or glued to a support, so a backing must be applied. The simplest method is to spray the back of the glass with gold, silver or aluminium paint – a process which has been simplified by the availability of small cans of metallic paint with spray nozzles attached, which can be obtained from paint retailers. If glass is to be used without further treatment in a kiln, the piece may be sprayed before cutting, or the pieces may be cut and then reassembled face downwards on a newspaper and the backs sprayed – some of the decorative pressed glass makes useful material if treated in this manner. A large cardboard box with one side cut away makes a useful spray booth. Individual fired pieces may be backed with foil or silver paper. The backing should be securely attached to the glass – PVC waterproof glue is a suitable medium – and then varnished. To obtain a degree of reflection equivalent to metallic smalti the most satisfactory material is metallic leaf applied to the back of the glass. This method requires quite a lot of skill but is well worth the time and trouble involved, particularly if special fired material is to be backed, or glass in shapes and sizes not available from the manufacturers.

A suitable adhesive is *isinglass*, which is a form of gelatine obtained from freshwater fish and used commercially to preserve eggs. All the metallic foils are supplied in paper books $5\frac{1}{2}$ in. square and each leaf is protected by fine tissue paper. It is advisable to remove leaf and tissue from the book together, as the leaf is so thin that even contact with apparently still air can destroy it, causing it to tear or contract into a crumpled mass. Eliminate currents of air as much as possible. When using leaf, keep all doors and windows closed; a very large cardboard box with one side removed makes a convenient booth to work in and reduces draughts.

The isinglass is applied to the back of the glass with a soft brush. A sheet of metallic leaf, still protected by the tissue, is laid very carefully over the coated glass and smoothed with a piece of soft cloth, and the tissue may then be removed. When thoroughly dry the leaf may be given a coat of clear varnish. Flat glass pieces may be coated with leaf and then cut to the size and shape required. If the glass has a textured face the leaf should be applied to that, leaving the smooth side free for cutting. If kiln-rounded pieces are to be used they may be embedded face downwards in a bed of plasticine or clay. Several of these pieces may be grouped closely together and pressed into the bed with a block of wood in order to present as flat an area as possible for the application of the leaf.

5 Clay and its applications

Clay is a useful material for the mosaicist provided a kiln is available. As it is malleable when wet, it can be prevented from returning to its malleable form only by firing it in a kiln to a specified temperature. If this is not done it can be resoftened with water quite easily. There are various ways of obtaining clay. It can be dug from a local deposit, but will prove troublesome to use in its unrefined state; it can also be bought in powdered form, but it is much easier to buy prepared clay from a supplier of pottery material. Great care must be taken, however, to maintain it in the good condition in which it is received, by means of proper storage.

Original clay is known as 'primary' clay and lacks the plasticity of prepared clays, of which the primary material forms only a part. The purest type of clay, known as 'residual', is kaolin or china-clay. As the term 'residual' suggests, it is discovered in the deposits where it was originally formed. In prepared clays plasticity is provided by the addition of 'secondary' clays which are found in places away from the original sites of formation. The plasticity is induced into 'secondary' clays by the agents of their removal, ice and water. A clay of this type in common use is 'ball-clay', an extremely useful body, firing white or cream owing to the fact that very little iron oxide is present. Ball-clays are not suitable for commercial use as the extreme plasticity of the material causes shrinkage and warpage. To overcome this disadvantage ball-clays are mixed with china-clay, a residual material which lacks plasticity, and two other materials, flint and feldspar. Feldspar is the original material from which clay is formed, the product of decomposed feldspathic rock, and is present in most prepared clay-bodies and in most glazes. All feldspars contain alumina and silica (sand) with another ingredient; for instance, some contain lime, others potash or soda. These ingredients are dissolved out of the feldspathic rock during the weathering process and the alumina and silica remain to form clay.

Earthenware clay will be the most generally useful type for use in the mosaic studio, as the temperature range, which is between 950 and 1150 °C., is suitable for the small studio-type pottery kiln. This clay is non-vitreous; even after firing to maturity it retains its soft and porous nature and will not hold liquids unless it is glazed. Stoneware clay has a higher firing range than earthenware, 1260 °C., is hard

(*Opposite*) Pieces of textured clay after firing.

and vitreous and will hold liquid without being glazed. At such a high temperature, however, most natural clays would melt, consequently few of these clays can be included in the composition of stoneware. China-clay, another type used commercially, is never made from natural clays alone. The usual composition is: kaolin, ball-clay, flint, feldspar and an essential flux to lower the melting point, such as talc or ground glass. The first firing, the 'bisque', or 'biscuit', is 1280 °C., but the glaze firing is lower, at 1165 °C. The type of clay with the highest firing temperature is porcelain, which is fired to 1410 °C. and is known as 'hard paste'. Fireclay, not normally used for pottery, is a dark, rough-textured clay, lacking plasticity. It is an ingredient in stoneware bodies and is used commercially for the manufacture of refractory brick.

Plasticity

The term *plasticity* when used in connection with clay means the property which makes it workable. Exposure to air or to heat or even excessive handling causes clay to lose this plasticity, without which it would crumble when worked. Plasticity can be increased by a process of ageing; the clay is kept very moist in an airtight container for several months and the action can be aided by the addition of a teaspoon of weak hydrochloric acid. If plasticity is not improved by this maturing process the addition of up to ten per cent of ball-clay is recommended. Sand and 'grog' can be added to clay to reduce shrinkage, and for the mosaicist the textural qualities introduced by these ingredients are extremely pleasant. Grog is clay which has been fired, ground and sieved and when added to clay (in proportion of between fifteen and twenty per cent) it provides openings through which moisture can escape. It helps to minimize cracks which may occur during drying and firing, and is useful in the prevention of warping. Before being mixed with the clay, the grog should be soaked in order to facilitate the process.

The working condition of clay must be suitable for the job in hand. The following list gives a summary of the various conditions obtainable and the purposes for which they are suitable.

CONDITION	CONSISTENCY	PURPOSE
Liquid clay		
slurry	thin, free-running liquid	easy to sieve
slip, thin	consistency of cream	thin coating obtained by dipping
slip, medium	consistency of thick cream	ideal for coating

CONDITION	CONSISTENCY	PURPOSE
slip, thick	easily stirred but sluggish	good for slip-trailing
slip, heavy	very heavy to stir	suitable for jointing

Plastic clay

sticky	sticks to bench and hands	
soft	sticky, difficult to model	suitable state for adding grog
ideal plasticity	does not stick, retains shape	suitable for coiling and pinching and rolling out
stiff	workable, but tendency to crack	ideal for cut-out shapes, pressing and incising

Leather-hard clay

damp	can be handled but not modelled	can be carved, suitable for coating with slip
dry	shrinkage apparent due to loss of water	can be scratched, incised and scraped

Hard clay

white-hard	light colour at edges, damp inside	
bone-dry	'green' ware, very brittle	can be sandpapered

All work with clay requires a disciplined system of procedure and storage. If clay is kept in an airtight container it will keep moist and in good condition indefinitely. New clay, wrapped in polythene, should arrive in perfect condition, but for convenience of handling it is advisable to cut the clay into smaller pieces before storing, using a length of fine wire for the purpose in the manner of a cheese-cutter. Lead-lined clay-bins, suitable for the storage of fairly large quantities, are manufactured, but for smaller quantities plastic buckets with snap-on lids are satisfactory. Small pieces of clay which may be left over after work should be collected and wedged into cubes, and holes should be made in them with the thumbs. These holes should be filled with water after which the cubes may be stored in the usual way.

The term *wedging* has a particular meaning for the potter; before clay is used it must be wedged and this applies to new clay also. The purpose of wedging is to create a uniform

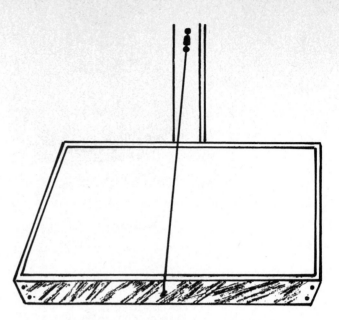

A wedging slab.

texture throughout the clay, and to eliminate air-pockets which may cause pottery pieces to explode when heat is applied. The process is also useful if the clay is too damp, as it reduces excessive water content. If a slab of clay is cut in half it is possible to see if air-pockets are present. It is well worth the trouble to make a wedging slab for permanent use in the studio. The slab should be made from plaster of Paris and held in a wooden frame with a piano wire attached for cutting through the clay (see diagram). A slab of clay should be cut in half with the wire. One half should be slammed on to the wedging slab as hard as possible with the cut side pointing away from you; the second half should then be slammed down hard on to the first piece with a twist to the left in a kneading motion. The whole piece is then picked up, cut with the wire and the process repeated. This should be continued until the clay achieves an even texture throughout and repeated cutting does not reveal a single air-pocket.

A point to remember about clay is that shrinkage can occur up to sixteen per cent of its bulk after the drying and firing processes, and allowance must be made if the finished size is important. Clay should be allowed to dry very slowly, and large pieces should be hollowed out from the back to allow moisture to escape during firing. Fresh clay should never be added to harder clay as the rates of shrinkage will be different, which will cause the pieces to separate. Before joining, wet the hard clay thoroughly, roughen the joint with a modelling tool and coat it with slip. After the fresh clay has been added, cover the work with a damp cloth until both the old and the new areas are equally damp. Different kinds of clay may prove to be incompatible, so one should be cautious about such additions. Incompatible material may crack during firing.

FIRING

The kiln is an expensive investment and should be carefully maintained. A thick coat of kiln-wash should be applied to the base of the kiln to prevent the adhesion of molten glaze which may drip from the clay units during the course of firing. When the firing has been completed and the kiln has cooled, drops of glaze may be removed fairly easily. The top side of kiln shelves may be treated similarly.

There are various types of kilns, none of them cheap: they include oil-fired, gas-fired and – perhaps the most useful for work on a small scale – small studio kilns operated by electricity. Electric kilns are easily installed and give off comparatively little heat, which is an important consideration when a separate kiln room is not available. They can be controlled thermostatically and have the capacity to heat and cool evenly. For general use, especially when extra-high temperatures are not required, they are unbeatable.

When articles made from clay are fired, physical changes are effected in the clay body, and the procedure is precise and invariable. The term 'biscuit' or *bisque firing* is applied to

An electric kiln.

an initial slow firing which brings about the physical and chemical changes in clay in the following order. The water of plasticity is driven off at a temperature of 120 °C. (which of course exceeds the boiling point of water). The drying process should have been completed at a temperature of 150 °C. but it is wise to continue with a slow firing, since water expands as it evaporates and may cause the ware to shatter. To be absolutely safe, the bungs should be left out of the kiln until the temperature reaches 600 °C. or slightly higher, after which the firing may proceed more rapidly, until the kiln becomes a dull red colour.

The changes which will have occurred are as follows. At 283 °C. there is a change in the volume of chrysabolite; between 450 and 600 °C. chemically combined water is driven off and at 573 °C. there is a change in the crystalline structure of quartz, which leads to a sudden increase in volume; between 200 and 900 °C. organic matter and sulphur compounds are driven off. It is essential that a temperature of 900 °C. is reached during the bisque firing in order to ensure that all organic matter is completely burnt out. The final temperature is determined by the nature of the clay and the preference of the artist: a temperature of 1000 °C. is the lowest limit (although the ware would be very porous). It is possible to have a hard-fired bisque and a softer glaze, or a soft bisque and a harder glaze, but it is essential that one firing reaches a temperature of 1080 °C. When the required temperature has been reached it should be held, or 'soaked', for several hours before the kiln is allowed to cool as slowly as possible. The kiln should never be opened until the temperature drops below 200 °C. and if possible the kiln should be allowed to cool completely. During the bisque firing clay tiles may be densely stacked, or stacked on top of each other, provided the pieces are not too heavy. A good general rule is that the thicker the form the slower the bisque firing.

Glaze firing has fewer risks than bisque firing and may proceed with more speed, although the ware must be completely dry before the firing commences. A number of chemical changes occur: between 0 and 200 °C. the glaze shrinks, and at this stage 'crawling' may occur, especially if the glaze is physically unbalanced. To counteract this the heat should be kept down for a few hours until the interior of the kiln looks red. Between 500 and 600 °C. organic matter is released and waxes, adhesives, etc. are burnt out, also the chemically combined water in the clay content is driven off. At 700 °C. the frit particles of some fritted glazes start to soften and from 700 °C. upwards other constituents begin to dissolve, quartz being the most resistant. The final temperature should be held for up to two hours before the kiln is allowed to cool, with the bung in. Holding the temperature in this way ensures that the heat is even throughout the kiln. As with bisque firing, the kiln should be allowed to cool to below 200 °C., or preferably to become completely cool before being opened. A quick cooling, induced by removing the bungs, increases the glossiness of the ware.

Preheating the kiln helps to reduce the danger of cracking the ware. Glazed pieces must always be separated from each other during firing, and should be set on stilts, bat wash or silver sand. The ware must be packed in such a manner that the pieces do not touch even during thermal expansion. Bisque ware should never be fired in the same kiln as glazed ware, as air-pockets may explode and deposit fragments on glazed surfaces.

COLORANTS AND GLAZES

There are several ways of adding colour to clay, all of which are useful for the manufacture of mosaic material. One of the most straightforward methods is the application of coloured *engobe* (slip), that is, clay in liquid form. It is possible to buy plastic containers of slip and as this keeps indefinitely in good condition it may prove to be the best way of obtaining it, especially if it is only required for limited use. Remember that slip must be applied to wet clay in order to combat unequal shrinkage, which would occur if liquid slip were added to leather-hard or bone-dry clay. The following recipe gives a standard method of making 100 grams of white slip:

INGREDIENTS	WEIGHT (gm.)
china-clay	25
ball-clay	20
feldspar	17
flint	30
whiting	2
magnesium carbonate	6

The material must be carefully weighed, mixed with a small quantity of water, and finely ground with a pestle and mortar. After grinding, the engobe should be sieved through a 100-mesh sieve and stored in an airtight container, clearly labelled. This basic white slip may be coloured by the addition of metal oxide in the proportions given below.

COLOUR	AGENT	PARTS PER 100 PARTS OF WHITE SLIP
blue	cobalt oxide	2
dark blue	cobalt oxide	6
iron-red	iron oxide	24
crimson	pink oxide	40
yellow	antimony oxide	9
green	copper oxide	9

COLOUR	AGENT	PARTS PER 100 PARTS OF WHITE SLIP
grey-violet	manganese carbonate	12
grey-green	chromium oxide	3
grey	iron chromate	6
purple {	cobalt oxide	2
	pink oxide	20
black {	copper oxide	5
	manganese carbonate	20
	cobalt oxide	8

These metal oxides should be ground with a little water and mixed into the prepared slip, which may then be stored in an airtight container. Red clay can be used without any addition (save that of water) to form a useful slip, although care must be taken to ensure that it is applied to a suitable body with a similar shrinkage rate. Red clay makes a useful base for black slip, which may be made by the addition of cobalt or manganese. Accumulated scraps and trimmings should be collected, crushed, and then soaked in water for several days. After draining off excess water the residue should be stirred until absolutely smooth. A ten per cent solution of sodium silicate should be prepared and added to the slip in a proportion of 1 tablespoon to 1 gallon of slip. The slip should be sieved and may be added to new slip in a proportion of one to three.

The oxides which are used as slip colorants are also used in the manufacture of glazes. Cobalt oxide is a very strong colorant and may be used in the form of black cobalt oxide or as cobalt carbonate. When used in glaze, very little cobalt oxide is required to produce a fairly strong blue and it should never be added in excess of three per cent. Iron oxide, which is usually present in clay, is usually added in the form of red iron oxide. It can be used to produce a wide range of colour from warm tan to deep reddish-brown. Antimony can be used to produce a yellow glaze but is not altogether satisfactory as the glaze tends to blister. Copper is generally added in the form of black copper oxide, or copper carbonate, to produce green, which varies according to the quantity used. An overcharge of copper in glaze can produce an odd grey, metallic surface. Manganese can be used either as manganese carbonate or as manganese dioxide, the former being the most suitable. When added to glaze it will be found that a variation of quantity produces a range of purplish-browns although, like antimony, too much can cause glaze to blister. Chromium may be used in the form of green oxide of chromium or iron chromate and forms a base for a number of underglaze colours. When used in glaze it reacts rather oddly, for instance in a lead glaze it ranges from red at a low temperature, through brown, to green at a high temperature.

Making patterns in wet slip by 'feathering'.

Application of coloured slip

Coloured slip may be applied in a number of ways to the still-damp body, either by a brush, or sprayed, or trailed with a special tool known as a 'slip-trailer'. When slip is to be painted on, it should be of a fairly thick consistency. The brush should be soft and not too small, kept fully loaded with slip, and applied to the clay body in a dabbing motion. When slip is to be applied by means of a slip-trailer the consistency should be fairly thick but not so thick as to remain in lumps after application. The rubber receptacle which is attached to the nozzle of the slip-trailer, and which contains the slip, must be kept full in order to maintain a regular flow. Clay objects may be coated with slip by means of pouring or dipping; the slip must be of the consistency of thin cream.

It is advisable not to 'touch up' the surface once the article has been coated, although there are exceptions to this rule. For instance in the technique known as 'combing', which requires a wet surface, a design is formed by means of a wooden comb which is drawn over the surface of the wet slip. Another method, a process known as 'feathering', is also carried out in wet slip. The surface of the article is coated with a slip of the required colour and while it is still wet, parallel lines of a different colour are trailed across the surface. The next part of the process requires considerable speed and dexterity, as a feather is drawn across the lines to produce the typical and traditional pattern while the slip is still pliable.

A form of inlay decoration may be produced by means of slip. An intagliated design should be applied to the ware with a wooden modelling tool, and thick slip brushed over the surface. When the article has become leather-hard the surplus slip may be scraped away. Interesting patterns and textures may be achieved by the use of a *sgraffito* technique. Coloured slip, of a different colour from the body, is applied and when it becomes leather-hard, areas of slip may be removed, care being taken not to incise the underbody.

A simple but effective form of decoration is a process known as 'masking'. Areas which are to remain uncovered by the slip are masked by newspaper shapes which are damped and applied to the clay body. The piece is then coated with slip and allowed to become leather-hard, after which the paper stencils may be removed.

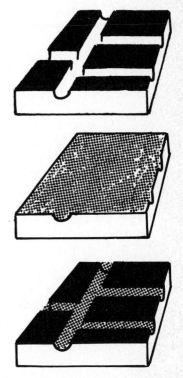

Clay inlay: (*top*) a criss-cross design is cut out of the clay; (*centre*) coloured slip is applied; finally, when slip has been scraped away a contrasting design is left.

95

Underglaze

An important colouring agent for clay is a type of pigment known as underglaze colour, which can be obtained prepared for use. It is an invaluable method of decoration for clay pieces which are to be used for mosaic. Underglaze colour may be applied to bisque ware, that is, clay ware which after a single firing has not reached maturity. After the colour has been applied, the article is glazed with transparent glaze and fired for a second time. The colour may also be applied by brush or spray to the surface of an article before the glaze has been fired. The technique of applying the colour to a white opaque glaze before firing is that used for *maiolica*. In order to ensure correct firing, the colour must be mixed with a flux, which may be glaze or a proprietary frit. A vehicle is required to assist the flow of the colour; either gum tragacanth or glycerine mixed with water is suitable.

To make a medium-thick solution of gum tragacanth 1 teaspoonful of powdered gum tragacanth should be added to 1 ounce of alcohol, and 1 pint of water should then be added to the solution. If it is required to keep for some time, add a little oil of cloves. The gum should be added in the proportion of 1 tablespoonful to 1 pint of glaze. To ensure a good consistency all the ingredients must be thoroughly mixed on a plate-glass slab or a glazed tile: first, the underglaze colour to which is added the flux of glaze, then a drop or two of water and finally the vehicle. All the ingredients should be mixed together until a smooth and creamy consistency is reached.

If the maiolica technique is to be used, the raw or bisque ware should be coated with a lead glaze, to which a proportion of tin has been added to give opacity. The glaze can be applied by dipping, brushing or spraying. The application of the colour is rather tricky as it will be absorbed very rapidly into the glaze. A thin coat of gum tragacanth applied over the glaze may make the application of colour easier. Underglaze painting on bisque ware requires the use of an oil medium: a suitable vehicle may be made from equal parts of turpentine and fat oil of turpentine. When oil has been used, however, the pieces must be fired to a red heat not higher than 895 °C. before glazing, in order to burn out the oil, which would resist the glaze if it were left. It is possible to decorate raw clay and then apply a clear glaze over the decoration, and so complete the work in a single firing, although it is difficult to cover large areas unless the glaze can be sprayed. It may be found necessary to fire to a red heat before applying the glaze after which the objects can be fired to an appropriate temperature.

Overglaze

Another type of pigment, known as overglaze colour, is, as the name suggests, used over fired glaze, after which the ware must undergo a third firing. It is essential that the glaze firing be taken to the full maturing temperature before the decoration is applied, as overglaze must not be fired in excess of 900 °C. Such a temperature is high enough to soften the glaze sufficiently to bind the colours. Again, fat oil of turpentine and turpentine may be combined to produce a suitable vehicle for the pigment. An advantage of the overglaze technique is that it allows mistakes to be easily rectified as the colour which has been applied to the glazed and fired surface may be removed with a damp sponge.

GLAZING

The use of glaze presents something of a problem as it is far too wide a subject to be within the scope of this volume. Anyone particularly interested in the possibilities of using glazed ceramic as a mosaic material should consult a pottery manual of a more specialized nature.* However, the following information may lead to an understanding of the materials involved.

* See, for instance, the *Thames and Hudson Manual of Pottery* by David Hamilton.

Glaze is basically glass. Two oxides have the property of producing glass when they are cooled from a molten state: silica (silicon dioxide) – a major constituent of most rocks and minerals (including clay) – and boric oxide, which is a constituent of borax. But the melting point of silica at 1713 °C. is above the normal working temperature required for the production of pottery, and the melting point of boric oxide at 577 °C. is below.

In order to overcome this difficulty another group of oxides are involved, which have the property of reducing the melting point of silica. These oxides are known as *fluxes* and are found, in combination with silica, in a number of minerals and rocks, although the most powerful, lead oxide, is found in isolation.

Simple combinations of fluxes do not produce workable glazes but certain oxides may be used to introduce a stabilizing factor which controls the liquid quality; if not controlled this would prevent the combination of glaze and body during firing. The introduction of these oxides provides viscosity. Included in this group, which are known as *basic oxides*, are aluminium oxide, one of the most important stabilizers, which is present in a high proportion in clay, and fluxes such as sodium oxide, potassium oxide and lithium oxide. Among the glass-formers are silicon dioxide, boron oxide, germanium oxide, antimony oxide, phosphorus pentoxide and arsenious oxide.

It follows that the vitrification range of clay bodies is governed by the presence of glass-forming oxides in varying proportions. The importance of following the manufacturer's instructions cannot be over-emphasized; just how important this is becomes obvious when one realizes that a clay body which is classified within a low firing range would melt if exposed to a temperature greatly in excess of its maturing point. For instance, a temperature in excess of 1300 °C. would reduce a low-firing earthenware body to a molten mass resembling a crude glaze. Logically, this would mean that glaze could only be applied to clay bodies with an equal maturing point. Obviously some means of controlling the vitrification temperature must be adopted, and this is the function of the flux.

Glazes take their classification from the type of flux used in their composition, for example alkaline, borosilicate, lead and feldspathic. An additional classification indicates whether a glaze is raw or fritted. A frit is a glaze which has been heated to the point of vitrification and, after cooling, has been pulverized. Impurities in the form of organic matter are present in the raw material from which glazes are compounded. During the firing process they are driven out in the form of gases, which may adversely affect the surface of the glaze or cause it to 'crawl'. The inclusion of frit in glaze overcomes this problem as the impurities have already been eliminated, and the result is more predictable.

One of the most ancient types of glaze is lead glaze, in which both red and white lead may be included as a fluxing agent. Glazes in this category have the advantage of a fairly low firing range, between 900 and 1180 °C., although those which fall within the higher range will almost certainly include other ingredients in addition to lead. Unfortunately lead glazes have two major disadvantages: they have a tendency to yellow and the raw material is poisonous. They cannot be used in establishments of education, although pre-fused mixtures of lead and silica may be permitted. Alkaline glazes also fall within a low temperature range. These glazes are compounded with a flux of soda and potash, from which brilliant colours may be produced, although they are rather difficult to use. Soda and potash are added to the glaze in the form of water-soluble ingredients such as borax, soda ash, potassium bichromate or sodium bicarbonate, and the bisque ware tends to absorb some of the soluble ingredients. The glaze should be ground in a small quantity of water for immediate application and in general it is more satisfactory to use the fritted variety. Borosilicate glazes contain boric acid which unites the silica content during the course of the firing, although they present the same problem as the alkalines since boric acid is soluble in water. Usually an insoluble form of boric oxide, which is found in colemanite (hydrous borate of calcium from California), is substituted.

A wide range of prepared raw material may be obtained from a number of stockists, and mixing glazes is quite easy when using standard recipes. The powders are carefully weighed according to instructions and are then stirred into sufficient water to produce a mixture of creamy consistency. The mixture should be brushed through a 120-mesh sieve (or 'lawn') into a plastic bucket and stored. The type of bucket which has a snap-on lid makes an ideal container and should be of a suitable size to hold approximately 8 lb. of dry glaze powder and the appropriate quantity of water. The water content may require adjusting after the mixture has been sieved, although the most suitable consistency for a specific purpose can only be established by experiment. A thinner application will be suitable for transparent glazes and a thicker application for matt opaque glazes. Glazes must be thoroughly stirred before use as the heavier compounds tend to sink to the bottom of the container, indeed glazes should be stirred even when not in use, to prevent the ingredients from settling too heavily. Clay pieces may be dipped, or the glaze may be poured or applied with a brush, and a brush should be used for touching up if required. For initial brush application a solution of gum arabic or gum tragacanth may be added to the glaze in order to improve the flow.

PLASTER OF PARIS

Plaster of Paris is useful in the studio (see p. 58) as a separator for glass-firing, to absorb moisture from clay, and in the production of moulds suitable for use with both clay and slip. The source of plaster is gypsum rock (sulphate of calcium) which has been burnt; the heating process reduces the rock to a soft crushable material which can be bought in powder form, the best kind being known as 'dental plaster'. This plaster is fine and white and is excellent for the manufacture of small sprig moulds from which attractive mosaic material can be produced. When mixed with water, plaster of Paris powder sets to a hard solid, and if it is to be kept for any length of time it must be stored in an airtight moisture-free container. It should be used as fresh as possible and will prove more economical if bought in sufficient quantities as required, to avoid long storage. Industrial and building grades of plaster are coarser than dental plaster and are usually pink or cream in colour.

To achieve a satisfactory mix the plaster and water should be measured to correct proportions. The plaster should be strong enough, when set, to withstand frequent use, yet remain sufficiently absorbent to draw moisture from clay and slip. For this purpose 1 quart of water combined with $2\frac{3}{4}$ lb. of plaster will be admirable. If it is necessary to retard the setting, cold water should be added and the volume of water increased slightly. The setting may also be retarded by reducing the amount of stirring as the plaster is added to the water, or a solution of glue size may be mixed with the water before the plaster is added. Other useful retarders are a solution of sugar added to the water, or about five per cent of citric or acetic acid. Conversely, the setting rate may be accelerated by adding more plaster to the water, or by increasing the rate of stirring as the plaster is added. Both the water and plaster may be heated, or common salt added to the water before the plaster is added. Another method is to add lime to the plaster before the mix. Use a bowl or a bucket large enough to contain the quantities required and with room to spare. Measure the water first, and then the correctly weighed plaster should be sprinkled into the water as gently as possible (never add water to the plaster). Allow the plaster to absorb the water for a minute or two – a process known as slaking, which helps to avoid the formation of lumps in the mix. The mixture should then be stirred in such a way as to drive out air-bubbles, which, if allowed to remain, will be present in the hardened plaster as troublesome airholes. To avoid creating air-bubbles in the mixture place the hand at the bottom of the mixing vessel with the palm uppermost and wiggle the fingers rapidly for several minutes until the mixture thickens. When pouring plaster, try to do so as smoothly as possible so as to avoid creating further air-bubbles.

Anyone inexperienced in the use of plaster should begin by making plaster bats, which are essential equipment in the studio. For this purpose a sheet of glass (preferably plate glass) will be required and this should be placed on a level surface. A simple butt-jointed or hinged wooden frame should be made from wood strips $\frac{3}{4}$ in. wide. The frame should be oiled or coated with vaseline on all surfaces except the underside, which should be lined with moist clay, after which the frame should be pressed firmly on the glass. The clay lining adheres to the surface of the glass and prevents the mould from lifting when the plaster is poured. After pouring the plaster the bench top should be jarred to assist the flow into the mould and so force any air-bubbles to the surface, where they should be burst by blowing on them. The first setting stage is known as the 'cheese state', as the plaster has the consistency of cream cheese. The next stage is a period of crystallization during which heat is generated. When the slab becomes cold the wooden frame may be removed.

For accurate quantities it is useful to remember that the proportion of 1 quart of water to $2\frac{3}{4}$ lb. of plaster is equal to 81 cu. in. A 9 in. × 6 in. mould, $1\frac{1}{2}$ in. deep, can be filled by the standard mix. Similarly a mould of the same dimensions but 3 in. deep would require double quantities, that is $5\frac{1}{2}$ lb. of plaster to 2 quarts of water. Freshly made plaster must be allowed to dry for several days before it is ready for use. Slight heat can hasten the drying process but excessive heat must be avoided as this weakens the plaster. When thoroughly dry, plaster gives a slight ring when it is tapped with a pencil.

Working with plaster should not pose any great difficulties provided several important points are remembered. Never allow pieces of dry plaster to float down the drain of the sink. Carefully measured quantities of water and plaster should be used to ensure a correct mix, and plaster must always be added to the water, never the reverse. Never leave plaster in an open container; if lumps are present, sieve it before use but the best method is to use it as fresh as possible. Clean all tools, bowls and work surfaces immediately after use, and never allow old plaster to accumulate, especially if clay is to be used in the same area.

TILES

The manufacture of tiles is closely related to the manufacture of pottery, as clay is the basic raw material of both. Common ground also exists in a number of decorative processes which may be applied. Early Egyptian tiles contained only small amounts of clay. The body consisted largely of sand quartz in which very small quantities of clay and alkalis were incorporated. It is thought that fairly large quantities of common salt were added to aid workability and to ensure that the finished object retained its shape. The method of tile manufacture seems to have been substantially the same as hand methods employed today. After the wedging process the clay mass would be rolled into a flat slab of even thickness, and individual tiles formed by means of a knife and templates of the required geometric shape. The drying process was critical, the tiles being partially dried and then regularly turned to ensure even drying throughout. Generally speaking, early tiles tend to be less flat than those manufactured today, the reason being that a rolling process has been introduced which flattens and smooths the tiles before they are dry and before the final cutting takes place. In comparison with modern products, older examples are generally much thicker.

Ancient techniques

A wide variety of decorative processes were developed in the ancient world. Marvellous examples of the decorative possibilities of tiles when applied to architecture can be seen in such works as the Ishtar Gate of Babylon and the bodyguard frieze from the Palace of Artaxerxes II at Susa, the winter residence of the king which can be dated to about 350 BC. The Ishtar Gate was built about 580 BC and 152 of the animals from the frieze have been recovered. These tiles have been treated in the manner of sculptural relief, each one individually produced, fired and glazed and then assembled as a unit of composition. Babylonia was conquered by Cyrus the Persian in 539 BC and the decoration of the palace at Susa is from the period of Persian domination, although the superb tile architecture of Persia was the product of the Islamic period, notably of the Abbasids (AD 750–1285) whose capital, Baghdad, was open to Persian influence.

Turkey and Syria were directly influenced by the Persian mode and gradually the technique was introduced into a number of countries under Mohammedan domination. Asia, Africa and notably Spain were strongly influenced in this manner. The 'azulejos' tiles of Spain (from the Arabic *zuleija* meaning burnt stone) were developed during the

(*Top*) Detail of tiled pavement, Bylands Abbey.

(*Above, centre*) Cuenca tile showing characteristic 'raised line'.

(*Above*) Four cuerda seca tiles.

twelfth century A D. They were originally quite small and set mosaic-fashion on to wall surfaces. Later a style known as 'cuenca' was developed: larger tiles were used and interstices were impressed into the still-damp tiles to give the impression that they were composed of smaller tiles. Another form known as 'cuerda seca' gave an illusion of mosaic also. The interstices were suggested by the application of a dividing line made from a dark composition which included manganese and had a fairly high firing temperature. The cells within the lines were filled with enamels of brilliant colour, a technique reminiscent of *cloisonné* enamel (see diagram).

In Europe, at least until the twelfth century, decorative tiles appear to have been entirely confined to floors. The patterns were assembled from numerous small tiles which were manufactured in various geometric shapes and fitted together on a cement bed in the manner of mosaic. Some of the patterns are reminiscent of Cosmatesque decoration, tiles being substituted for marble and porphyry. An excellent example of this type of tiled pavement can be seen in the Cistercian House of Bylands in Yorkshire (see diagram). Sometimes a number of tiles were assembled to form one complete unit, each tile bearing a portion of the design.

Decorative finishes

The decorative processes were varied. Relief decoration was a common form and was carried out by two methods. The design was stamped on to the surface of the tile, while it was still in the frame, by means of a block which had a negative relief decoration on its surface or the negative relief decoration formed the base of the moulding frame. The frame was made of wood or fired clay into which the clay mass was pressed and then flattened. After being released from what was in effect a mould, the tile would be allowed to become sufficiently dry to handle before being trimmed to the final size and shape. Such a method was, of course, unsuitable for high relief and sculptured reliefs of a more intricate nature, which would be produced individually as mentioned earlier in reference to the Ishtar Gate and the Palace of Artaxerxes II.

During the thirteenth century A D a transparent lead overglaze was developed in Persia. The glazed elements were embedded in mortar on the exterior face of buildings, in the manner of mosaic, the decoration often extending over whole walls. Examples of lead-glazed tiles have been found in Syria, Turkey and Egypt. Underglaze painting was developed in North Syria, in a town called Raqqa, notably a scheme of black and blue on a white ground. But production of these tiles ceased in A D 1259, the date of the town's destruction by the Mongols. The fourteenth century saw the imitation of Chinese ware, which was being imported in considerable quantities, with underglaze decoration which was primarily blue on a white body. Beautiful examples of hexagonal tiles of AD 1423, decorated in this fashion, may be seen in Damascus.

A number of processes suitable for tile decoration were developed which required one, two or even three firings. The single firing process was popular in Europe between 1300 and 1500. A simple lead glaze compounded of clay and lead sulphide in suspension was applied to the 'green' (unfired) tile, although the presence of impurities in the lead prevented the glaze from being absolutely transparent, and more commonly the ware acquired a yellowish tinge. The addition of manganese oxide to the basic glaze produced black, which was generally used on red clays, or clays which fired red. The addition of copper oxide produced green, although this process was used only on white clay bodies or ware with a white slip coating, in order to preserve the colour of the glaze. Slip was often used for a number of decorative processes which were suitable for a single firing. Sgraffito was popular and variation was introduced by the application of dark slip to a light body, or light slip to a dark body. Slip-trailing was popular, and also a very effective inlay technique.

Two firings required much greater skill, although in spite of the uncertain chemistry of ancient times, beautiful results were achieved. A clay body of unsuitable colour was often coated with white slip in order to preserve the colour value of the glaze, or slip was applied to selected areas only, so producing a two-tone effect. Because of their absorbent nature, slip grounds were not very suitable for brush decoration and a technique was evolved in which the tile was fired and then glazed with an opaque glaze. Polychrome decoration was applied to the unfired surface of the glaze, after which the ware was fired for a second time. This process developed into a style known as *faience* or *maiolica*. In principle, the white opaque glaze was a transparent lead glaze, the opacity being induced by the addition of the much more expensive tin. Various proportions of lead and tin were employed although opacity could not be ensured without a minimum proportion of one part of tin to four parts of lead, and a more suitable proportion was one part of tin to two parts of lead. The pigments used for painting the design on to the opaque ground were basically of the same composition as the glaze, with a colouring agent substituted for the tin oxide. Apart from the direct painting, which required considerable skill, the pigment was also applied by means of a sponge, or spattered or stencilled.

A form of decoration known as *lustre* is an example of a decorative technique requiring three firings. The metallic lustre was applied as an overglaze to pieces which had already been glazed and fired. Lustre firing requires a temperature lower than normal and a reduced atmosphere in which smoke is allowed to develop. The presence of smoke in the kiln caused the metallic oxides, which produce the lustre, to assume a metallic state at a temperature low enough to leave the previous work unaffected. The Persian potters brought this technique to perfection. The soluble metallic salts which are used in the process include copper sulphate, silver nitrate, bismuth sub-nitrate and gold chloride. Alternatively copper carbonate and silver carbonate can be substituted. Silver nitrate produces a range of lustres between yellow and ivory; copper produces a range between red, salmon-red and gold; a beautiful reddish-purple is obtained from gold, and bismuth produces an iridescent finish.

Another type of lustre is produced by an oxidizing fire, and the inclusion of a reducing agent in the composition of the lustre. This reducing agent is formed by the combination of sodium resinate, which is made by boiling lye and rosin together, and the addition of oil of lavender which is used as a medium. When this is fired to red heat, carbon is formed by the resinate and oil, which 'reduces' the metal and allows it to form a thin film on the glaze. Prepared lustres are now obtainable from a number of manufacturers for application over matt and glass glazes, and are attractive and predictable.

An inexpensive but effective material for use in mosaic can be obtained from commercially manufactured tiles, both glazed and unglazed. They are in general supply and very little work is required to convert them into useful material. There are two kinds of tile, ceramic and encaustic, and the difference between them is fundamental. Ceramic tiles are glazed and have a wide range of colour, size and finish. Encaustic tiles, designed primarily for use as a flooring material, are coloured throughout the body and have a matt finish, and the colour range is limited.

A range of glazed porcelain tiles, specifically designed for use as mosaic material, is now available. The most common is a square tile approximately 1 in. square, although a variety of shapes may be supplied to order. The colour range is wide and includes colours of considerable brilliance. A useful addition to the range is of Japanese origin and consists of a variety of shapes both geometric and of free form which are supplied pasted on to backing sheets. They can be removed from the backing quite easily by immersion in warm water.

Tiles manufactured from earthenware bodies are porous, and glazes are necessary to render the material waterproof. Commercial glazes are now much more varied and richer colours are available, which increases the value of these products to the mosaicist. Local contractors are often willing to sell random selections of left-over tiles at considerably reduced prices, and off-cuts, damaged tiles and fragments may be obtained at a nominal charge. In practice, fragments may prove to be more useful than whole tiles which are often difficult to cut with accuracy. Many mosaicists reduce these tiles to random shapes by covering them with sacking and tapping them sharply with a hammer.

When tiles are required for use as essential elements it is much better to produce them in the studio, although the process is fairly laborious and is probably more suitable for non-commercial or small-scale work. When tiles of a uniform nature are required for large-scale work it may prove to be false economy to expend a great deal of time and labour in their production. Depending upon the area of the tile, the most suitable thickness will be between $\frac{1}{2}$ in. and $\frac{3}{8}$ in., unless there are precise requirements. A simple rule to follow is that the thinner the slab the greater the possibility of warping, and the thickness or thinness of a slab should be relative to its surface area. If thick pieces are required for a special purpose they should be carefully hollowed out from the back.

Interesting material can be produced by imprinting the surface of damp tiles with a variety of pattern and texture before they are fired. Nothing special is required in the way of tools as almost any object of a harder consistency than the clay can be used for the purpose. Interesting patterns may be obtained from keys, buttons, nuts and bolts, screws, thimbles, indeed almost any common object. The only requirement is that the objects should be of reasonable thickness, otherwise they are difficult to handle, and may not be easily recovered from the clay after imprinting. Small objects can be glued to a block of wood or a piece of dowel and kept in the studio for permanent use. Stick printing forms are useful and small linocuts can be glued to blocks of wood and used in a similar fashion although care must be taken to ensure that the incisions are not undercut and that waterproof glue is used. Undercut forms cannot be removed from the clay without damage to the surface. Small blocks of plaster and fired clay make excellent and fairly permanent press moulds, and the pattern can be cast or incised, care being taken to ensure that it is in the negative form. If the pattern is incised in plaster the blocks must be carefully washed in order to remove all fragments of plaster, before being put aside and allowed to become thoroughly dry. Plastic castings make excellent forming material, as for instance plastic doilies which may be lightly rolled into the wet clay and then carefully peeled away.

Numerous textures can be introduced in a more random fashion by means of combs, wire brushes, saw blades, rough wood, crumpled paper. Plastic spreaders, of the kind supplied with the mastic which is used for fixing floor tiles, can be drawn across the face of the tile or clay slab, before it is cut into smaller pieces of the required size and shape. Inevitably tiny crumbs of clay will be left on the surface of the slab, although they are easily removed after the clay has become thoroughly dry. Interesting effects may be obtained by rolling the fragments lightly but firmly, so that they attach themselves permanently to the surface of the tile. Coarse sand can be applied to all or part of the clay surface and lightly rolled, and materials of an inflammable nature can be similarly used. Material of this type, such as sawdust or crumbs of polystyrene or cork, will burn away during firing and leave craters in the surface of the clay. Surfaces of this type are especially useful if the pieces are to be glazed, as the glaze runs into the craters and forms deep pools of colour. Crushed glass and metal filings can be applied to the surface of the clay although care must be taken to ensure that the particles are not inhaled. Materials which are pressed into the surface in this way must not be too large as they may cause the tile to crack.

A most useful mosaic material can be made from small balls of clay pressed on to a plaster bat with the ball of the thumb to produce a domed shape, or pressed with the tip of a finger with sufficient pressure to form a cup shape. All manner of decorative finishes may then be applied; the cup shapes are beautiful if filled with coloured glass or glaze and then fired. Small pellets of clay may be pressed into sprig moulds, a form which was developed to a remarkable degree of refinement by Josiah Wedgwood (1730–95). His raised figure ornaments were made by pressing white clay into a block of plaster which contained an incised negative impression of the ornament. These sprigs were then attached to a coloured background by means of slip. Many of Wedgwood's moulds were designed by the outstanding sculptors of the day, for instance Flaxman, who was associated with Wedgwood from 1775.

Similar moulds may be made by incising a block of plaster or by casting the block over a modelled clay positive. If clay is used it should first be moistened and firmly applied to a glazed tile or a piece of polished plate glass in order to prevent it from floating in the casting plaster. It is advisable to blow a thin coating of plaster over the clay form in order to remove air-bubbles. This is done by pouring a small amount of plaster over the clay form and spreading it over the surface by gently blowing, with the mouth a few inches away, until the modelled unit is completely covered, after which the remainder may be poured. If it is desired to experiment with decorative finishes a great deal of useful information may be derived from applying a random selection of substances to the glazed surface of a tile, as for instance salt, soap, paint and even foodstuffs. Many unexpected results occur, and if records are kept a surprising number of commodities may be utilized.

Formal patterns can be applied to slabs and tiles by means of paper stencils. The paper should be damped and pressed firmly on to the surface of the tile and the exposed areas sprayed with underglaze. This may be done by dipping a toothbrush into the prepared colour and holding it near the surface which is to be sprayed. The colour-laden bristles are then stroked with the edge of a knife blade which causes the colour to spatter on to the surface of the ware, the paper acting as a resist. If several colours are to be used, protect all exposed areas from unwanted colour by means of paper, or thin card which may be less inclined to lift. Apart from paper any open-textured material may be used as a resist, such as

Clay shapes.

Detail of sprig decoration.

netting and perforated metal (including metal mesh). It
should be remembered however that it is almost impossible
to spray small areas if the stencil material is thick as the 'walls'
of the cavities will tend to protect the surface from the spray.

Rolling and cutting

The production of clay tesserae is quite a simple process. The
clay should be in good condition and free from impurities. The
slab of clay should not be over-large as it is very difficult
to roll large pieces of clay satisfactorily. The rolling process
is very similar to pastry-making; the clay should be rolled
out on a backing of newsprint laid on a smooth, level surface.

Several manufacturers offer a simple rolling frame made
from a sheet of Formica-covered plywood with wooden
strips screwed along two opposite edges of a rectangle on the
longest dimension. These strips serve as a guide for the
rolling-pin and ensure the even thickness of the slab. The
clay should be pressed by hand into the tray and then beaten
flat with a smooth, heavy piece of wood. Alternatively, two
battens can be screwed on to the surface of a wooden bench
and the space between sprinkled with fine silver sand, which
forms a good surface for rolling the clay. After the slab has
been rolled, tiles and tesserae may then be cut to the desired
shapes. Special tile-cutters are available for use when regular

Hungarian stove tile from Buda
castle: openwork with green glaze.

107

Tile cutters and adapted shapes.

shapes are required. They are made in two sizes for square tiles, and a useful octagonal shape. Otherwise the tiles should be cut with a sharp knife of a size and shape to suit the requirements. Care must be taken to maintain the cut at right angles in order to avoid bevelling the edges; a smooth strip of wood makes a useful guiding edge for the knife blade and if it is of a reasonable thickness it will help to maintain the right angle.

Clay tiles must be allowed to become thoroughly dry before being fired. If the glaze has been applied to wet clay it should be possible to cut the slab into pieces within two hours or so, depending on the room temperature.

Ceramic shapes.

SUMMARY

When ceramic tiles or tesserae are to be manufactured in the studio all the conditions concerning working procedures which have been mentioned in the foregoing part of this chapter should be observed. The following instructions analyse the main points which have been made:

1 Whenever possible the work should be covered with a damp cloth until it has been completed, to prevent the clay losing its plasticity (see p. 88).
2 If two pieces of clay are to be joined their moisture content must be equal (see p. 90).
3 All clay must be wedged and should be kept away from plaster fragments (see pp. 89–90).
4 If warping or shrinkage is a problem the addition of grog may prove helpful (see p. 88).
5 Ageing is beneficial as it allows even distribution of the water content of the clay mass (see p. 88).
6 All containers used in the pottery studio should be water-proof and manufacturers' instructions should be carefully read and closely adhered to if a predictable result is required.
7 All materials should be carefully labelled, especially oxides which are difficult to identify by appearance in the raw state (see p. 94).

6 Stone, metal, plastic

Among the humbler materials available to the mosaicist the most plentiful is the pebble. The pavimental mosaics of ancient Greece, which were largely composed of pebbles, are evidence of the skill with which the material has been used. When using pebbles one is obliged to concentrate on the general rather than the particular, and even quite simple geometric patterns require a disciplined approach. Although pebbles are freely available, a considerable amount of time and effort can be spent on their collection, but it is a pleasurable activity. When making a collection of pebbles time should not be spent selecting stones for special qualities: when each pebble takes its place as part of the whole, individual beauty will have little significance, indeed colour and contour will be found to be of more importance than veining and striation. This rule, however, does not apply when pebbles are used in comparative isolation or in contrast with other materials, especially when the work is on a small scale. During the process of selection the material should be sorted into categories of colour, shape and size. When pebbles are to form the principal material in a mosaic, it is often an advantage to collect them specifically for the job in hand, as random collections rarely produce sufficient usable material. If beautifully marked pebbles are to be used in isolation, and are to be polished or varnished to enhance their qualities, they should be treated on the exposed surface before being set in place, as considerable tonal changes can occur, owing to the darkening effect of the varnish.

Apart from the ubiquitous pebble which has been worked by the elements into a usable form, other types of stone and rock may be considered as potential material for mosaic. One should have an understanding of the nature of such material, for some stones are difficult to work and polish and others, contrary to their appearance, weather badly. The term 'stone' is often applied too generally and it is important to realize that distinction should be made between minerals and rocks. Rocks are aggregates of various minerals, and there are three main classifications: sedimentary, igneous and metamorphic. Minerals, on the other hand, have a chemical composition which is specific and has constant characteristics. Rocks classified as *sedimentary* include limestones and sandstones, the latter being formed from the deposits of older rocks, such as quartz and feldspar, or from accumulations of matter of organic origin, bound together by natural cement. Various types of sandstones are classified according to the composition of this natural cement, which imparts specific qualities and colour. Limestone is composed mainly of calcium carbonate formed by deposits of solution or solids in water. Typical limestones are travertine, and the Portland stone and Bath stone which are two of the most commonly used stones in England. These oolitic★ limestones are formed from minute spherical shells which vary in size and, incidentally, in their relative hardness, which can cause variations in a single block. Bath stone is one of the softest of the oolites, but samples do occur which are of a considerable hardness.

★ From the Greek; literally, 'egg-stone', from its resemblance, under the magnifying glass, to fish roe.

The *igneous* group includes volcanic, hypabyssal and plutonic rocks, the various structures being controlled by the rate at which the crude molten mixture (or magma) cooled. Those classed as volcanic include basalt and pumice, which cooled very rapidly, and are consequently non-crystalline in structure. Those of the hypabyssal group, which includes porphyries, cooled fairly slowly and reveal a crystalline structure of medium size which can be polished. Plutonic rocks resulted from an extremely slow cooling process, and are of a markedly crystalline structure, a typical example being granite.

As the name suggests, *metamorphic* rocks were formed from older stones, which, having been subjected to intense heat, actually changed their structure. Marble is metamorphosed limestone, crystalline in structure, whereas slate is metamorphosed clay which was subjected to intense pressure. Rocks may be composed of several species of minerals or from a single species, in which case they are known as 'simple'. For instance white marble, which is simple, is composed solely of limestone (calcium carbonate); granite, on the other hand is largely composed of quartz, feldspar and mica. A wide variety of colour and veining can occur in marble, including black, grey, cream, beige, honey, brown, green, red and pink, and is caused by the presence of various minerals. Subject to their ability to reflect light, rocks can offer visual as well as textural variety, their qualities of colour and marking being dependent upon smoothness of surface which, in turn, depends upon the workability of the stone.

Minerals which have been sought after and treasured since ancient times have been attributed with miraculous properties, supposedly conveying benefits and protection to those who possessed them. A relic of this regard lingers on in the designation of birth stones. Certain gems were believed to possess healing powers, and, although incredibly costly, were crushed and taken as medicine. They were also admired for their intrinsic beauty, and hoarded both as a symbol and a source of wealth. Hard stones and softer minerals such as lapis lazuli have been employed in commesso, intarsia and mosaic for centuries, and even small scraps of such materials are of inestimable value to the mosaicist, especially in the field of small-scale and miniature work.

MINERALS

Minerals are constituents of rocks, ores and meteorites, and almost all are crystalline, but there are exceptions – as, for instance, opal. The scientific study of minerals began in the nineteenth century, although since early times man has speculated upon their nature. Part of a treatise on mineralogy by Theophrastus entitled *On Stones*, which was written sometime during the first half of the fourth century A D, survives today. Pliny concerned himself with mineralogy in his *Natural History*; the last five chapters are devoted to the subject, although these are typically undiscriminating as to the difference between fact and hearsay. From the sixteenth century onwards a number of works have been preserved which exhibit a more scientific concern with the subject. The material was largely descriptive, the most important of the early works being *De Natura Fossilium* by Georgius Agricola which was published in 1564. Chemical analysis of the properties of minerals commenced at the beginning of the nineteenth century, and was considerably assisted by the development of improved instruments. Today the classification of minerals is based on their chemical composition, and the molecular or atomic structures which are exhibited in crystal form.

The physical characteristics of minerals are described under the headings of cleavage, fracture, tenacity, hardness, elasticity and specific gravity. Hardness is the most important characteristic from the point of view of the worker in hard stones. The durability of minerals was an important aspect which contributed to the regard in which they were held, being symbolic of their actual worth. The term 'hardness' defines this quality, but in practical terms the hardness of minerals is variable. The old yardstick of measurement, although it established a ratio of hardness and softness, was far from accurate. It was based on the ability of a stone to withstand a scratch from steel, which established a ratio of hardness; the inability of stone to withstand a scratch from a finger-nail established a ratio of softness. A more practical, though still unscientific method, was devised by a German named Friedrich Mohs in 1833, after whom the system is named. The Mohs test was based on the principle that: 'Of two minerals the harder is the one that scratches the other.' Ten degrees of hardness were established, hard stones being those which fall in the sixth to tenth categories. However, the Mohs system is in reality a more sophisticated rule-of-thumb method and basically imprecise, as it fails to establish the variations which can occur on different facets of the same stone. Modern techniques which include the use of instruments are able to establish the hardness rating of a given example with great precision. Unfortunately, in order to do so the stone has to be pierced, so from a practical standpoint the Mohs test retains its validity, and the following scale is acceptable:

1 Talc — soft
2 Gypsum — soft
3 Calcite — semi-hard
4 Fluorite — semi-hard
5 Apatite — semi-hard
6 Orthoclase (feldspar) — hard
7 Quartz — hard
8 Topaz — hard
9 Corundum — hard
10 Diamond — hard

Minerals vary greatly in colour owing to the presence of impurities, even in quite small quantities. Other qualities, such as iridescence and opalescence, are present in certain minerals, a well-known example being the opal. Those hard stones which are most commonly used in commesso work come from the families of granites, quartzes, porphyries, jaspers, agates and chalcedonies, each family producing several varieties. Granites make up a large family group, which is metamorphic and composed of quartz, feldspar and mica, and ranges in colour from white through pinks to red. Quartz, which is hard, may be obtained in a colourless transparent form or in a variety of colours, each with a different name. A yellow variety is described by the rather misleading name of topaz quartz, and another gem, the amethyst, gives its name to a violet variety, known as amethystine quartz. The well-known rock crystal is a white variety, and, when white and opaque, is termed milky quartz. Porphyries are volcanic and extremely difficult to work, but take a very fine polish. They range in colour from red to green, and were exceedingly popular in the ancient world for sculpture and as a building material. They were also incorporated in many Cosmatesque works (see p. 45). The chalcedonies are a form of quartz which may be transparent, or assume a wide range of variegated colour when impurities are present. Both agate, and cornelian with its intense red colour, are of the family of chalcedonies. Jasper is a variety of quartz which is opaque, but may have decorative striations formed from an admixture of minerals, although these examples should more properly be classified as rocks. Other minerals, though lacking hardness, have been employed since ancient times because of their special qualities of colour, among the foremost being lapis lazuli, which was obtained in a wide range of blue.

Apart from the expensive range of hard stones (which are rarely used in unlimited quantities today), other types of stone can be successfully used as a mosaic material. This is true of marbles, which formed the basic material of pavimental mosaic throughout the Roman period; however, even the coarser, non-reflective varieties can be used either in large-scale work or in contrast with more colourful material. All stones are capable of being worked more easily when freshly quarried (when they are referred to as 'green') and a number of stones, including such varieties as Portland and Cotswold, tend to harden considerably on exposure to the atmosphere. When the strata formed by the deposits can be detected, care should be taken to set the stone with the strata in a horizontal position in order to reduce the action of rain on the softer areas, which, when exposed to frost, may cause the stone to flake. If stone is to be used extensively, it is good practice to complete the work in summer, and then submit it to a gradual weathering process. All stones tend to lose colour in time, although some of the harder sandstones retain their colour longer. Certain limestones are rather chancy if exposed to a polluted atmosphere, particularly the creamy Caen limestone. On the other hand, a number of sandstones have a considerable degree of resistance to many conditions, including the action of frost, although they can be rather difficult to cut owing to the presence of a high proportion of silica in their composition. They are obtainable in a pleasant range of colour from a milky brown to a brownish-red. Among the well-known English varieties are Runcorn, Red Midland, Robin Hood, White Hollington and the York stones, blue, brown and grey. Other, less gritty varieties include a blue and grey Forest of Dean, and brown and blue Hornton. Another variety, Hopton Wood stone, is in reality a form of marble, but is extremely hard to work. It is also important to remember that stone can weigh up to 140 lb. per cu. ft., which can pose considerable problems.

METALS

Metal can be used to add interest and variety to mosaic, and has several advantages, being easily obtained in a variety of colours and capable of modification by a number of processes. It is, in fact, one of the most amenable of materials, being adaptable to processes of moulding, extruding, cutting, forging, piercing, stamping, welding, and riveting. Metallurgy, which is the art of extracting metals from their ores, is of very ancient origin, although the scientific study of the nature of metals commenced as late as the nineteenth century, and today the term 'metallurgy' embraces a number of highly specialized branches. Obviously the first metals to find application in the ancient world were those which occurred in a natural state, such as gold and copper. The softness of natural gold precludes its use for offensive or utilitarian purposes, although copper, which is fairly soft, tends to harden when worked by beating, and so lends itself to the production of weapons and cutting tools. Consequently, from early times copper retained a utilitarian function and gold remained specifically ornamental.

For domestic and artistic use, gold, silver and lead were available. Gold is always found in a metallic state, even when alloyed with other metals, and the extraction of gold was never a great problem. The metal was extracted from the dross by sluicing, although various means of carrying out this process had to be devised, as for instance when the metal was discovered in the form of dust. Electrum, which was employed by the Greeks for coinage, was a natural alloy of gold and silver. It was semi-purified by heating the alloy in a crucible with the addition of common salt. This converted the silver into silver chloride, which was further purified by a repetition of the process. The removal of base metals from gold was achieved by a method of very ancient origin known as cupellation, in which gold and lead were melted in a porous crucible in the presence of air. The lead oxidized and formed a molten slag, and such base metals as were present in the gold passed into the slag and were absorbed into the porous 'cupel', leaving behind the precious gold and alloys. Unlike gold, silver was not abundant in the natural state, and remained relatively rare until the recognition of the presence of silver in lead ores. The extraction of lead from ore is a very simple process. The commonest variety, lead sulphide, was mixed with charcoal and heated in a primitive furnace erected in the open air. Further refinement, to remove impurities which existed in the form of copper, tin or arsenic, was achieved by melting lead (which retained its silver content in solution), a process which could be carried out at a low temperature. The molten lead could then be drained away, leaving the dross behind.

Properties

All metals fall into two main groups; the ferrous group which consists of iron and alloys in which iron is present, and the non-ferrous group which includes all remaining metals. A further subdivision classifies gold, silver and platinum as 'noble' metals on account of their resistance to corruption (although silver is, in reality, semi-noble as it can be attacked by sulphurous fumes). Certain features are common to all metals – they are of crystalline structure, and are all capable of assuming a liquid form, provided the correct temperature for each is established. Further, they all share the quality of opacity, can be united to other metals by various means, expand in all dimensions when heated and contract when cooled, although the cooling or 'freezing' temperature differs and is specific to each variety of metal.

A number of qualities are sought for in metals and are defined in various ways. 'Malleability' is the ability of the metal to be pressed, hammered or rolled and so extended in all directions from its original form, without fracture. Gold

(*Right*) Flashed antique glass; (*below*) how to combine it in an attractive design (*Fish* by C. Bingham).

(*Left*) *Jester* by Joan Haswell: detail of a mosaic using clay pieces (see p. 177).

(*Below*) *Night Owls* by Joan Haswell: detail of a mosaic showing the copper gaskets used for the eyes (see p. 178).

is the most pliable of all metals and can be beaten into foil
0.00001 mm. thick. Silver is the next most pliable metal,
followed in order by aluminium, copper, tin, platinum, lead,
zinc (only when hot), iron (when wrought) and soft steel.
The quality of malleability is not present to any degree in
cast iron or hardened steel.

Another term, 'ductility', has a general meaning akin to
malleability, but technically, when applied to metals, refers
to the ability of metals to be drawn out into wire. Gold
possesses this quality to a marked degree: one gram may be
drawn to a wire two miles long. It is followed, in order, by
silver, platinum, iron, copper, aluminium and nickel. Lead,
which is malleable but not ductile, can only be drawn by
extrusion, yet gold thread, which is drawn silver thread
coated with gold, can produce 1,400 yards per ounce.

Other qualities are described in terms of 'compression',
'tensile strength' and 'shear'. Compression and tensile
strength are opposites: compression refers to the degree to
which metal withstands the effects of squeezing; tensile
strength refers to the degree of strain metals can stand while
being stretched. Shear is the degree of resistance offered by
metal to the action of two blades meeting with the design of
penetrating the metal from each side.

Gold, as well as being the most malleable and ductile of
metals, is also the most resistant to the effects of corrosion by
both atmospheric and chemical attacks. However, natural
gold is much too soft for general use, and various alloys are
added which give special characteristics to the product in
terms of stress, melting point and colour. The amount of
alloy present in gold is expressed by the term 'carat', a
twenty-fourth part. Pure gold is 24-carat, whereas 18-carat
gold contains 18 parts of gold and 6 parts of silver and/or
copper; 9-carat gold consists of 9 parts gold and 15 parts of
copper and/or silver. The colour of the alloy is conditioned
by the type of metals used, and they also impart special
characteristics in terms of stress and melting point. Pure
silver is characterized by a beautiful lustre and, as already
mentioned, is second only to gold in terms of malleability
and ductility, but less resistant to the corrosive action of
certain chemicals. Electrum, the alloy of gold and silver, is
a pale metal, although the name is sometimes misleadingly
given to an artificial gold which is really a form of brass.

Gold and silver

Although innumerable gold artefacts have survived, it has
proved difficult to establish the historical sequence of very
early examples with certainty. Great losses have been sus-
tained, as the intrinsic value and portable nature of these
precious objects made them an obvious target for plunder.
Even when they have not been melted down, their removal
to lands far from their place of origin has tended to confuse

the issue. It is certain, however, that the goldsmith's art was very widespread in ancient times, and most of the products were of high quality. From the point of view of the mosaicist, however, the most interesting examples are those in which gold or silver is used as a base for inlay. The tomb of Queen Hetep-heres, the mother of the Pharaoh Cheops, which was discovered at Giza contained a great number of beautiful objects, including silver bracelets inlaid with delicate butterflies made from precious minerals such as lapis lazuli, turquoise and cornelian, dated to the Fourth Dynasty, approximately 2613–2492 B C. Beautiful examples of gold and silver inlay have been discovered in Mesopotamia, of a period between 2494 and 2345 B C, which are obviously products of an established tradition. Two well-known versions of the same theme, 'A ram caught in a thicket', are typical products in which gold foil, silver, lapis lazuli and shell are combined. The royal graves at Ur have yielded a quantity of inlaid jewelry including crowns, ear-rings and figurines. Hoards have been discovered in burial sites over a wide region and in places with legendary names – Thrace, Uruk, Troy, Mycenae, Paphos, Delos, to mention but a few. But the supremely sophisticated examples of goldsmiths' work from Etruria are devoid of inlay, the gold being decorated by means of granulation and filigree, carried out with great technical virtuosity.

The sumptuary laws of ancient Greece were responsible for the scarcity of objects of precious metal. It is to the eighth century B C that we must look for the consolidation of a style of ornament which reached a peak of brilliance in the seventh century B C. A similar prohibition was responsible for the late development of luxury artefacts of gold and silver, in the rather severe social climate of republican Rome. However, contact with the luxurious and opulent products of eastern manufacture inexorably eroded the somewhat puritanical conventions which obtained. A considerable taste for precious objects spread throughout the western Empire during the Imperial period. The ancient proclivity for polychrome inlay as a form of decoration on articles of gold and silver persisted in the east and finally triumphed in the west. During the period of barbarian invasions, precious metals were used as little more than mounts for other materials. Ultimately, regional schools developed, each with special characteristics. One of the most interesting aspects of gold and silver work is the way in which a popular or folk tradition has persisted. Many of the articles which fall within the realm of popular art incorporate, apart from gold and silver, a variety of metal. Although not strictly apposite to the monumental aspect of mosaic, many of these inlaid articles are of great interest, and may stimulate those craftsmen who have a specific interest in miniature mosaic and mosaic jewelry, as well as being in line with the contemporary tendency to incorporate a number of materials, other than the traditional ones, in mosaic.

Base metals

Among the base metals, the first to be used was copper, which was subsequently alloyed to produce bronze and, with the incorporation of zinc as an alloy, brass. These brass alloys have been extensively used in the production of jewelry, for instance in the well-known pinchbeck. Copper has a number of innate qualities which make it a suitable material for inclusion in mosaic. It is easy to work, although cold working by beating induces the metal to harden, but it can be restored to softness by heating and quenching. It is soluble in sulphuric and nitric acid, a fact which provides a basis for a number of decorative processes, and it is also a beautiful colour. It responds well to polishing, but the high surface shine is impermanent unless it is treated with varnish, although a very attractive patina can be obtained on exposed copper.

Copper-working probably developed in Egypt, and weapons and implements have been found in graves of as early as 5000 B C. The skill was developed to a point when the material could be hammered into thin sheets. One of the great centres of production in the ancient world was the island of Cyprus, a fact which made the island a prey to successive conquerors. Rome drew almost her entire supply of the metal from the island; the name copper is derived from *cuprum*, a corruption of the Latin *aes cyprium*, ore of Cyprus.

Today the greatest part of the world's copper is used to supply the electrical industries, or to form alloys. Copper can be obtained as wire, sheet or strip. Copper strip is usually less than 2 ft. wide and supplied in long lengths, although it is more commonly used in strips 1 ft. wide. When in excess of 2 ft. wide the material is termed copper sheet, which may be obtained in specific degrees of hardness. Specially cut blanks are sold for enamelling purposes and a considerable amount of material which can be of use to the mosaicist can be bought from scrap.

Lead also has many qualities which make it useful to the mosaicist. It is soft enough to cut with a knife, and has a low melting point of 327.5 °C. It was probably the first metal to be used in the practice of smelting. Lead coins and medallions of lead have been discovered in ancient Egypt, small votive figures cast in lead have been discovered in Troy and Mycenae, and it was extensively used by the Romans. Ornamental lead castings of Roman origin have been discovered which are at least two thousand years old. Apart from a purely domestic or utilitarian function, lead has been widely used for architectural purposes largely because of its great resistance to climatic conditions. Its low melting point, coupled with the fact that it does not contract, makes it an ideal material for casting purposes.

The casting process was highly popular in the Middle Ages, when lead was often used as a substitute material in place of more precious metals, yet the monk Theophilus makes no reference to the ornamental use of lead in his treatise. Pilgrim badges cast from lead were sold at all the great medieval pilgrimage shrines; the Musée Cluny in Paris has a fascinating collection of these small religious articles. During the Renaissance many replicas of metal articles and goldsmith's patterns were cast in lead and extensive use of the material was made in the seventeenth and eighteenth centuries for garden sculptures and ornaments. Their excellent state of preservation is due to the protective oxide which very quickly forms on the surface of lead upon exposure to air, although it is bright when newly cut. It has the disadvantage of weight (709 lb. per cu. ft.) with the advantage of being relatively inexpensive. Tin, a white metal which is soft and with a high degree of resistance to corrosion, is available in considerable quantities in the form of scrap, and is worth considering as an addition to the range of mosaic material.

The intrinsic beauty of most metals makes them a desirable addition to the materials available in the mosaic studio. In some cases a high degree of polish can be given; they can be coloured and a number of them can be allowed to acquire a beautiful patina by a natural process of oxidation induced by exposure to the atmosphere. Those which are not easily worked may be obtained in the form of scrap, the accumulation and processing of which is now an important industry, as the supply of metals is not inexhaustible. Scrap pieces often occur in forms suitable for direct use, as for instance metal parts from machines, as well as nuts, bolts, screws, nails, buttons, tins and bottle tops. Many of the ancient craft processes are still employed today – for example casting and hammering, which includes a process known as 'repoussé' work (from the French *repousser*, to push). This is a form of embossing, which involves the raising of a relief decoration from the reverse side of the metal. Other types of decoration are accomplished by 'chasing', inlay, engraving and enamelling, all of which are very ancient practices.

Metals may be coloured by the application of certain chemicals, which should take place after the metal has been shaped or formed. But specific results cannot be guaranteed as there are a number of unknown factors which can influence the final result, as for instance the nature of the alloy which may be present in the metal, which also has a bearing on the temperature range. Metal pieces must be thoroughly cleaned prior to the colouring process. Copper, brass, bronze, iron and zinc may be cleaned by rubbing with a paste made up from pumice powder and water, or by boiling in a solution of caustic soda (sodium hydroxide), or potash (potassium carbonate). The solution may be made up in a fairly large quantity to a proportion of 1 lb. of soda or potash to 1 gallon of water, which may be stored and kept for some time. The pieces should be placed in the solution and then removed with tongs, and immersed in cold water. If iron and zinc are to be cleaned in a caustic solution, they should be immersed for only a short period. The following recipes are standard and do not present great difficulties but care must always be taken when handling chemicals, and special directions should be observed. All chemicals should be clearly labelled and kept out of the reach of children, pets and foodstuffs, and good ventilation is essential at all times.

If an antique green is required on copper or brass, the following solution should be made up, and warmed:

ammonium chloride	2 oz.
copper nitrate	2 oz.
calcium carbonate	2 oz.
water	$\frac{1}{2}$ gall.

The article should be thoroughly cleaned and warmed immediately prior to stippling the solution on to the copper with a sponge.

A yellowish-green may be obtained by immersing brass or copper in the following solution:

calcium chloride	32 grains
ammonium chloride	32 grains
copper nitrate	32 grains
water	2 oz.

A range from yellow to a fairly bright red may be obtained on brass by dipping until the desired colour is obtained in the following solution:

caustic soda	1 part
copper carbonate	2 parts
water	10 parts

A process known as 'water gilding' may be applied to brass and copper. A solution should be prepared from:

gold chloride	$1\frac{1}{2}$ parts
hydrogen potassium carbonate	60 parts
water	200 parts

This should be boiled in an ovenproof glass container until the solution turns green, which may take several hours. The brass or copper articles should be immersed in the hot solution for no longer than half a minute.

Enamelling

The process of enamelling on metal is a valuable technique for the mosaicist, as it can be carried out with a minimum of equipment. The enamel itself is a compound of vitreous materials, and can be applied to the metal in a number of ways. An exhaustive survey of the craft is beyond the scope of this book, but the brief instructions which follow should be found adequate for the production of small-scale flat pieces in a variety of shapes to make an attractive addition to the material available for mosaic. The initial outlay can be kept to a minimum as a small hot-plate kiln is currently available which can be used on a table and run off the domestic electricity. Enamels can be bought in the form of chunks, threads or pre-ground into powder, and are obtainable in a range of colours, and in fairly small quantities. The price varies according to colour. Opaque and transparent colours are available, and a basic collection should include both types; the grade described as '50-mesh' is most suitable for a beginner.

Enamel is in reality a form of glass with a low melting temperature which has been established by the addition of a number of fluxes, such as borax, potassium or specially prepared frits. Opaque enamels do not transmit light because of the addition of opacifying agents during the manufacturing process, although they do reflect light from the surface. Transparent enamels transmit light; in fact, some are absolutely clear, and will allow the metal of the base to shine through. Semi-transparent enamels can be obtained which exhibit a milky quality, although the firing temperature is critical if the opalescent effect is to be retained. The most important enamel in the range is white opaque, necessary as a base for transparent colours. It is obtained by compounding opacifiers such as titanium, antimony or zirconium oxides with clear glass during the melting process. When a white opaque enamel base has been used, only transparent colours of a lower firing temperature can be applied, so ensuring that the base remains stable.

Sheet copper (20–22 gauge B+S or 22 S.W.G.) is the most suitable material for enamelled units which are to be incorporated into a mosaic. It can be easily cut and shaped or alternatively metals of this gauge can be purchased from a manufacturer in the form of prefabricated units known as 'findings'; brass, silver and gold findings are also obtainable. Only pure copper can be enamelled successfully; therefore, when forms are to be cut from sheet metal, it is vitally important to specify this when ordering. Strip copper is usually supplied in rolls of various widths between 6 in. and 16 in. and sheets 30 in. × 60 in. or 20 in. × 90 in., and is also obtainable in tube form. If copper is to be worked in any way, the most suitable thickness is 18 gauge B+S or 20 S.W.G. (the larger the gauge number the thinner the metal); this applies also to pieces which are to undergo several firings.

When using ground enamel it is important to ensure that all impurities are removed, otherwise the quality of the colour cannot be guaranteed. The enamel powder must be washed, a rather tedious operation though larger quantities can be prepared at one time, if so desired. A separate bowl will be required for each colour; ordinary earthenware kitchen mixing bowls are suitable. The enamel is placed in the bowl, and ordinary tap water is added and then stirred for a few moments before the enamel is allowed to settle. This process is repeated for each colour. The water will become slightly discoloured owing to the presence of extraneous matter, which, if allowed to remain, would seriously affect the clarity and brightness of the colours when fired. After the enamel has been allowed to soak for some time, as much of the water as possible should be poured away, care being taken not to allow any enamel to flow out with it. Fresh water should then be added to the enamel, stirred and again left to settle before the water is poured away (a process which must be repeated several times). The procedure should then be repeated once or twice with distilled water substituted for tap water. Finally, as much water as possible must be poured away, and the enamel transferred to foil pie-dishes, preferably by means of a large wooden cooking spatula which allows more water to drain away (a spoon tends to conserve the water). The trays may then be placed in a preheated kitchen oven on the lowest possible setting, and allowed to become thoroughly dry. This process may take up to ten or twelve hours, depending on the amount of enamel in each container, as the door of the oven should be left slightly ajar. When thoroughly dry, the enamel should be stored in airtight containers, although it is better to complete the process by sieving and grading the washed enamel, than to do it immediately prior to use.

An 80-mesh sieve and a 200-mesh sieve will be required and it is important to ensure that sieves, receptacles and any other implements are absolutely clean in order to prevent the inclusion of foreign matter in the washed powder. One should work away from draughts, handle the material gently so that it does not float in the atmosphere and, if it does so, the powder must not be inhaled. Always remember that the material is ground glass, and it is essential to keep enamels away from children, pets and foodstuffs.

Sieve the enamel through the 80-mesh sieve into a scrupulously clean receptacle. The enamel that will not go through the mesh should be stored in another container, with a clear indication on the label that it is residual material suitable for sprinkling. Sieve the enamel again through a 200-mesh sieve, and store the residue with an indication that it is suitable for inlaying. The main batch may then be stored in another container and will be suitable for painting; remember that all storage vessels must be completely airtight.

Before the application of the enamel coat, the copper blank must be given preliminary treatment, and these processes cannot be omitted if satisfactory and predictable results are desired. After the copper has been cut (and the edges filed if necessary) it should be placed on a trivet or an asbestos mat and heated until it assumes a dull red glow, which may be done by allowing the flame of a small blowtorch to play over the copper. The piece should then be firmly gripped between the jaws of a pair of pliers and plunged into a receptacle of cold water – a process known as 'quenching', which is only applied to fresh pieces of copper, and is not required when a piece has been partially enamelled and is being prepared for a second coat.

The second process, known as 'pickling', must be repeated before each application of enamel, no matter how many coats are applied. The pickling solution consists of one part nitric acid to five parts of water, and never add water to the acid – always add acid to water. A clean glass container is quite suitable for the acid solution, and the pieces should be handled by means of a pair of brass tongs. Tongs and receptacles must be rinsed several times in clean water after use. The copper blank should be completely immersed in the solution, and a cover placed over the receptacle; the pickling should continue until the piece assumes an unmistakable pinkish colour. The pickling process is designed to remove all dirt and grease in order to produce a suitable surface for the application of the enamel; it is essential therefore that the surface should not be subsequently handled. The copper should be removed from the pickle by means of brass tongs, held for a short while under running water, then thoroughly washed in detergent and water, and allowed to drain on a clean paper towel. Alternatively 'Perfon', a proprietary metal-cleaning solution, may be used. This product is quite harmless, and should be used according to the manufacturer's instructions. Always work in a well-ventilated room when handling acid; never inhale the fumes, and treat all acid burns seriously. If burns do occur, the affected parts should be placed under running water immediately, then thoroughly washed with soap and water, and covered with an application of bicarbonate of soda.

The third process, which is applied to all pieces that are to be enamelled, is the production of a reflective surface, achieved by polishing the copper with very fine steel wool; this enhances the effect, especially when transparent enamels are to be used.

A number of techniques can be employed to produce decorative enamelled units, which may be incorporated with other materials or assembled in sections to form complete panels. None of these processes is particularly complicated, but etching is probably the most laborious. The process of etching is really a controlled extension of the pickling process, and the etching solution is the same, one part nitric acid to between five and seven parts of water. Having decided which areas are to be left in relief, the design should be sketched lightly on to the surface of the copper with pencil. Those areas which are to be in relief should be coated with a substance known as 'stopping-out varnish', thinned to a suitable brushing consistency with benzine. In addition to selected parts of the design the varnish should be applied to the back and sides of the piece, and then allowed to become thoroughly dry. The copper should then be immersed in the nitric acid solution, and allowed to remain until the etch is judged to be of sufficient depth; the timing is governed by the freshness of the solution and the required depth of the etch. When the piece is removed from the acid solution, it should be treated in the same manner as that described in the pickling process.

If the copper is to receive a complete coat of enamel, this may be applied in several ways. The copper must first be coated with a solution of gum tragacanth consisting of 1 dessertspoonful of concentrated gum solution to $\frac{1}{2}$ pint of distilled water. A concentrated solution can be obtained from 1 heaped tablespoonful of gum to 1 quart of distilled water. If the powdered gum is lumpy, it should be sieved before use. The gum should be mixed with a little of the distilled water, and worked with a spoon until the granules are reduced. The remainder of the water may then be added, and brought slowly to the boil in a clean saucepan. (Gum tragacanth is harmless and an ordinary kitchen saucepan may be used.) After the solution has cooled, it should be strained through muslin or nylon into a clean airtight jar, which should be labelled, and can be stored in a cool place for several months. The gum coating may be applied to the copper by means of a camel brush, or alternatively, a fixative atomizer may be used. This is a simple mouth-spray which is used to apply fixative to charcoal or pencil drawings, and is suitable for the purpose of applying gum, although only to small areas.

The powdered enamel must be sifted on to the copper before it dries, so one must be prepared to work rapidly. The enamel should be sifted on to the gummed surface through an 80-mesh sieve, and in order to conserve surplus enamel, the copper piece should be placed in a small plastic dish (a photographic developing dish will be suitable). The enamel may clog the sieve, so do not over-fill; about one-third full will be found to be a reasonable amount. If the flow of enamel is obstructed, a sharp tap on the rim of the sieve with the blade of a knife should clear it. The enamel can also be applied to the copper in the form of paste made from ground enamel, thoroughly mixed with gum solution made from 1 dessertspoonful of concentrated gum solution to $\frac{1}{2}$ pint of distilled water. The paste should be very smooth, and is applied to the copper with a small spatula or one of the tools specially designed for the purpose.

Beautiful pieces can be produced by a technique known as 'sgraffito'; the design is created by scratching away the unfired enamel, either from the surface of the copper or from the surface of an opaque, pre-enamelled piece. The ground enamel should be sieved on to the surface of the copper and allowed to dry, whereupon certain areas may be carefully removed. Interesting designs may be created by the use of stencils, although one must work on fairly broad lines, and the result is more mechanical; it is possible to work over the piece using the sgraffito technique after the main areas

(*Right*) The masking process: (*top*) two stencils are placed in position and coloured enamel applied and fired; (*centre*) the stencils are replaced by another one and another colour applied; finally, the stencils are removed leaving the finished design.

The simple fish shape (*far right*) was produced by 'masking' with a stencil, and the fish's features were scratched out using the *sgraffito* technique.

have been laid down. The stencils should be made from absorbent paper which, after being soaked in gum, are then applied to the prepared surface of the copper. If small, they are tricky to handle, and it may be necessary to use tweezers. Once they have been satisfactorily placed, they should be firmly smoothed down on to the copper with a clean dry brush, after which the piece can be coated with gum solution, and the enamel sieved on to the surface in the usual way. The stencils should be removed when the gum has become semi-dry. It may be necessary to prise loose the corner of the stencils with a needle before carefully removing them entirely with a pair of tweezers, care being taken not to damage the surface of the enamel. After the piece has been fired, further stencils may be applied, and the process repeated with a different colour.

Another method is to apply the enamel in the form of paste; different colours can be applied to selected areas at one time, but care must be taken to ensure that all the enamels have the same firing temperature. This technique, known as 'inlay', can be used to apply contrasting colours to those areas which have been protected by stencils. Other decorative processes make use of balls, threads, and chunks of enamel which are listed in manufacturers' catalogues and are ideally suited to the decoration of flat pieces, which should be pre-enamelled. When the location of threads, chunks or balls has been decided upon, the area should be coated with gum solution and the piece of enamel placed in position with a pair of tweezers. During the firing process, progress should be watched very carefully and the pieces withdrawn the moment the enamel is seen to be satisfactorily melted.

Pieces of solid enamel should never be left too proud of the surface as they may crack when the copper cools. Similarly, if a very thick coat of enamel is required it should be built up in successive coats rather than in one thick application.

The firing process bonds the enamel to the metal in a smooth coat, and enamelling kilns are available from several manufacturers. It is possible, however, to use a small pottery kiln, provided it is of a type with a single door (one hand must be kept free to handle the enamel pieces). If a pottery kiln is to be used, remember that the elements are exposed. Never open the door without first switching off the kiln, switching on again only after the door has been closed. A certain amount of heat loss is inevitable, but the danger involved in opening the kiln with the power switched on is too great to be ignored. Unlike pottery firing, the time required for the process of enamelling is quite short. Enamels have specific fusing temperatures which are recommended by the manufacturers; the kiln should be brought up to the required temperature beforehand and maintained for a time in order to ensure an even distribution of heat throughout the kiln. Small flat pieces can be fired adequately by means of a blowtorch or a small hot-plate kiln, which are probably the most suitable methods for the mosaicist whose requirements are limited. The hot-plate kiln is inexpensive, and has the advantage of reaching sufficiently high temperatures very quickly, and, since it is small and portable, the work can be carried out almost anywhere. The chief disadvantage of this type of kiln is that pieces cannot be counter-enamelled as they are placed directly on the hot-plate. The process of counter-enamelling is employed as a means of counteracting warping, which may cause the enamel to crack away from the metal. Copper expands when heated, and upon cooling takes a greater length of time to contract than the enamel takes to harden. The enamel follows the expansion of the metal but is unable to contract, and in consequence tends to break away. The application of a coat of enamel on to the reverse of the piece, before decoration is applied to the upper surface, helps to balance the stresses.

If a blowtorch is to be used, heat must be applied evenly over the whole area of the copper; therefore the maximum size of the piece to be fired will be strictly limited, nor can the piece be counter-enamelled, as it is placed directly on a rack. A piece of heat-resistant nichrome mesh of a suitable size should be supported on two bricks, and the copper, with the enamelled side uppermost, placed directly on the mesh. The flame is directed from below upon the under-surface of the copper, and should never be allowed to make contact with the enamel. Enamelled pieces should be carefully watched during the firing process, which is usually completed when they assume a bright red glow, and the grainy enamelled surface disappears to be replaced by one which is smooth and glossy. Special enamelling forks are useful as they facilitate the removal of the mesh racks. The racks should be placed on asbestos mats, where the pieces may be left to cool very slowly, protected from draughts. Always ensure that the enamelled pieces are cool before attempting to pick them up.

PLASTICS

Research into plastics has developed since the end of the nineteenth century, and various forms are available which offer the mosaicist a completely new range of materials. The thermoplastic group of synthetic resins includes acetates, vinyls and acrylics. The thermosetting group, the most useful from the point of view of the mosaicist, includes polyesters and epoxies. On a comparatively simple level, interesting results can be obtained with these materials, even by people with little or no experience within the field of plastics. A basic understanding of the properties of the latter group may be useful.

Briefly, to achieve a solid state the liquid ingredient must be activated by heat. The heat may be physical or chemical, although spontaneous hardening will be effected over a period of time by general exposure to sunlight or the atmosphere. In order to control the heat reaction, a catalyst is added which promotes a process known as polymerization. In its liquid state resin is made up from molecules which resemble minute beads. The process of polymerization causes the molecules to join together in long chains, which can be compared to threaded beads. Hardening is effected when these chains become so entangled that further movement is impossible. This process can be induced by an ingredient known as an 'accelerator', or by oven temperature. In the liquid state, polyesters are translucent, and have a rather treacly consistency.

Liquid resins should be bought only in sufficient quantity for immediate use; even when these products are purchased in prime condition, a storage period of about three months should be considered to be a maximum, although if stored in a cool, dark place, their shelf life will be prolonged. The lid of the container should never be left off; however, the unpleasant smell which is associated with these products usually precludes this possibility. When working with polyester, good ventilation is essential, and any allergic reaction on the part of the user or others present should be noted. If such reactions are found to be extreme, and cannot be counteracted by means of ventilation, it is not wise to continue with the use of these products. In any event, avoid inhaling the vapours which are given off by the resin, and take precautions to avoid all contact between resin or catalyst and the skin. If this does occur, the affected part should be washed immediately in a solution of boric acid and water. However, if normal precautions are taken, resins are perfectly safe to use. The catalyst should be stored in a container which bears a label indicating that the contents are poisonous and inflammable. In fact all solvents, cleaners, and thinners should be kept away from naked flames.

The additives have specific functions, but if failure persists, even when care has been taken in the use of the ingredients, the fault may lie in the physical conditions in the workshop; for instance, dust, humidity and constant extremes of temperature may have an adverse effect. The catalyst which is supplied with the resin at the time of purchase is fairly expensive. It is sometimes referred to as the hardener and at other times as MEKP (methyl-ethyl ketone peroxide). The catalyst, which is colourless and odourless, does the actual work by causing the molecules to form chains. The chemical (cobalt naphthenate) which causes the dispersal of the catalyst into the resin is the accelerator. It makes curing possible without the application of heat, and is considerably cheaper than the catalyst. Sometimes the accelerator is introduced into the resin by the manufacturers, when it is referred to as 'pre-accelerated' resin. Accelerators must always be mixed with the resin prior to the introduction of the catalyst. The resin acts as a buffer, and prevents the violent chemical reaction (causing combustion) which would take place if catalyst and accelerator were mixed together.

Casting resin changes colour very little under normal lighting conditions, but a tendency to yellow may be detected if the material is exposed for a considerable length of time to strong sunlight. It resists the action of weak acid, although weak acetone and cleaning fluids can cause a slow rate of disintegration. It is highly resistant to the effect of water, lubricating and vegetable oils, gasolene, kerosene, alcohol and soap. When cured, the material has neither odour nor taste, exhibits a marked degree of heat stability and will not craze or crack even when exposed to extremes of temperature. It also has a very slow rate of burning. Colour may be added by the use of specially prepared paste pigments, which are normally added before the process of catalysis. When using resins it is advisable to protect clothing and other surfaces.

The material may be mixed in bowls or containers made of pro-polythene or polythene, as resin does not adhere to these surfaces. Moulds for casting can be made from almost any non-porous surface provided it will resist attacks from the solvent content of the resin, although release agents can be obtained which ensure the separation of the cast from the mould. Almost any dry material can be embedded in casting resin, and recipes can be worked out which make it possible to work with extremely small quantities, provided the ratios remain constant. When the depth of the cast exceeds $\frac{1}{2}$ in. the resin should be poured in layers of less than that amount and each layer allowed to cool before the next one is poured, in order to reduce the effect of the heat which is generated. The solid cast may be drilled, machine-cut, sanded or polished.

Cast resin shapes are suitable for use as mosaic material, either coloured or with inserts of various materials. The process of casting shapes using polyester casting resin is quite simple, and the material can be prepared in small amounts in the following proportions:

RESIN VOLUME	AMOUNT OF CATALYST
1 tablespoonful	3 drops (using an eyedropper)
2 tablespoonfuls	6 drops

The gel time should be from thirty to sixty minutes depending on the room temperature, and when the cast has hardened it should be cured by placing it in hot water. Slabs can be cast in aluminium trays, glass tumblers or wooden forms; in fact, most non-porous materials of a suitable shape may be used. Care must be taken to avoid the use of articles with undercuts, or which are narrower at the top than they are at the base, as the casting will be locked in the form. Moulds can be made from glazed earthenware, disposable cups, aluminium cake tins and even tin cans, although glass remains one of the best materials for the purpose. It is important to remember that any form of textured surface will imprint on the cast.

Liquid polyesters are packaged in two parts, one container of resin and another of the catalyst, and manufacturers' instructions are usually included. When mixing resin it is advisable to use disposable materials for the purpose. However, if the containers and mixing implements are required for further use, they must be immersed in hot water and detergent after use and before the resin begins to harden. When the resin is ready to pour it will be fairly thick and syrupy, and should not be stirred too vigorously at this stage as air-bubbles may be trapped. The resin should be poured into the centre of the mould, which may then be tilted in different directions to allow the sides to be coated: when the first coating has gelled, a second coat should be poured and suitable inserts added, which will ensure that they are firmly anchored. When the material has gelled and cooled, a thicker layer may be poured over the inserts, although not in excess of $\frac{1}{2}$ in.

Allow at least twenty-four hours to elapse before removing the casting from the mould. Cast blocks may fracture, an occurrence usually caused by the addition of too much catalyst, which generates the heat to enable polymerization to take place. When polymerization is speeded up by the addition of larger amounts of catalyst, tensions are set up, as, for instance, rapid expansion or contraction. The best way in which to avoid sudden fracturing is to build up the cast in successive layers, although the heat may be countered to some extent by placing the mould in a refrigerator or in a bowl of iced water. Another fault may be observed when a variety of materials have been embedded in polyester. The inserts appear to be surrounded by a slightly metallic skin which is caused by the separation of the embedded objects

Twelfth-century book cover, Limoges enamel, Musée de Cluny, Paris: detail showing how the retaining strips of metal accentuate the lines of the drapery folds (see p. 177).

Dionysos on a panther: detail of pebble mosaic floor, Pella (see p. 185). Compare also the use of random coloured pebbles almost in the 'pointilliste' manner of Seurat (see detail overleaf).

from the surrounding resin, usually owing to the presence of dust, grease or even moisture. Another common cause is the inability of some materials to absorb the liquid resin sufficiently quickly, a fault which is particularly noticeable with certain fabrics. This can be prevented by using the minimum amount of catalyst and building up the cast to the required thickness in several thin layers, or coating the embedments with resin before use and allowing the coating to gel, after which the material may be set into the resin in the normal way.

Resin panel with embedments.

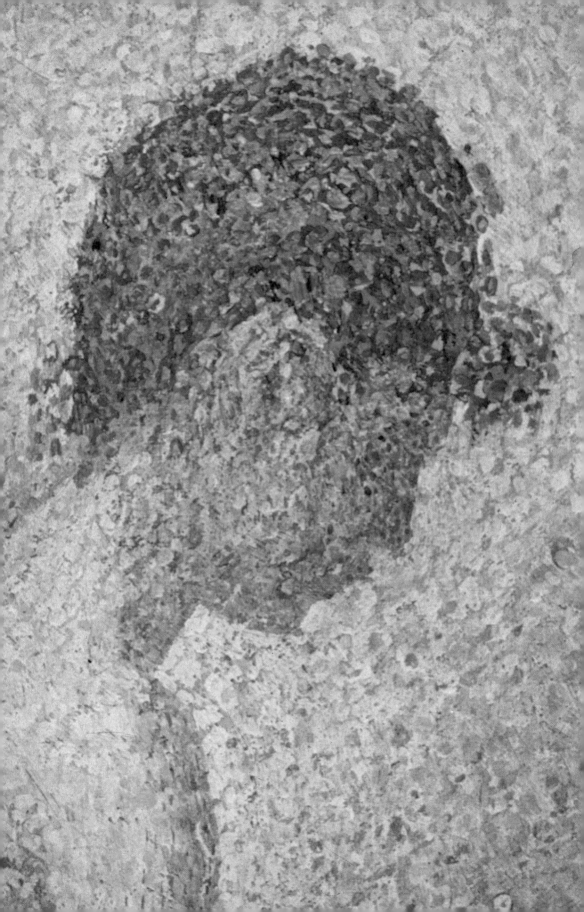

7 The Studio: practical procedure and elements of design

It is possible to undertake the production of small-scale mosaics without the amenity of a workshop, provided one has access to a fairly large kitchen sink, and a working situation in which projects can be left undisturbed. Work which includes a limited range of materials can be carried out successfully in a domestic environment provided vulnerable surfaces are protected (as fragments of glass will be scattered and accidents may occur with glue and mastic). Many people find that a garden hut, part of a garage or an attic can be adapted for use as a mosaic workshop, although the lighting arrangements must be adequate. Attic rooms impose certain limitations, as difficulty may be experienced when negotiating stairs and doors, especially when carrying panels of more than average size (after tesserae have been added the weight of a panel will be considerably increased).

When the serious mosaicist progresses beyond the modest requirements of small-scale work, it will be necessary to acquire or adapt a room which is used solely for the practice of the craft. The acquisition of space invariably leads to expansion, and it will be found that in most mosaic studios space is at a premium, especially for storage purposes. This is inevitable, as, in order to undertake fairly large-scale work (which may involve a considerable variety of material), stocks must be kept above the minimum. Working space must be allowed for, and one ought to bear in mind that even when large mosaics are carried out in sections, one should have sufficient space to view the work *in toto* from time to time if over-all control is to be maintained.

Good lighting is essential, preferably north light, which minimizes the effect of cast shadows. Mosaic has a strong light-reflecting capacity, and neither sunlight nor artificial light should be allowed to shine directly on to the surface of the work. The effect of excessive sunlight can be controlled by the introduction of blinds, but artificial lighting poses a considerable problem. If one is likely to spend long periods at work in artificial light, it may prove to be a sound economy to introduce fluorescent lighting of the 'daylight' type, which diffuses the light but does not change the colour of the tesserae. The size of the workshop ultimately depends on the scale of work which is to be undertaken, although even for normal work a room of at least 20 ft. on the shortest

(*Opposite*) *Les Poseuses*, ensemble by Seurat: detail of painting (see p. 142). Private collection, Switzerland.

137

dimension will be the minimum requirement. A sink with running water is essential, and if this is to be specially installed, choose the largest you can afford.

STORAGE

If your workshop is of sufficient size, it should be planned to include the following areas: storage for tesserae and other materials and general storage; a working area containing a mosaic table; a design area; and an area for pinning up cartoons and sketches. These are basic requirements; the inclusion of extra activities such as glass or ceramic work or carpentry will involve special planning. A system of wall-shelf storage is suitable for mosaic material, with a space underneath to accommodate bags of sand, cement and plaster, buckets for the storage of made-up glaze, and clay bins. Open storage for plaster and cement is preferable to enclosed storage (unless there is adequate ventilation) as a humid atmosphere will cause deterioration. Resins and acids should be stored according to the recommendations of the manufacturer, and indications of the presence of dangerous properties should be clearly written on the outside of the container. Containers for storing tesserae can be made from a number of materials, as they are chiefly required for the purpose of keeping each colour separate. Cardboard boxes are cheap and easily stacked if storage space is limited. They are light to handle, but tend to wear out quickly, and are of course unsuitable for the accommodation of damp material. Mixing bowls, wide-necked jars, metal, wooden or plastic boxes, plastic plant pots (with the drainage holes covered) or even deep aluminium, earthenware or metal foil pie-plates are suitable receptacles for tesserae. If possible, containers should not be stacked: it is much more satisfactory to mount wall shelves with sufficient space between each to accommodate a single container. A sample of the contents should be glued to the outside of each storage unit to indicate the colour and type of material which it contains.

If sheets of coloured glass are to be stocked, it is advisable to construct sturdy but simple racks at ground level in which to store them. Glass sheets should never be stacked one on top of the other, nor should they be stored on shelves above the floor.

A tool-rack is a useful addition to the workshop, and the correct place for each tool should be indicated by means of a painted profile on the wall behind the rack. Electric power tools should be used and stored in a position which allows for the recommended safety precautions. All work-tables should be as large as possible and completely free-standing so that they can be approached from all sides. Occasionally a very large working area may be required and it may be useful to introduce one or two trestle tables of suitable dimensions into the studio. The work-table should be strong and rigid with a flat surface, and easily movable. Whenever possible, the design area should be isolated from the practical area of the workshop so as to avoid the nuisance of dust and splashes and fragments of material infiltrating into what should be a clean area. A panel of composition board fixed to the wall adjacent to the design area will help facilitate the production of large cartoons. Full-scale designs for mural panels should always be drawn up in a vertical position.

A concrete floor is most suitable for this type of workshop, but whatever the flooring material, it should be kept scrupulously clean, particular care being taken when fragments of glass have accumulated.

ORIGINAL DESIGN

Sketches which explore and demonstrate various ideas are a vital part of the design process. The exploratory and experimental nature of such sketches should not altogether eliminate the relationship which must exist between the sketch and the proposed work. Consideration of the proportion and function of the mosaic should be included even at the sketch stage, otherwise there may be a tendency to force a design, which is seen to be attractive, but may be otherwise unsuitable. There are those who can transpose ideas into practical reality spontaneously; others need to plan the finished work in detail. Commissioned work must, in fairness to the client, bear some resemblance to the sketch design, which presumably he has seen and approved. Rough sketches should explore such aspects of design as the organization of shapes within a given space, colour and spatial relationships and textural contrasts. Later, sketches should develop these elements with reference to the material which is to be used (probably one of the most difficult aspects of the design process). A design prepared to a reduced scale and suitable for presentation to a client must not only synthesize the elements of design in order to produce a work of aesthetic merit, but should, in addition, take clear account of the function of the work, the architectural setting, the source of light, and the materials to be used. Several detailed drawings may be necessary before a satisfactory design is achieved, but the time will be well spent. A drawing in full colour and to a suitable scale should be prepared for submission to a client, and an identical copy on squared paper should be retained in the studio. This will be useful when the time comes to enlarge the design to full scale. If the work is to form an integral part of an architectural setting, a simplified cardboard scale model of the relevant section of the building (with the coloured design to a similar scale in place) may enable the client to gain a clearer and more sympathetic idea of the concept of the artist.

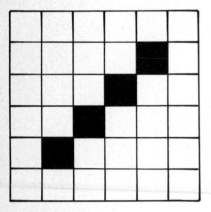

'Squaring up': the above design is an
enlargement of the top one in the
same proportions.

The term 'cartoon' denotes the full-sized drawing upon which the finished mosaic will be based. The amount of detail which is to be included in the drawing is a decision for the individual artist. Ultimately, the quality of the work depends upon the artist's ability to interpret his idea in practical terms. This should be a highly creative process, and for this reason many artists prefer not to work from a detailed cartoon. On the other hand, the cartoon can enable one to detect weaknesses of concept and construction, and, when assistants are to be employed, a fully developed design on paper will be essential if the artist is to maintain over-all control. With experience it is possible to work from a well-developed cartoon without unduly sacrificing spontaneity of expression.

A process known as 'squaring up' is used to facilitate the enlargement of the small-scale drawing prepared on squared paper. The paper upon which the cartoon is to be drawn should be divided into squares which are proportionately larger than those of the scale drawing, and the design transferred square by square. If the design is very large, and there are a great number of squares, it may be found convenient to mark the squares of the scale drawing and the cartoon with corresponding numbers. As a general rule, the more complicated the design, the closer should be the grid (and consequently, the greater the number of squares). The main lines of the design should be accurately drawn and boldly emphasized to form a strong linear pattern. A felt-tipped pen will be useful for this purpose, although in the case of a very large cartoon, bristle brushes of various sizes may be more suitable.

A small mosaic panel can be considered as a self-contained unit without external relationships; a mosaic mural, however, should never be designed without close reference to its setting. Apart from the structure of the building, other factors must be taken into account. The colour and texture of the building materials may exert a considerable effect upon the work. The nature of the surrounding landscape, the possible shapes of shadows, the direction and duration of sunlight, and the height and position in which the mosaic is to be set are also of importance with regard to the final effect. The intensity of light is another factor which must be considered, especially when glass smalti are to be used, because of their high degree of light reflection. Conversely, a number of materials absorb light, and dynamic design depends to a great extent upon the control and exploitation of the effects of light on all types of mosaic material. For instance, the manipulation of cast shadows from areas which are set in relief, the device of angling individual units in order to catch or reject light, the use of recession, and the exploitation of contrasts of shape, size and colour are factors which can introduce both liveliness and order.

Colour can be used to convey emotion, although there are no unchanging laws to assist the designer. The master works of one generation often express aesthetic values in direct opposition to those established by the previous one. There are, however, a number of factors common to all periods, differing only in the manner in which they have been used. Balance, for instance, is concerned with the manipulation of the size, shape and weight, of line, form, colour or tone in purely visual terms, in order to maintain the equilibrium of the whole. This visual congruity may be expressed by symmetry, which is achieved by the distribution of parts (exactly similar in size, shape and position) equidistant from a central fulcrum. When a design is asymmetrical, it will be found that visual balance has been established by a process of compensation. When planning a design for a mosaic, many factors which are to do with compositional balance will come under consideration. For example, a small area of texture may present more visual weight than a large unbroken surface. Similarly, the visual weight of colour varies considerably, and the preservation of balanced areas of colour is made more difficult by the fact that colour variations in a mosaic can only be achieved by what is known as 'optical mixture'.

Optical mixture

The principle of optical mixture was perfectly understood by the old master-craftsmen, although it was left to a painter, Seurat (1859–91), to evolve the theory which included consideration of colour. Seurat's theory was based on a number of scientific and theoretical writings on the subject, particularly on the work of Michel-Eugène Chevreul's *De la loi du contraste simultané des couleurs*, some of the writings of Delacroix, and *Grammaire des arts du dessin* by Charles Blanc. Blanc wrote that the role of colour 'is to tell us what agitates the heart, while drawing shows us what passes in the mind'. Chevreul had discussed optical mixture in his book, basing his observations on the occurrence of the phenomenon in weaving. He noticed that threads of two complementary colours became grey when viewed from a distance, and that this effect could only be rectified by increasing the quantity of one. The grey then became tinged with the colour which was present in greater quantity. He ruled that: 'The greater the difference between the colours, the more they mutually beautify each other; and inversely, the less difference there is, the more they will tend to injure one another.' Blanc made use of Chevreul's work in his book, which was written to supply information which he considered was not otherwise available. Blanc noticed that two colours, if placed side by side, generated a third colour when viewed from a suitable distance. Of equal importance, he devised a series of diagrams which illustrated optical mixture conclusively. Some of these theories undoubtedly influenced Seurat (he had read the book while still at school), and served as a source for his theory and practice of 'Divisionism'. Blanc also put forward important theories in connection with colour vibration. For instance, he pointed out that 'by putting tone upon tone in a pure state, blue upon blue, yellow upon yellow, red upon red, colour could be made to vibrate'. He also made important observations on the colour of light and its effect upon objects.

Seurat's early work was concerned with a search for a formula and was analytical in intention. In his own words: 'Art is harmony. Harmony is the analogy of contrary and similar qualities in tone, colour and line, considered with reference to a dominant, and under the influence of a scheme of lighting in cheerful, calm or sad combinations.' He goes on to explain that 'Cheerfulness of tone results from a luminous dominant; of colour, from a warm dominant; of line, from angles above the horizontal. Calmness of tone results from a balance of dark and light; of colour, from a balance of warm and cold; of line, from a horizontal. Sadness of tone results from a dark dominant; of colour, from a cold dominant; of line, from angles below the horizontal.' Much of the work of Seurat is of great interest to the mosaicist although few would care to proceed so rigorously.

Colour

Emotional reaction to colour can spring from an infinite variety of associations. For instance, it may have symbolic associations in accordance with the conventions of a particular cultural background. In such a case the meaning of colour has, like the meaning of words, been established by common agreement. Western civilization, for example, associates white with purity for it was the colour worn at baptism in the Early Christian Church. A direct association between colour and feeling is very common in human beings, and was a significant factor in the emotive use of colour exploited by Expressionist painters. Strong reactions and emotional responses may be sparked off by the casual juxtaposition of colours; indeed, many colours invoke liking or are disliked by direct association with previous events or feelings. Such reactions may be so strong that, when confronted with associated colours, the original event may be recalled or re-experienced by the spectator. Other senses may be stimulated by means of colour association. Indeed, many of these reactions were examined by Seurat. Colour may be hot or cold, soft or hard, fast or slow. It can soothe or disturb, calm or excite, appear agreeable or repellent. In spite of these theories, the best way to understand colour is to use it, and to learn how others have used it as an instrument of expression.

It may be useful at this juncture to include a brief explanation of the terms which are used in relation to the theory of colour. The optical theorist's term 'hue' refers to the ability of pigment or other material to reflect certain wavelengths

Form and rhythm expressed in line.

of light and energy and to absorb others. The term 'value' indicates the position which a given colour occupies within the scale of light and dark. The lower the position on the scale the nearer a colour approaches black; the higher in value, the nearer it approaches white. Colour in pigment may be altered by the addition of black or white, or both. The intensity of colour, that is, its saturation, is conditioned by the amount of hue present in the material or pigment, which, in theory, may be altered by the addition of black or white, or both. Obviously, in terms of mosaic, such an admixture would be impossible; the effect of pigmental mixture can be achieved only by optical mixture.

The impression of movement can be expressed in a number of ways, although line (which describes movement graphically and is itself the product of the movement of the hand) is the paramount method of kinetic expression. Movement, direction, form and rhythm may be indicated by the use of line within areas of apparently solid colour. Many painters have used this device, it is commonly used in embroidery and it is fully exploited by mosaicists throughout

Detail of gold embroidery enlarged eleven times.

(*Above*) Detail of mosaic from Imperial Palace, Constantinople, showing tesserae set in the form of shells.

(*Right*) Detail from apsidal mosaic, S. Clemente, Rome, showing directional lines for setting tesserae so as to express form and movement.

144

the long history of the craft. The device of filling areas with monochromatic tesserae set in the form of shells (or fans) was commonly used in classical pavimental mosaics.

Texture, in the context of mosaic, refers to qualities of surface which may be not only seen but felt. Apart from the tactile qualities of mosaic material, the variations which create visual texture do so because each material absorbs or reflects light in a particular way. The inclusion of different materials in a single work creates a source of both kinds of texture by means of broken surfaces, colour contrast, and contrast between opaque and transparent, or rough and smooth materials. However, it is important to realize that texture largely depends on scale for its effect. The seashore, when seen from a distance, appears to be perfectly smooth, an assumption which conflicts with our knowledge of its composition. Similarly, texture which may be eminently suitable for a small panel of mosaic in a domestic setting would be insignificant in a large mural situated above eye-level. Texture can define space and shape; it can give a sense of movement to form or introduce a static element. It can induce mood and variety, but should at all times be used with discretion; it must never become uncontrolled, indeed excessive texture can be self-negating.

SETTING

There are two basic methods of setting tesserae, which are fundamentally different. The direct method is the oldest, and was used even for the megalography of the classical, Byzantine and medieval periods. The reverse or indirect method (which is also known as 'parcel mosaic') was developed in an attempt to industrialize the process in order to reduce the expenditure of time and labour. Unfortunately, greater efficiency resulted in loss of flexibility in technique, and loss of quality and expression in design. The direct method is a time-consuming process, as each stone is individually embedded in mortar, or attached to some form of base with an adhesive. The *indirect method* involves a reversal of the image on to a strong paper backing (see diagram). Each tessera is pasted face downwards on to the paper, using a water-soluble paste or a solution of gum arabic. This method does not allow any variation of setting and the exposed surface will be fairly flat, whatever the material used, particularly in the case of Italian vitreous tiles.

One of the advantages of the method is that the work can be completed in the studio, then cut into sections and transported to the site. In spite of the smooth surface finish it is possible to work creatively once the difficulty of setting tesserae in a reverse direction has been overcome. It is advisable to check the progress of the work at intervals through a looking glass (which reverses the image) as it is

Parcel mosaic is 'buttered' with cement before reversal into setting bed.

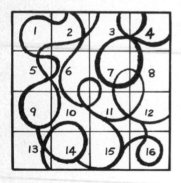

Random shapes painted on backing paper of parcel mosaic and numbered to ensure a close and correct fit when the mosaic is reversed.

possible unconsciously to adjust the setting so that the obverse image looks correct. If lettering is included in the design it is essential to check the reverse image frequently.

The tesserae may be cut and fitted in exactly the same way as in the direct method, although care must be taken to ensure that very small pieces have sufficient face contact with the paper backing, otherwise they may become detached during the fixing process, and float into the cement bed. Quite large areas may be set (limited only by the paper size) which upon completion can be cut with a craft knife into a random jigsaw pattern. These random pieces are preferable to regular squares, for, if carefully set, the lines of mortar which occur between each section seem to be less obvious. Before the panel is cut into sections, an irregular linear pattern should be painted across the backing paper, as this enables the pieces to be correctly and closely fitted when reversed into the mortar. The sections are surprisingly strong when pasted up in this manner, but care should be taken when handling those areas which are made up from predominantly small pieces. In spite of the disadvantages of the method, it does make possible the creation of large-scale works at a reasonable cost. An added advantage is that mistakes can be seen and rectified before the mosaic is fixed into the mortar bed.

Gum arabic may be bought in solution or obtained in crystal form. The crystals should be dissolved in hot water and then strained through fine muslin into a storage jar, to ensure the removal of extraneous matter. A fairly thick solution can be made and then diluted as required. For flour

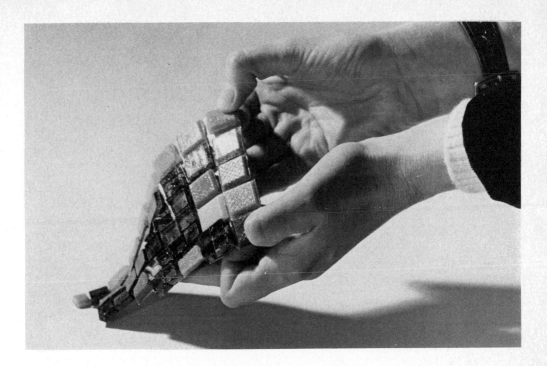

Jig-saw 'parcels' as used for Stockton Church of England Grammar School mosaic (overleaf).

paste, a solution made from one part of flour to six parts of cold water is suitable. This flour should be mixed to a thin cream with a little of the water, and the remainder may be added very slowly, stirring all the time. The mixture should be brought slowly to the boil until it thickens. Proprietary brands of cold-water paste are suitable for reverse mosaic. For small-scale work, the more expensive forms of water-soluble glues, which are supplied in tubes, are useful. The adhesive may either be applied to each tessera with a brush, or brushed on to the surface of the paper. The tesserae should be applied to the glued area while it is damp. Sufficient glue should be applied to ensure that each tessera is held firmly, but surplus glue should never be allowed to seep into the gaps between the pieces, as it could prevent the tessera from making full contact with the setting bed.

It would be wrong to pretend that setting 'parcel mosaic' on a vertical surface is easy, and large projects should be handed over to a professional tile-setter. If possible, the artist should be present when the mosaic is fixed, not only to answer queries which may arise, but to benefit from the experience of watching a difficult process made to appear easy in the hands of an expert craftsman. If the wall has been previously plastered and is in good condition, it should be thoroughly cleaned and then scored diagonally to provide a key for the setting bed. If the wall surface is of brick, it must be given a screed coat of one part Portland cement to five parts of sharp sand, which must be thoroughly mixed with water. After the screed has been applied, it should be scored diagonally before it is completely dry. Again, it may be more

Mosaic mural by Joan Haswell,
Stockton Church of England
Grammar School (see p. 175).

(see p. 175)

suitable to leave this part of the job to a professional builder. When the first coat has set, the second screed may be applied, consisting of one part of Portland cement to one part of slaked lime and six parts of sharp sand. The application should be approximately half the thickness of the tesserae if they are fairly large, or about $\frac{1}{2}$ in. thick. The screed should not cover more than 10 to 12 sq. ft.; if the total wall area is in excess of this amount, it is general practice to start at the top and gradually work down. The first section of mosaic should be 'buttered' with a thin layer of cement mortar composed of Portland cement and water, with the addition of cement colour if required. The mortar should be thoroughly worked into the spaces between the tesserae with a mason's small tool. The buttered sheet should be held gently but firmly by the top corners and placed in position on the wall with the backing uppermost. The section may then be patted gently with a flat wooden board to encourage the amalgamation of the two layers of mortar, and to ensure a flat surface. This operation should be carried out with care, as excessive pressure may bring the water content to the surface, causing the sheet to slide down the wall.

Care must be taken to ensure that the first section is correctly placed, that it is not upside down, and that the right angle of the corner is true with the right angle of the wall. Inaccuracies are cumulative, and a setting error of as little as $\frac{1}{16}$ in. on each of sixteen sections will cause the panel to be noticeably off-centre. If the sections have been cut in jigsaw fashion, even minor inaccuracies can accumulate to such an extent that it may be impossible to fit the last panels correctly, and adjustments are difficult to make at this stage. After the first section has been correctly placed, the remainder of the sections can be assembled, and the beating process repeated when an area of approximately 4 sq. ft. has been laid, to ensure that all the tesserae are embedded in the mortar and that the surface is level. When all the sections have been fixed, the panel should be left undisturbed until the mortar begins to harden, when the backing paper may be removed. Warm water may be applied, liberally, with a large brush to facilitate the removal of the paper. After the paper has been thoroughly soaked, it should peel away easily. If the moment has been judged correctly, and the cement bed is firm but not completely set, it should be possible to correct minor mistakes, such as straightening tesserae which have become twisted or tilted, or retrieving pieces which have sunk into the mortar. The panel will then be ready for grouting and cleaning.

Proprietary brands of premixed cement suitable for grout are available although they are fairly expensive if used in large quantities. A satisfactory grout can be made from one part of lime putty to five parts of Portland cement. If coloured grout is required, the cement colour should be thoroughly blended with the dry ingredients before the water is added. The natural colour of cement sometimes robs coloured tesserae of their brilliance, and the judicious use of colour in the grouting mixture can counteract this tendency, and even emphasize the brilliance of certain colours. Weatherproof cement colours are available from local builders' merchants under various trade names. When the dry ingredients have been prepared, they should be mixed to a creamy consistency with clean water, and worked into the interstices between the tesserae. As much surplus cement as possible should be removed, while it is still fluid, from the surface of the mosaic. After the grout has hardened a film of cement may be found on the surface which should be removed with a solution of hydrochloric acid (sometimes referred to as muriatic acid) and water. The solution should be weak, made up of no more than twenty per cent of hydrochloric acid, and may be applied by brush or a thick pad of soft cloth. After the application of the acid solution, the panel must be washed down several times with clean water to ensure the complete removal of the acid. After the panel has dried, it may be polished to a brilliant finish with ordinary floor wax. The hands should be protected with strong rubber gloves when handling cement and acid.

The indirect method is very suitable for functional surfaces, but the flatness of finish is not very appealing in other situations. The double reverse method helps to overcome the over-reflective monotony of a completely flat surface, although its use is confined to small-scale work or sectional murals made up from small units. The tesserae are set into a bed of moist sand, which is contained within a wooden form.

The advantage of the method is that the tesserae may be set at various angles and to different depths. When this has been satisfactorily completed, a layer of boiled fish glue should be poured over the surface and one or two layers of fine muslin or scrim pressed into the glue, and carefully moulded over the surface of the panel, care being taken not to displace the tesserae. The panel should be allowed to dry and can then be treated as an ordinary parcel mosaic. The removal of the glue and muslin will require more patience, but can be done successfully by repeated application of hot water.

Damp sand moulds are used in another process known as sand-casting. A container of adequate proportions is required to retain the sand. A wooden frame is the most suitable, although a stout cardboard box can be used for small panels. The container should be filled with damp sand firmly packed. If a free form is to be cast, the shape should be scooped out of the sand to the required depth, and the sand firmly tamped and smoothed. The tesserae are pressed into the sand and a standard concrete mix is poured into the mould, and reinforcement introduced if necessary, as described later. After the cast has been cured it should be cleaned with a wire brush. The advantage of the method is that an irregular shaped form may be produced without difficulty, although care must be taken to ensure that the base is level and the sides straight.

The direct method is a much more interesting process, as each tessera is placed individually and with due regard for its contribution towards the total effect. Angles of reflection may be considered; indeed, light can be engaged as a material element. Areas can be recessed or built up in relief, and surface texture introduced to give vitality and richness. It is possible to work in the direct method using the wide range of adhesives which are available, and in conjunction with base material other than cement mortar. Mosaics produced in this way have the advantage of comparative lightness, and panels may be prefabricated at home or in the studio, and eventually transported to the site. The materials are less messy to handle than cement, and are probably easier for the beginner to use. It should be remembered, however, that when using this method variety of surface can only be achieved by the use of materials of different thicknesses (as the base is inflexible) or by actually building up the base, unlike cement mortar which is flexible and which enables surface variety to be achieved by adjusting the depth of setting of the individual tesserae.

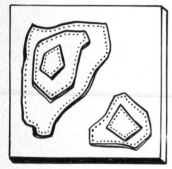

Building up a background.

(*Below*) Cutting boards: if the boards overlap and the cut goes through both, they will be bound to fit accurately.

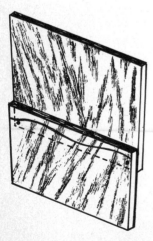

Cement mortar beds

The advantages of cement have been discussed in Chapter 3 and in certain situations cement mortar is unrivalled as a bedding material. It is cheap and gives unity to the mosaic surface, a unity which cannot be obtained to the same degree with any other material. Another considerable advantage is that concrete can be shaped and moulded, but its chief disadvantage is its weight. A panel in excess of 3 ft. × 4 ft. cannot be moved without mechanical aid. If large panels are required, and are to be prefabricated away from the site, they must be constructed in sections and reassembled. As explained previously (see p. 57), cements and mortars are extremely sensitive to temperature; they should never be exposed to a temperature lower than 10 °C. (50 °F.), and exposure to frost will render them useless.

The dry ingredients should be assembled, carefully measured, and thoroughly mixed together with a trowel on a base of wood or linoleum. It is essential that each particle of sand and aggregate is coated with cement powder. This initial mixing should never be skimped, as the final strength of the concrete could be jeopardized. The mixed dry ingredients should be formed into a heap, and a hole resembling a crater should be trowelled into the peak. Water should be poured very slowly into the crater and allowed to soak into the mixture, after which it can be trowelled until it reaches the consistency of stiff dough. A drier mixture is stronger than a sloppy one and is less likely to shrink, although the rough bed, which generally contains an aggregate or is reinforced with steel mesh or rods, may be of a softer consistency than the setting bed.

A wooden form should be constructed to contain the mortar, and if a panel is to be assembled in sections, a separate form will be required for each. The form, a wooden frame, should be at least 3 in. high and placed on a wooden base. All areas which are to come into contact with the mortar should be greased to facilitate the removal of the form when the concrete has set. A suitable mixture for the rough bed consists of one part Portland cement, two parts of clean sharp sand, and aggregate to about three parts, never in excess of four parts. It is advisable not to use too coarse an aggregate – about $\frac{3}{8}$-in. mesh is suitable. The mixture should be poured into the form and the flow assisted by means of a small trowel to ensure that the mortar is pressed well into the corners. To reinforce the panel expanded metal mesh should be cut with metal shears to a size slightly smaller than the form, and carefully laid into position on the bed, after which a second layer of mortar may be poured to cover the mesh completely, the flow again assisted with a small trowel. Sufficient mortar should then be added to bring the slab to the desired thickness and at least 1 in. above the reinforcing material.

Another method of filling the form is to place the reinforcement on the greased wooden base, and pour sufficient concrete to fill the area completely. The fingers, protected by rubber gloves, are then inserted into the mortar and the mesh pulled up into the desired position. The mixture should begin to set in a few hours, after which the surface can be roughened with a small trowel to provide a 'key' for the setting bed. The slab should be allowed to 'cure' very gradually by being kept moist for at least a week. This may be done by sprinkling the slab with water and covering it with a polythene sheet or a wet sack. When the curing process has been completed, the slab should be set aside and allowed to become thoroughly dry.

Before the setting bed is laid, the concrete slab must be soaked with water and a bonding coat applied to the surface. This can consist of a soupy mixture of cement and water, or a mixture of cement and a proprietary brand of cement glue diluted to half strength with water. The ingredients for the setting bed should be mixed in the same manner as those for the rough bed. A suitable mixture can be made from one part of the Portland cement to three parts of sharp sand, to which ten per cent of lime putty should be added. Experience will help to establish a recipe suitable for individual requirements, as a certain amount of latitude is possible, provided all the ingredients are thoroughly mixed before water is added. If a coloured setting bed is required, the colouring agent must be mixed with the dry ingredients before water is added. It is preferable to use a weatherproof, limeproof variety of cement colour. Setting time may be retarded by the addition of no more than two per cent of plaster of Paris. Alternatively, a setting bed may consist of Portland cement mixed to a dough-like consistency with plastic cement glue diluted to half strength with water (a number of proprietary brands of cement glue are sold by builders' merchants). A typical Italian recipe consists of eight parts of Portland cement to one part of aged lime putty and one part of marble dust, to which water is added to form a 'fat' mixture.

The thickness of the setting bed is dictated by the nature and thickness of the tesserae. If the bed is too deep, the tesserae may sink, and if too shallow, adhesion may be insufficient. It is impossible to lay down hard-and-fast rules as to the amount of material which may be set at one time. The working speed of the individual and the intricacy of a particular area have to be considered before a decision can be made. As a general rule it is wiser to attempt too little rather than too much. Too great a margin of error can leave one with a rapidly hardening area of mortar and too little time left to set the remaining tesserae. If such a situation arises the excess mortar should be removed completely with a trowel. Having decided on the position and the area of the first section, it must be walled off so that the mortar can be contained. This may be done by means of a pliable strip of metal, or metal edging strip which is especially useful if an irregular area is to be set. The cement mortar should be poured into the form, trowelled into the corners and finished to a smooth surface. When the tesserae have been set, the wall must be left in place for an hour or two until the mortar is sufficiently hard for the form to be removed. The process must be repeated for each successive section, the frame being set adjacent to the area which has been previously set (which must be moistened before fresh mortar is poured, to ensure adhesion).

When the panel has been completed it should be set aside and allowed to cure very slowly, following the same procedure as suggested for curing the rough bed. If required, the panel can be damped and grouted before the final cleaning with hydrochloric acid. If the mosaic surface is very irregular, the acid solution should be applied with a stiff brush and the surface well scrubbed, and then details may be further clarified by scraping away surplus grout with a surgical scalpel. Remember to wear stout rubber gloves and to remove all traces of acid solution from the work with successive applications of clean water.

This basic method may be developed in a number of ways. An obvious relationship can be seen between the classical emblemata, and an elaborate panel used as a centre-piece and incorporated within an area in which cheaper material has been laid in a random fashion. Blocks may be fabricated in a variety of shapes and assembled to form a whole, or cast to a regular shape and laid like bricks. Each block should not exceed 8 cu. ft., otherwise it will be extremely difficult to move. If smooth pebbles are used, care must be taken to ensure that they are firmly bedded, especially when they are to be included in a floor mosaic. A sound foundation is essential for pavimental mosaic, and if a large area is to be prepared, professional assistance may be required. A concrete bed at least 4 in. thick should be laid, the mortar being mixed in the proportion of one part Portland cement to three parts of sand. After the bed has been allowed to cure, a setting bed should be prepared consisting of one part of Portland cement to two or three parts of sand, to which may be added lime putty and a bonding agent. Although the work may be on a different scale, the procedure is identical with that which has been outlined for the production of a small mosaic panel. Both the direct and indirect methods may be used.

Panels which are intended for indoors can be prepared by an indirect method involving some of the adhesives and base materials which were described in Chapter 3. All types of board should receive several coats of a waterproofing agent, and particular attention should be paid to the edges; even marine ply should be treated with further coats of waterseal. As a general rule, panels up to and including 2 sq. ft. can be carried out on a $\frac{1}{2}$-in. baseboard; for panels between 2 sq. ft. and 16 sq. ft. in area, $\frac{5}{8}$-in. material will be suitable, and for those over 16 sq. ft., use $\frac{3}{4}$-in. board. If the material is to be used for seating, the baseboard should be at least 1 in. thick.

Transferring the cartoon

After the waterseal has dried, the cartoon may be transferred to the base, using sheets of carbon paper. When very large-scale works are undertaken, it may be found necessary to divide the panel into sections in order to expedite handling after the tesserae have been applied. If the mosaic is to be transported, the sizes of entrances and exits must be carefully considered; even the means of transport have a bearing on decisions concerning the size and shape of the sections. When this has been established the cartoon should be divided into irregular sections by means of a clear line drawing, for which a felt-tipped pen is best. The cartoon, including the dividing lines, should be transferred accurately on to the baseboard. This must be done with precision to ensure that the panel is reassembled correctly on the site. The panel may then be cut into sections, using an electric drill with a jigsaw extension. All cut edges should receive two or three coats of waterproofing compound.

Setting agents

When glue and plastic adhesive are used, the setting process is straightforward. An area of suitable size should be coated with the adhesive, and the tesserae pressed into it. Alternatively, each unit may be 'buttered' individually and applied to the dry base, or both base and tesserae may be coated with adhesive. The choice of method will be influenced by the type of work being undertaken: if it is very intricate and likely to proceed slowly, 'buttering' individual tesserae will be the best method of application, and this also applies if the operative habitually works slowly. Rushing to complete an area can set up tensions and cause wrong decisions; when running out of time, always scrape away some of the adhesive from the board rather than make an attempt to complete the section.

It is possible to use cement mortar as a setting agent on a board though this adds considerably to the over-all weight. The board must be given several coats of waterseal and allowed to dry. The design should then be transferred to its surface, the main lines being emphasized more strongly than usual. A sheet of expanded metal mesh is then laid over the drawing, and trimmed to size with metal shears. The mesh can be attached to the board with rust-proof staples, which should be hammered in at intervals of not less than 3 or 4 in. A wooden frame of suitable thickness should be nailed around the base in order to contain the mortar, which can then be applied in the normal manner. The setting procedure is identical with that adopted for a concrete panel, as outlined earlier in the chapter.

When plywood or composition boards are used, provision for hanging should be made before the tesserae are set, in order to avoid disturbing the surface. The most suitable hangers are those which allow the board to remain flat against the wall. If the panel is to be fixed to a wall of hollow construction, toggle bolts should be used. The toggle bolt is a bolt with a swing joint which is inserted into a hole in the wall, and is then straightened, perpendicular to the bolt and across the hole. When the bolt is tightened, the swing joint is pressed against the interior of the wall. Keyhole bolts and

Setting in cement mortar on a metal mesh on board.

shields may also be used for fixing wood-based mosaics. The bolt is fixed to the wall, and the keyhole shield screwed on to the baseboard, which is then slipped over the bolt. The most suitable bolt for concrete construction is the lag or expansion bolt. Lag bolts are screwed into expansion shields; this shield expands as the bolt is screwed into it, and the expansion bolt has a shank which expands as it is screwed into place. When a sectional mosaic has been erected on the site, or tesserae have been deliberately omitted to allow bolt holes to be drilled, exposed areas may be made good after assembly.

If a panel is to be framed, various materials may be used, such as aluminium, brass, copper or wood strip (which must of course be sealed like the base). Wood can be readily obtained, and is very easy to treat, handle and stain, but has the disadvantage of adding to the over-all weight. When metal strip is used, it must be laid flat on a workbench and carefully marked out for drilling. Nails should be placed along a line which is equivalent to half the thickness of the baseboard. For small boards the nails should be spaced out at fairly small intervals; for larger boards the intervals may be increased, although not in excess of $1\frac{1}{2}$ in., and 1 in. from each corner. The marks are then punched and drilled, and the strip fitted, using $\frac{5}{8}$-in. tacks (preferably of brass). If the strip is reasonably strong, it may be necessary to hammer it round each corner; when doing so, the metal should be protected, for example by glueing a piece of leather to the head of the hammer.

8 Modern developments and techniques

The decline of the craft of mosaic began during the fifteenth century, coinciding with new developments in painting and sculpture. Craftsmen were tempted to abandon the forms of expression which had been developed and consolidated in the past out of a profound acceptance of the nature of fragmented design. Presumably, in order to meet the challenge of changes which were taking place, the mosaicists allowed themselves to be seduced by notions of plasticity which were more properly the province of the painter. Not only were the effects of painting sought after (the period saw the beginning of this approach which subsequently became common), but also famous painters were commissioned to design the cartoons which were then executed by experienced mosaic craftsmen. Few of the painters had themselves any real experience in the technical aspect of the work; as a consequence, the craftsman was relegated to an inferior position and set to carry out designs which were unsuitable. Many well-known painters, including Mantegna, Raphael, Titian, Veronese and Tintoretto, produced designs which were subsequently executed by others. Mosaics carried out after cartoons by Titian can be seen in the church of St Mark's in Venice. The dome decoration of the Chigi Chapel in Sta Maria del Popolo in Rome were executed by a Venetian, Luigi da Pace, after cartoons by Raphael. The current idea was that the mosaic medium constituted a means of producing 'painting for eternity', and mosaic remained in great demand. During the nineteenth century Italian mosaic workers were employed in a number of capital cities including London, Paris and even St Petersburg. The process of industrialization had already begun during the nineteenth century with the introduction of parcel mosaic. The substitution of glass composition tiles for the traditional glass smalti hastened a changing technique.

The contemporary revival of the craft demonstrates some interesting new aspects. The traditional function, and some of the traditional modes and techniques related to the practice of mosaic, which have been considerably revitalized, may be set alongside a number of experimental aspects, primarily concerned not with the introduction of new materials, nor with the utilization of mixed media, but rather with function and style. Perhaps the most remarkable development is the widespread adoption of mosaic as an amateur activity, as a form of expression rather than as part

(*Opposite*) Spire of the church of the Sagrada Familia, near Barcelona, designed by Antoni Gaudí (see p. 159).

of a commercial programme. As a consequence, a form of mosaic picture has emerged in which techniques are used which were previously reserved for monumental works. Portable miniature mosaics were produced in the past, although differing from larger works in that minute tesserae were employed, and the setting bed was usually mastic or occasionally wax. Of equal significance is the extension of the craft into the sphere of general education. Here a genuinely experimental aspect has been engendered, often as a result of the change-over from traditional materials to those which can be manufactured or salvaged.

USE OF TRADITIONAL METHODS

Traditional requirements are served by such concerns as the Vatican workshop, which was founded in the eighteenth century. The workshop still operates within the tradition which originated at the time of its foundation, a tradition based on the technique of painting rather than on that of mosaic. Originally, glass smalti were manufactured in a small factory within the Vatican city, although this has ceased to operate. A wide colour range, in excess of 28,000 shades, necessitated an elaborate filing system and made the copying of painting a practical possibility. Mosaic versions of paintings by Raphael, Leonardo, Guido Reni and many others were exported in great numbers. These works were deprived of the true qualities of both painting and mosaic, although they were technically superb. Subsequently the workshop undertook the production of replicas of classical mosaics as a source of revenue. Coincident with the revival of interest in the superb mosaic schemes which are to be found in a number of Roman churches, the Vatican craftsmen extended their activities into the field of restoration work. The fact that the well-trained Italian craftsmen possess undeniable technical expertise accounts for the fact that they are still employed in workshops and studios which exist in many European cities. The organization of these studios seems to be remarkably similar to those of the Byzantine period. General supervision is exercised by one man who allocates work according to the skill of the craftsman. The design is fully organized and presented in the form of detailed cartoons and must be strictly adhered to when work commences. Colour selection is the responsibility of the supervisor – even to the extent of mixing the tesserae for backgrounds.

The process of indirect setting played a large part in the semi-industrialization of the craft. Large mosaics were prepared in workshops, cut into sections and transported to sites, distance being of little importance. On the credit side, however, the supply of parcel mosaics to a widespread international marketing area increased the awareness of the craft. The Salviati workshop, which was founded in Venice during the 1860s, played a significant part in the industrialization of mosaic. Similarly, the Wagner workshop, which was founded in Berlin towards the end of the nineteenth century, played a major part in the popularization of the technique. Apart from the fabrication of parcel mosaic, the company manufactured glass smalti. A branch of the company was established in America in 1923, where they extended their activity into the field of secular decoration.

ANTONI GAUDÍ

Apart from the activities of workshops and companies, a number of individual artists began to show interest in the medium. Perhaps one of the most original was the Spanish architect Antoni Gaudí y Cornet (1852–1926), who developed a unique method of covering large exterior surfaces, both plane and formed. That so much of his decoration was applied to exterior surfaces gives him a unique place as one of the pioneers in a modern idiom. He was trained as an architect in Barcelona, and his first completely independent work was the Casa Vicens. This building is of particular interest as it bore what was to become the characteristic decoration of polychrome tile, in combination with stone and brick. Gaudí's method of introducing colour into his architecture by means of polychrome tile was a restatement of Arab forms. His work was remarkably expressive, owing a great deal to both the medieval and the oriental, and played a vital part in establishing a romantic reaction against the overplayed forms of neo-classicism.

He was extensively employed by a wealthy industrialist named Eusebio Güell y Bacigalupi, for whom he designed the Palacio Güell upon which he was engaged between the years 1885 and 1889. One of the most important commissions of this period was the design of the church of the Sagrada Familia (the Holy Family) which was to be constructed in the suburbs of Barcelona. Although he received the commission in 1884, the building occupied him until his death. The decoration of this church is of particular interest to the mosaicist. In his reaction against the rationalization of building methods (with the attendant danger of standardization) he used ceramic and glass pieces in a completely inventive way to provide a scheme of decoration. His argument against rationalization is set down clearly in the following passage:

> But if in the present day labour is expensive, and one needs to avoid this expense, one can only economize on the methods of procedure – any other way would be mutilation and not economy; every thing depends upon making abundant use of what is easily available, and utilizing in small quantities, or avoiding altogether, that which is expensive to obtain.

Gaudí considered that 'colour complements form and gives it light'. He gave practical expression to his ideas by means of an almost extravagant polychrome. He wrote, 'ornamentation has been, is, and will always be polychromatic', and he also gave a highly personal symbolic role to colour. Examples of the inventiveness with which he applied a coloured 'skin' to the fantastic forms which he created can be seen in numerous works: the façade of the Casa Batlló; the fanciful spires of the Sagrada Familia, and the serpentine benches on the terrace of the Park Güell. Of considerable interest are a number of ceramic medallions by a collaborator, Jose Maria Jujol, which decorate the ceiling of the hypostyle hall of the Park Güell. Here Jujol developed a form of mosaic collage, brilliantly coloured tesserae being set against ceramic objects such as the bases of bottles, cups and dishes, which he arranged in dynamic forms of stars and spirals. The decoration of the Casa Battló was added as part of the conversion of the house which Gaudí undertook between the years 1905 and 1907. The theme of the exterior mosaic was concerned with the elements of sky and water, and was described by Salvador Dali in the following words:

> . . . it is a real building and the true sculpture of the reflections of twilight clouds in the water, which was made possible by recourse to a huge and insane multi-coloured mosaic, shining with pointillistic iridescence from which the forms of water emerge, water that has spread and is spreading, forms of stagnant water, forms of shimmering water, forms of wind-sprayed water.

The spires of the Sagrada Familia demonstrate the meaning of Gaudí's words: 'Colour complements form and gives it light.' The brilliant encrustation of white, gold and red shimmers and sparkles, yet is balanced by contrast with stone and brick. He wrote: 'These other materials should include unpolished ashlar, brick, and terracotta for ornament, and sometimes bronze, iron and lead, but rarely wood.' He was one of the first of the Spanish architects to make use of reinforced concrete. The open-air theatre of the Park Güell has an arrangement of cement benches which undulate like an enormous exotic snake across the terrace. The brilliantly flamboyant decoration is achieved by encrustations of glass and fragments of ceramic and porcelain.

OTHER ARTISTS

Inevitably, the technique of fragmentation attracted a number of painters, notably the Futurist painter Gino Severini, who was concerned with the interdependence of art and architecture. After the collapse of the Futurist movement he moved to Paris, where he associated with a number

Serpentine bench in Park Güell, Barcelona, designed by Antoni Gaudì:
detail.

Totem by Joan Haswell (see p. 177).

Ritual King by Joan Haswell (see p. 177).

Angel by Joan Haswell (see p. 177).

Flying Fish (detail) by Joan Haswell (see p. 177).

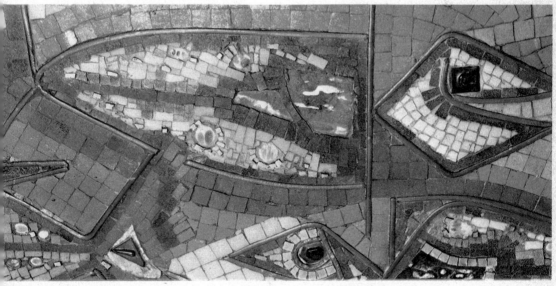

(*Above*) *World Shaker* (detail) by
Joan Haswell (see p. 178).

of the leading experimenters of the time, among them Braque, Picasso, Dufy and Utrillo. He was also greatly influenced by Divisionist theories of colour. In his writing Severini exhibits his deep awareness of the principles of mosaic. These he attempted to express through his own work in the medium, although, because of this, he must be seen as a reviver rather than an innovator; his understanding played no small part in the revival of interest in the basis of the technique which had for so long been neglected and despised. He wrote:

> In each form of expression, but especially in mosaics, design and technique are inseparable. . . . In the mosaicist's hands everything takes life, from the hammers and chisels to the stones and enamels.

Again:

> If I have so much interest and I might add so much love, for that marvellous form of art, mosaics, it is because I have so much respect for the materials which characterize it. Mosaic can be a powerful force in introducing clarity and purity into art. . . .

The Russian Boris Anrep (1883–1969) was a significant figure in the revival of mosaic, although a considerable amount of his output was archaicizing, as, for instance, his work for the Roman Catholic Cathedral of Westminster. However, when given the opportunity to undertake work which required a contemporary solution, he proved himself more than equal to the task. His pavimental mosaic for a house in Upper Brook Street in London was a demonstration of his ability to come to terms with contemporary requirements. So much so that the 'high priest of modernism', Roger Fry, commented most favourably on it. He habitually undertook pavimental work, examples of which can be seen in the Tate and National Galleries in London. His importance is due to the fact that he understood the essential nature of the fragmented medium, and that he consistently worked from his own designs. He was assisted in his work by a number of young artists who were enabled to share his insight. The American artist Jeanne Reynal, who played a vital part in the revival of mosaic in America, was an assistant in Anrep's studio. She mastered the traditional disciplines, and upon returning to America undertook work of a genuinely experimental nature. She investigated the possibilities of a technique whereby fragments of glass and stone were dribbled upon a surface of damp mortar, after which a process of selective adjustment took place, so emulating to some extent the work of the Action painters.

Contrary to the principle expressed by Severini, a number of modern painters have designed for the mosaic medium, and then handed over the cartoon to an executant, who was obliged to interpret the design in terms of mosaic. That this was not always successful was less the fault of the craftsmen than that of the designer, who more often than not submitted a design in his normal style. Many of these works were in fact painter's drawings and not true cartoons, and inevitably the finished work failed fully to exploit the qualities of the medium. Examples of this practice can be seen in the work of Chagall in the Knesset building in Jerusalem, which was executed *in situ* by Italian craftsmen in 1960. Hjalmar Boyesen has executed work from designs by Picasso and Jean Lurçat.

The work designed by Gustav Klimt for the Palais Stoclet, known as the Stoclet Frieze (*Stocletfries*), was executed between 1909 and 1911 by the *Wiener Werkstätte* under the direction of Leopold Forstner and Klimt himself. Josef Hoffman was commissioned by Adolphe Stoclet to design the Palais in the modern style, and the interior design, in the hands of the *Wiener Werkstätte*, was to be considered as an integral part of the scheme. The house was erected in the Avenue de Tervueren in Brussels, and was enthusiastically praised by those who were attracted to new architectural forms. A. S. Levetus said: 'There can be no doubt that the Stoclet Palace in Brussels represents a landmark in the history of modern architecture.' Klimt produced a series of detailed cartoons in mixed media including gouache, gold and silver leaf, tempera, watercolour, chalk, and pencil. The work was carried out on a ground of honey-coloured Paonazzo marble, again in mixed media, which, in addition to gold smalti, included coral, semi-precious stones, coloured faience, silver plate, and copper plates. The murals are located in the 'large dining room' which is 45 ft. in length, with a simple source of light at the far end. This provides a subdued light of a strength exactly right for the seductive surfaces of the murals and the furnishings. Klimt's decorations comprise three themes which are entitled 'Tree of Life', 'Expectation' and 'Fulfilment'. There are a great number of motifs made up from borrowings of art forms of diverse origin from such places as Japan, Egypt and Byzantium.

THE MEXICAN REVIVAL

That the revival of mosaic is an international phenomenon is borne out by such events as the international conventions which have been held in Italy, sponsored by the Italian Rotary Club, the Chamber of Commerce, the National Museum of Ravenna and the National Society of Tourism. Such gatherings allow for discussions, addresses and exhibitions, and, perhaps even more important, the interchange of ideas between craftsmen of many nations. The Mexican revival has been of great significance as it has led to the production of a number of mosaic schemes on a large scale. The Mexican architect, Juan O'Gorman, was responsible for the

University City library, Mexico, with mosaic murals by Juan O'Gorman.

design of the largest external mosaic of modern times. The mosaic is sited on the walls of the library block at University City, Mexico, and covers a total area of 4,400 sq. ft. Before undertaking this immense work, O'Gorman had devised natural stone mosaics for his home in San Angel, and later in Pedregal. The stone units were applied directly into a bed of mastic, and the decoration was allowed to flow over the surfaces of walls, ceilings and floors in a manner reminiscent of that of Gaudí. The decoration of the University Library was also carried out in natural stone, collected from many parts of Mexico. O'Gorman was well aware of the dangers inherent in over-all decoration of this type. He wrote:

> ... the first thing was to find a scale of plastic values to fit the building, one which would be correct in size when seen from various points of view, without over-small details or over-large figures which would have destroyed the monumentality of the building. The second thing was to relate the material of each wall to the composition of the four walls so that they would be regarded as one unit plastically and aesthetically. In the third place, it was necessary to bring each of the four walls into dynamic symmetry so that the total composition would form one geometric structure in three dimensions. ...

The method of fabrication and of fixing the individual units was very interesting. Black-and-white drawings were made and the ideas were further developed by means of coloured sketches. The full-size cartoons, in black and white, were drawn in reverse upon a huge, specially constructed drawing area. The cartoon was cut up into sections about a yard square. Each section was laid in a form, and stones up to 2 in. in size were placed in position on the cartoon. The forms were then filled with concrete, and reinforced with steel rods. Hooks were fixed to the reinforcing rods, and the finished slabs were attached to the exterior walls of the library by engaging the hooks with a steel grid which had been erected upon the surface of the building. The interstices were subsequently made good by the application of additional concrete.

Other Mexicans have responded to the availability of a vast range of natural materials which are to be found in their country. José Chavez Morado has combined natural stone with glazed and unglazed ceramics. Diego Rivera (1886–1957) has produced one of the most important experiments in the mosaic medium, obviously indebted to the work of Antoni Gaudí, which takes the form of an environmental mosaic sculpture situated outside the waterworks of Mexico City. The subject-matter appropriately depicts the rain god Tlaloc. Another important work by Rivera is a mosaic relief which depicts the merging of the Spanish and Indian races to form the Mexican nation, sited on the lava walls of the Mexico City Stadium.

OTHER MODERN WORKS

A number of Swiss artists have worked in the mosaic medium. One of Hans Erni's major works, for the broadcasting building at Berne, owes its technical expertise to the master craftsmen of the Ravenna school. Another Swiss, Hans Stocker (born 1896), was responsible for a Christ in Majesty for the Kaiser Friedrich Memorial Church in Berlin. Stocker used the traditional iconography of the subject, and combined it with a non-linear broken technique to produce a work in which the materials figure with a sparkling intensity. Giulio Padoan of Italy has been responsible for work as far afield as Belgium and Dallas, Texas. Gert Marcus of Stockholm has produced abstract works that greatly emphasize the textural possibilities of the medium, which, in spite of the lack of specific subject-matter, are strangely moving. The Scandinavians have made a notable contribution to the use of mosaic as a decorative feature of modern architecture, especially in public buildings.

In England the Greater London Council and London Transport have been active in their support for architectural decoration, and mosaic has been utilized for the purpose.

The work of Antony Hollaway has been notable in this respect. He has produced many decorative schemes under the aegis of the London County Council Architects' Department, and to comply with the restrictions of a very limited budget, Hollaway has frequently used cheap materials. Hans Unger and his colleague Eberhard Schulze have been responsible for works in mixed media, one of the most important being a mural for the headquarters of Penguin Books Limited at Harmondsworth, Middlesex. Glass smalti are combined with ceramic tiles upon which coloured glass was used. Polished typefaces, printing blocks and linotype pages were also included in the design and set against areas of slate.

A genuine 'folk' aspect has developed, and, rather surprisingly, a number of works of monumental intention have been produced. Among the better-known works are the towers of Simon Rodia, an untrained tile-setter, who is a true folk artist in that he works to satisfy an inner compulsion which allows him to produce works which are neither commercial nor functional. These extraordinary edifices are neither architectural nor purely sculptural but strange hybrids born of a singular talent. They are situated on the fringe of a somewhat run-down area of Los Angeles, rising 100 ft. into the air. These structures, which comprise towers, pavilions and archways, form an extensive and mysterious labyrinth, the result of nearly half a lifetime of patient labour. All the material has been salvaged, the structures being created from metal pipes, steel rods, and even salvaged bed frames. After assembly the frames were coated with concrete into which were embedded innumerable fragments of shells, pebbles, glass and broken pottery. The inventive variety of pattern creates areas which sparkle and glitter on a framework of structural intricacy. The reason for the creation of these remarkable edifices was apparently to satisfy the artist's desire to create something big. They are monuments to persistent and creative craftsmanship, and exhibit that responsiveness to colour and form of which so many are capable even if completely untrained.

Examples of a similar type of folk art which appear to have been inspired by the same desire for expression can be seen in the work of two Frenchmen, Fernand Chevel at Hauterives in France and Raymond Isidor who created the *Châteaux des Assiettes Cassées* (Châteaux of Broken Plates) at Chartres. The attraction of these works lies in the fact that they exemplify an almost universal response towards colour and decoration, and find expression with a directness and individuality which is fresh and unfettered. Juan O'Gorman expressed his admiration of these works:

> These breaths of freshness and pure creation, where the imagination is applied for the expression of freedom, are a wonderful relief in the stagnant academic atmosphere of our pretentious commercial modern times, and reveal the aspiration of liberty of the common people, their love of decorative free expression, which is the beneficial character of the Baroque.

Changed conditions have radically altered the traditional alliance between religious art and architecture. Instances occur, although rarely, of the artist's assuming total responsibility for the scheme, as in the chapel at Vence which was devised by Matisse. Occasionally it is the architect who accepts responsibility for the total scheme, as Le Corbusier did at Ronchamp. The church of Assy represents an attempt to integrate the work of several artists. These cases are exceptional however, and the extent of their contribution towards a reasonable solution to the problem of the forms of religious art will be debated for some time to come. In reality, the artist is usually involved as but one of several specialists responsible for such things as lighting, heating, sanitation and fenestration. A similar situation existed during the medieval period when the 'fine arts' were not distinguished from the 'mechanical arts'.

The Assy Experiment

The facts attendant upon the erection of the church of Notre-Dame-de-Toute-Grâce at Assy in France provide a case history of the problems which arise upon attempts to achieve an integration between religious architecture and the arts. The Dominicans who formed the spearhead of the Sacred Art Movement were opposed to the revival of historical styles. Many people very properly realized that the great works of the Middle Ages were the outcome of fervent concepts which inspired new and daring forms, the essence of which could not necessarily be recaptured. Le Corbusier has expressed his awareness of the inspired daring of medieval building. He said, 'When the Cathedrals were white', the new men were seeking what he refers to as 'a brand-new, prodigious, madly rash technique' and he goes on to say that the application of this technique led to 'forms the spirit of which disdained the legacy of a thousand-year-old tradition'. The newly finished church of Assy, which was served by the Dominican Order of Preachers, was attacked in the most violent terms almost as soon as it was consecrated in 1950. Massive opposition was mounted from leading conservative Catholic groups, and the basic concepts of the Sacred Art Movement were criticized by the Vatican. Particularly virulent attacks were directed towards the sculptured crucifix by Germaine Richier. So bitter was the opposition to this particular work that it was eventually removed from the church.

A number of well-known artists participated in the Assy experiment, including Rouault, Matisse, Lipchitz, Chagall, Bonnard, Lurçat and Léger. Apart from the Catholic Rouault, the group included atheists, Communists and Jews. The tragedy of Assy was that although seriously misunderstood, a genuine attempt was made not only to revitalize sacred art, but to break through the terrible stranglehold of conformism and sterility. André Rousseau, writing in *Le Figaro*, stated the case: 'With respect to modern art the cries of scandal are so loud that the Bishop orders the removal of the scandalous object, the Crucifix of Assy; on the other side – oh, well, on the other side nothing happens.' It seemed that the weakness of the schemes was inherent in the fact that many of the individual artists were incapable of expressing the dogma of the Christian faith because of their inability to accept it. The individual contributions are simply works of art with a religious subject-matter, rather than works of religious art. Thus the continuity of the inconographic programme at Assy suffers considerably. The figures are depicted without employment, narrative is non-existent and, in consequence, dogma is unstated. The central protagonists of the religious drama are virtually removed from the cast; the figure of Christ appears only three times. Father Coutourier, one of the central figures in the Assy controversy, wrote:

It is clear that Assy, Vence and Audincourt . . . are antipodal to the Byzantine tradition and its spirit. At a time when the Church lives practically in diaspora and when immense sections of cultural and social life have eluded it – when at least its institutions and its people are in constant inferiority – conceptions, doctrines, and attitudes of a Byzantine type cannot but be fallacious.

Controversy aside, perhaps the most interesting aspect of the Assy decoration is the façade of the church which was designed by Fernand Léger, and executed by craftsmen of the Maison Gaudin in Paris. The subject is the Virgin of the Litany and the mosaic was designed to occupy the western façade – not an ideal situation from the artist's point of view. The area measured 20·6 metres (67 ft.) across the base with a gabled top which reached a height of 10 metres (33 ft.) at the apex, but the plane surface was disrupted by nine windows and a door, and obscured by six columns and two spur walls. The work was produced by the reverse method and carried out in brilliantly coloured glass tesserae and cubes of marble. The fact that Léger was a Communist caused consternation in conservative Catholic circles. This was hardly surprising as in 1931 Léger had publicly expressed the idea that something should be substituted 'for the sentimental and outmoded church'. He wished to see the emergence of something 'capable of liberating humanity from the interference of the religious'. Such words were hardly likely to endear him to the orthodox. Yet Léger was probably more capable of producing work which would integrate with the building than any of the contributing artists. He had studied Byzantine mosaics, and had found himself to be in accord with at least the formal solutions which the period offered. What he could not do, and indeed was not asked to do, was to emulate the spiritual unity of the period, although undoubtedly the idea of collective expression appealed to him.

MOSAIC IN SECULAR ARCHITECTURE

Fortunately for the mosaic artist, secular architecture provides a less controversial substitute for the traditional areas of patronage. The United States has seen a spirited revival of the craft as a form of architectural decoration. Civic, religious and educational establishments throughout the country have received mosaic embellishments in various forms. Joseph Young, a professional mosaicist, is one of the leading craftsmen in this field. He studied under the well-known teacher George Kepes at the Massachusetts Institute of Technology and at the American Academy in Rome. It is clear from his writing that he gained an insight into, and maintains a profound respect for, the work of the past, which has enabled him to approach his own work in a manner proper to one who regards himself as part of a continuing tradition. His large and ambitious decoration devised for the main exterior auditorium wall of the Los Angeles County Hall of Records,

(*Opposite*) *Clown* by Joan Haswell (see p. 178).

Trastevere by Joan Haswell (see p. 179).

which is a combination of mosaic and granite bas-relief and occupies an area 80 ft. × 20 ft., was installed in 1962. The design is based on an aerial topographical map, and portrays the water sources and the formation of the land areas in the Los Angeles area. The mosaic insert depicts the direction of the main waterways, including a representation of the Pacific Ocean. The technique necessitated the production of a large reinforced concrete bas-relief to which granite and mosaic veneers were attached, and water is allowed to flow down specially constructed channels.

His works include a mosaic mural for the Jewish Emmanuel Temple at Beverly Hills, California, and the mosaics for the Presentation of the Blessed Virgin Mary Church, Midland, Pennsylvania. This prefabricated glass mosaic occupies an area of 32 ft. × 34 ft. behind the main altar. The work represents a major act of patronage. Of particular interest is the way in which areas of grout have been stained to produce calculated effects.

The large mosaic mural which was designed and executed by the author for the combined assembly hall and chapel of a Church of England grammar school was carried out by the indirect method. The mural, which occupies a 12 ft. × 24 ft. area, had to be produced as economically as possible. In order to do so, while at the same time introducing gold smalti to add sparkle, and to make the scheme more telling from a distance, the cutting of tesserae was kept to an absolute minimum. This did not prove too difficult owing to the fairly large scale of the mosaic. The cutting was limited to those passages which could not be successfully expressed otherwise.

The theme of the mosaic was intended to express the spirit of the text from Isaiah, which had to appear prominently in the design. The work (p. 148) was carried out entirely in vitreous glass mosaic, with the exception of small areas of more expensive gold smalti within the panel itself, and the use of gold for all the lettering within the border. Again, in order to keep cutting to a minimum, the lettering was specially designed and was based on two sizes of gold smalti. The individual sections were not carried out on regular squares of brown paper, but were cut into intricate shapes, resembling the units of a huge jigsaw. This process was adopted in order to reduce the possibility of the joints being detected. This was not completely successful as the wall was out of true, and adjustments had to be made during the fixing process.

An attractive mosaic mural fascia of a public house adds colour to the redevelopment scheme of Edinburgh's Royal Mile, which, in spite of its picturesque appearance, was in a grave state of disrepair. Furthermore, the living conditions of many were squalid and insanitary, and the authorities were faced with the usual dilemma of many ancient cities both here and in Europe. A decision was taken to redevelop the area, and the difficult task has been undertaken with a considerable degree of sensitivity and concern for the local character of the area. The fascia of the *Blue Blanket* pub is in riven-faced Caithness stone panels, and the mosaic mural tells the story of the Blue Blanket, a rallying standard which was used when danger threatened the city. The name is sunk-raised in the granite in a large, strong letter-form. The figural design has also been sunk-raised in the Caithness stone, and the details filled with tesserae of stone, glass and ceramic. The background to the historical episodes consists of famous Edinburgh landmarks which have been carved directly into the Caithness stone. They include the Cathedral of St Giles and Edinburgh Castle.

MIXED MEDIA

The field of mixed media has been among the most productive and original aspects of the contemporary revival. Louisa Jenkins, a well-known American mosaicist, has undertaken a variety of projects which include architectural murals, patios and the decoration of interiors. Her work is especially interesting because of the variety of material and processes which she uses. Helen and Margaret Bruton were among the earliest pioneers of the revival. Apart from the importance of her role in reintroducing an awareness of mosaic in the United States, Helen Bruton has played a significant part as an experimenter, although she has never departed from the established procedure simply for experiment's sake. Another artist, Mary Bowling, has produced architectural decorations by a technique which she refers to as 'intarsia'. The term exactly describes the technique, mosaic units being laid into a plain wall area. Frans Wildenhain has been responsible for large-scale mosaic murals made entirely from clay units. His monumental mural for the Strasenburgh Laboratories, Rochester, N.Y., although based on conventional laboratory equipment, is an agglomeration of carved and decorated clay units which, in spite of their relationship to prosaic objects, have an air of exotic richness. The sun symbol which forms the central theme of the project is a *tour de force*. Each piece was created from a thick slab of clay to which every conceivable form of texture was applied; the slab was then carefully hollowed out from the back before being fired. Many sections were glazed and fired several times until the desired effect was achieved.

Charles Schlein, an American carver, has incorporated mosaic and woodcarving, the mosaics being inlaid into areas channelled out from the wood so that they are flush with the surface. A similar technique has been employed by Emmy Lou Packard, whose *Fighting Cock*, executed for the *S.S. Lurline*, was carved from a block of Japanese ash 2 in. thick which was then inlaid with tesserae. Three-dimensional forms may be decorated with mosaic, and a number of artists have experimented in this field. Many materials have been used to create the base – papier-mâché, cement, clay, breeze blocks, and even reinforced plaster, although the latter is only suitable for indoors. Preformed cells into which mosaics can be set are very attractive, with an obvious relationship to the emblemata of the classical period (p. 186). These can be made from clay or concrete, and a similar effect may be achieved by routing out the desired areas from the plaster rendering of interior walls, and inlaying the cells with tesserae or mixed media. The illustration entitled *Totem* was one of a series undertaken by the author which were purely experimental. The structure was built up from scrap wood and with a minimum of joinery. The recessed areas were created by what was in reality a built-up frame. Many materials were incorporated – vitreous glass mosaics which had been left over from various projects, lead, buttons and map pins. The wood moulding was painted with matt colour before assembly.

Prepared clay pieces may be incorporated with glass mosaic and other materials. The pieces illustrated, *Angel*, *Jester* and *Ritual King*, were again purely experimental. The use of lead was related to the cell-like quality of enamels and inlay, and also to the metal strips which were used to add linear emphasis to the ancient Greek pebble mosaics. The base material was $\frac{1}{2}$-in. blockboard, which was framed and waterproofed before work commenced. Care was taken to ensure that the frame would stand slightly 'proud' from the finished background. The clay units were modelled in brown earthenware clay, some of which were left unglazed while others received a coat of rutile glaze. The unglazed sections were waxed when the panel received its final polish.

The lead strips are calmes (more commonly used for leading up sections of stained glass) which in section resemble the letter H. Before these strips are used they must be stretched to ensure the correct tension. This can be done by nailing one end of the strip (about 2 in. from the end) to the side of a work-bench. The strip should be straightened along its length, and the opposite end gripped between the jaws of a pair of pliers. The lead should be firmly stretched until the length is increased by at least 12 in. Care should be taken not to bend or damage the strip after it has been stretched. When working on small projects, chop the strips into shorter lengths. If a full strip is required, stretch it immediately before use rather than leave it lying around the studio. A useful tool for cutting the lead can be made from a paint-scraper. The blade should be sawn down to about 3 in. in length and then carefully sharpened. The very sharp blade can be pressed through the calme without damaging the core.

All the ceramic units which were used in these experiments were set in place with epoxy glue which was allowed to become thoroughly dry before the lead strips were glued into place. When the lead was firmly attached to the base, the tesserae were applied in the normal way. I found that vitreous glass tiles could be inserted into the core of the lead,

Cross-section of calmes or lead strips (see also p. 133).

which ensured a very tight joint although this would not be possible with $\frac{3}{8}$-in. smalti. The lead 'pips' were formed from small sections cut from the strip with scissors, which produced the oval shape; they were then turned on to their sides and gently beaten with a wooden mallet.

The panel entitled *Flying Fish* was carried out in exactly the same way as the previous examples. The lead lines were intended to give emphasis to the suggestion of rapid movement. Apart from vitreous glass mosaic, the panel incorporates chunks of stained glass which were melted in a kiln, as described in Chapter 4 (p. 80). A similar procedure was adopted for the *Night Owls* panel. The hard outline of the trunk and leaves of the bush were made from lead strip, in contrast to the fluffiness of the young birds. The owls were composed from vitreous glass tiles, each tile being cut into six small rectangles, and used in an impressionistic non-linear manner to emphasize the softness of the birds. Copper, buttons and theatrical jewelry were used for the eyes, which when seen in diffused light appear to light up. The copper pieces were cut from discarded cylinder-head gaskets begged from a local garage. Some of the coat-buttons were iridescent and resembled the tail of a peacock, and the stars, set in silver smalti, appear as brilliant points of light in the deep blue of the night sky.

Roofing slate can be used most successfully in contrast with the brilliance of glass, and may also be used as a means of building up the level of certain areas to give textural variety.

The piece entitled *The World Shaker* was carried out on a base of preframed blockboard, and includes various materials. The most expensive materials were the cubes of gold smalti and the red smalti which were used in the cheeks, rather similar in treatment to the head of S. Agnese described in Chapter 1. The wand and the contour line of the face are set in glazed ceramic units of Japanese origin, and the wand is capped with a large decorative coat-button. The slate background, made from scrap material, is not built up; the different heights were achieved by the use of two thicknesses of slate. The textured slate was obtained from broken roofing tiles and the lovely, smooth, warm-coloured slate, which was somewhat thinner, was originally used in old writing slates. The background was given sparkle and contrast of colour and texture by the introduction of fragments of vitreous glass, dark-blue stained glass, gold smalti and coloured map pins which were hammered into the board.

A similar technique was employed for the *Clown*, although the slate background was built up in layers, using epoxy glue. An attempt was made to give the impression that the large, brightly coloured ball upon which the clown is balanced was revolving at considerable speed, and virtually throwing off sparks into the background. It was intended to contrast the insecurity of the clown, exemplified by his sad expression and precarious foothold, with the dynamism of the circus suggested by the ball and the background and the gay colour of the costume. It may be noticed that the kinetic aspects and the lack of equilibrium of the figure, which is composed asymmetrically, are compensated for by the introduction of several stable horizontal and vertical setting lines in the background. For example, the strong yellow line which runs along the outside of the left leg contrasts with the horizontal lines which may be detected in the background to left and right of the upper yellow disk which surrounds the clown's body. The small panel entitled *Trastevere*, derived from the name of a picturesque area of Rome, contains a development of the slate backgrounds. Areas of hardboard, sawn and then partly torn, were built up in layers, glued and pinned to the background. The panel was waterproofed and fragments of slate were glued to the built-up areas; the vitreous glass mosaic was set in the normal way. The forms were expressed by means of an 'impressionist' technique, although the limited tonal range of the vitreous glass made this rather difficult. The small pebbles which were incorporated into the background of *Trastevere* were collected in Rome itself, which was purely a matter of sentiment as they were quite unexceptional. This work, in common with the others which I have described, was grouted with a mixture of cement and 'Bondcrete', and polished with floor wax.

When vitreous glass mosaics are used in conjunction with other materials, care must be taken to ensure that they are not used simply as a coloured filling. In spite of their limited colour range they can be used expressively, especially when the material is cut into various shapes, for instance to form a contrast between the static square and the more dynamic rectangle, although they will never add the vivid colour and sparkle which can only be obtained from smalti.

An interesting although somewhat hybrid development, to which a number of artists have turned their attention, is transparent or translucent mosaic. This boldly combines the fragmented technique of mosaic with the brilliance and transparency of the stained-glass medium. The method brings its own problems concerning the relationship between the work and the passage of light. It is necessary to distinguish between the terms 'transparency' and 'translucency'. When a material is transparent, rays of light are transmitted without diffusion, and objects behind the material can be clearly seen. Translucency is the quality which allows the transmission of light through the surface, although bodies which lie behind the material are not clearly seen. Consequently, if transparent material is used, it is important to remember that bodies which exist outside play a part in the over-all effect; this applies to all elements, whether permanently to be seen or not. For example, moving clouds and the changing colour of the sky can radically alter the quality of the colour; the action of the wind on trees can disturb the balance and distribution of the design elements in the work. The light-level within the room must be taken into consideration as it conditions the effect of light on transparent material in terms of colour intensity. This phenomenon greatly influenced the development of stained and painted glass. Combinations of colour which were suitable for the tiny windows of Romanesque churches were unsuitable for the light interiors of the late Gothic period.

Several methods of assembling transparent panels have been developed. The most apposite from the mosaicist's point of view is that which employs a method basically the same as that of mosaic production and which uses epoxy adhesive. The base material consists of a sheet of plate glass, with mosaic units formed from transparent or translucent glass. The glass may be cut into regular geometric shapes similar to tesserae, or in free forms reminiscent of stained-glass sections. The pieces should be assembled and securely fixed to the base with epoxy glue. The pieces may abut or be set so that channels of varying widths are left between each piece, which may be subsequently filled with grout or mastic.

Miniature icons made from tiny cubes or rods of glass, and occasionally cubes of natural stone, were popular during the Byzantine period. Jewelry in the form of mosaic represents another tradition particularly associated with Italian craftsmen. The field of miniature work is an excellent one for those who are interested in the medium but are restricted by lack of space or time. It is especially suitable for those who wish to work only with the most expensive materials, but must limit their expenditure.

9 The historical development of mosaic

The place and manner of origin of the mosaic technique known as *opus tessellatum* has been a subject of controversy. The material from which mosaics of this type were made was natural stone which was cut into squares or tesserae, fairly coarse in size and shape. Pliny makes reference to pavimental mosaics of a similar type. He wrote 'paved floors [*pavimenta*] skilfully executed in the way of a painting, originated with the Greeks'. It would seem probable therefore that the genesis of *opus tessellatum* is to be sought in early Greek mosaics which, although largely composed of uncut pebbles, incorporated elements of cut stone in the later examples.

Prior to the development of pebble mosaic the only technique similar to true mosaic appears to have been the surface decorations dating from approximately 3000 B C, discovered in the ancient city of Uruk (modern Warka, Biblical Erech) in Sumeria. The mosaic units are long clay cones, baked and with coloured heads, which were driven into walls and columns while the mud coating was still wet. Clay mosaics appear to have been reserved for the decoration of important buildings such as temple complexes; at Warka a good example is to be seen in a courtyard in which columns and half-columns are decorated with quite intricate patterns. At Tell al-'Ubaid cones were discovered with heads of coloured stones formed into floreate patterns. Throughout the area examples of clay cones have been found in a variety of sizes ranging from 5 in. to 12 in. long. Some of the larger cones, which are made of gypsum plaster, are particularly interesting as the heads are plated with sheets of copper cemented to the plaster with bitumen. Some fine examples of decorative panels made from hollow clay cones were found on the ziggurat at Warka. The cones were quite large and formed like hollow vases. Examples of palm-wood columns covered with a mosaic decoration of pink limestone, mother-of-pearl and shell have been found at the temple of Ninkhursag at al-'Ubaid. The wooden columns were coated with bitumen and the individual units of mosaic were secured to the coating by a length of copper wire fixed to the back of each piece.

Bitumen was used extensively in Babylonia even as far back as 3500 B C. The material was obtained from the natural seepage of bitumen through the earth, which when combined with sand and similar matter formed a kind of asphalt which was extremely strong and with tremendous adhesive

Clay mosaics from Warka, made with clay cones as the mosaic units: detail.

Pottery head covered with mother-of-pearl mosaic, Toltec period, from Tula.

qualities. Bitumen deposits occur both in the earth and on the bed of the sea or of lakes; in the latter case the material tends to rise to the surface, from which it can be skimmed off or collected in lumps. The most important sources of supply were at Hitt in the neighbourhood of Babylon and the earliest known use was on houses excavated near al-'Ubaid dated to about 3500 BC. Rush mats, which formed the walls of these houses, were coated with bitumen and later it was used as a bonding material. Mixtures containing bitumen were also used for road building, especially for ceremonial roads. It has also been found as a waterproofing agent for floors, baths and drains.

Many ancient cultures used a technique of inlay which has an affinity with mosaic, although of a much more rigid appearance and lacking the colour modulation of mosaic. From pre-Columbian America there are examples which demonstrate a true mosaic technique, although in its simplest form. Stone mosaics have been found in Mexico over a wide area and the dates attributed to various examples suggest an old-established tradition. Among objects collected from various sites are to be found a number of masks decorated with mosaics of precious and semi-precious stones. A striking jade mask representing a Zapotecan bat god is an excellent example of the skilful fitting together of stone units. Another mask from Palenque, a Maya site, is of a remarkably realistic human face with a mosaic 'skin' fashioned from polygonal units of jade. Another interesting mask in Mixtec style, probably representing Quetzalcoatl, is of turquoise cemented on to wood, with units which project above the level of the turquoise. It is known that the Aztec king Montezuma II presented masks of gods to the Spanish conqueror Cortes, the mosaic units being principally of turquoise although other stones were included.

An interesting fresco from Tula depicts a god wearing a mosaic mask which is coloured blue and black, the blue no doubt representing turquoise. A pectoral ornament of the Mixtec culture, now in the British Museum, representing a double-headed 'Snake of Heaven' and dated to the four-

'Snake of Heaven' – a turquoise mosaic pectoral ornament of the Mixtec culture. British Museum, London.

teenth or fifteenth century A D, is completely covered with flakes of turquoise. Another Mixtec example from Tilan-tongo, Oaxaca, and now in the Washington Museum is in the form of a mask, wood-based and covered with the usual carefully worked flakes of turquoise combined with pink shell and mother-of-pearl. Other examples have been found in which lignite, iron and pyrites, garnet and shell have been used in addition to turquoise. As with the mask of Quet-zalcoatl, the base material of many of these examples was wood, although bone was occasionally used.

The Pueblo Indians of the south-west of the United States used turquoise in the manufacture of ornaments which no doubt were of ritual significance. These examples are very similar in technique to work of other regions, the base being generally of wood although examples occur in which stone forms the base material. The predominance of the mask in the art of Mixtec, Toltec, Aztec and Maya is an aspect of a head-worshipping cult common to most of the early cultures of the Pacific. Included in this cult was the venera-tion of the skulls of ancestors and actual head-hunting took place in certain instances. These heads (or masks) had a precise function, which was to protect by averting the evil eye. In some areas apotropaic additions are to be found which emphasize this function, as for instance the protruding tongue or the addition of antlers.

Apart from the mask with its religious and ritualistic significance, shields have been found bearing mosaic decora-tion. Peru has yielded up examples of articles of adornment, for instance pendants, earplugs, pectorals and forms of head-gear dating to the pre-Christian era, which bear mosaic decoration. Stylistically the Peruvian examples are related to the convention in textiles and other crafts, and seem to have been of secular use. Those from Mexico on the other hand were almost exclusively of religious significance. The only evidence we possess of the mosaic technique being employed in the decoration of buildings is to be found in literature, which suggests that the interior walls of palaces were decorated with mosaics of stone and shell.

'Bellerophon Fighting the Chimera' – a floor mosaic from Olynthos made from white, yellow and blue-black pebbles.

Rinceaux.

THE WEST

The earliest known examples of a mosaic technique in the Western tradition are a number of non-figural floor mosaics carried out in black and white stone, which were discovered in Gordium in Asia Minor and in Crete, and are probably of the eighth century BC. By the fourth century BC evidence proved the existence of a much more sophisticated tradition of pavimental decoration in the medium. Eighteen pebble mosaics which were found at Olynthos on the Chalcidice peninsula are especially fine, and although by no means the latest, mark a peak of achievement in the medium in spite of the illusionistic devices which were adopted later, for instance in a group at Pella.

The stages of stylistic development are uncertain, but the significance of the Olynthos group lies in the fact that they were numerous, were of an advanced technique and were discovered in private houses, which suggests that the style was popular and well established. They are of natural stone and the mortar in which they are embedded is clearly visible. The figures are two-dimensional and exhibit a sensitive grasp of the nature of fragmented design which demands a considerable degree of stylization to be fully effective. The drawing is simple, linear and lively and included among the motifs are foliated borders, hunting scenes, fighting animals and mythological themes with figures and pattern forms such as *rinceaux* and meanders. The areas between the main lines of the designs are filled with large pebbles which do not appear to have been graded for size or specially selected for shape, nor do they appear to have been worked in any way.

Coloured stones were used but the effect is monochromatic owing to the subtlety of tone. The diagram shows part of the central panel from a pavement discovered in a dwelling which has been named the 'House of Good Fortune', depicting the mythological hero Bellerophon mounted on his horse Pegasus, fighting the Chimera. The figural panel, approximately 51 in. in diameter, is dated to the mid-fourth century BC and depicts the figures in strict profile.

Although not very far removed in date from those at Olynthos, the Pella mosaics exhibit a number of stylistic differences. The graphic quality typified by the Bellerophon panel has given way to a style in which greater emphasis is placed on plastic values. The colour is much brighter and the effect of light on form has been observed and exploited to convey the illusionistic intention of the artists. Much smaller stones have been used – a common device when greater realism is desired as form can thus be expressed more satisfactorily and in greater detail. An interesting effect is achieved in the backgrounds of some of these mosaics by the use of random coloured pebbles set in a style reminiscent of the 'pointilliste' technique of Seurat. Another unusual feature is the introduction of strips of metal to emphasize certain outlines. Further examples of the style have been discovered at Athens, Assos, Corinth, Pallene, Sikyon, Sparta, Priene, Tarsos, Olympia and Sicily.

The advent of stone, cut to the required size and shape, was an event of considerable importance in the development of the technique which was to lead to the *opus tessellatum* style in which elements of cut stone were used throughout. An example in a transitional style was discovered in a house at Serra Orlando in Sicily in which roughly cut stone and pieces of terracotta were incorporated, and a similar transition can be detected in a group of mosaic floors in the vestibule of the Temple of Zeus at Olympia. The artists, in order

(*Below, left*) Mosaic made from cut stone or *opus tessellatum*. (*Below, right*) Pebble mosaic from Pella with metal strips to accentuate lines.

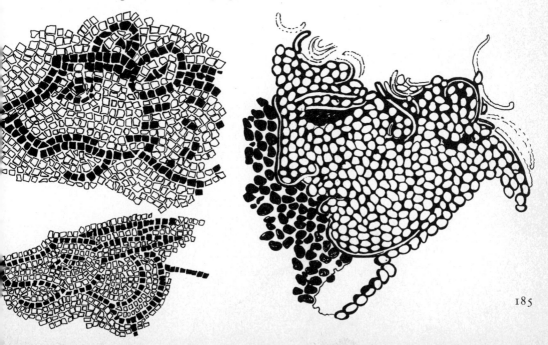

to convey form more realistically, were attempting to assume greater control over the medium. It has not been possible to establish with certainty the date at which cut stones were used throughout. The earliest textual information is contained in a description of a display boat which Hieron II of Syracuse (*c.* 270–216 B C), a relative of Archimedes, gave as a gift to Ptolemy III of Egypt (*c.* 246–221 B C); the cut stone with which the boat was decorated is specifically mentioned. Very little mosaic remains from the Hellenistic period; the earliest known example is a personification of Alexandria of the late third or early second century B C.

THE PERGAMON SCHOOL

An important centre for the production of mosaic in the fully developed *opus tessellatum* technique was the island of Pergamon, during the second century B C. The palaces of the Hellenistic rulers of the island contained refined polychrome mosaic pavements made from coloured marbles, limestone, and very occasionally glass, and characterized by the use of tiny closely set cubes. The fashion for these highly sophisticated pavements was in accord with the extremely luxurious tastes of the ruling tyrants of the island. The remarkably realistic figural subjects, obviously the work of highly skilled craftsmen, were more or less restricted to the central areas, the remainder of the pavements being composed of coarser work. These inserts, known as 'emblemata' ('emblema' in the singular), were intricately worked with very small tesserae which led to the development of a style known as *opus vermiculatum*, derived from the word *vermis* (a worm), which accurately describes the manner in which the tesserae were set so as to express form more realistically. Emblemata were products of considerable artistic ability, and the fact that they were incorporated as units into the main pavimental layout suggests that they were prefabricated away from the actual site. They were probably manufactured in the workshops of skilled craftsmen, and afterwards transported to the site to be combined with the remainder of the scene, which consisted largely of coarsely worked ornamental borders. In spite of changes in technique, the over-all layout of the pavements was similar to the pebble mosaics of an earlier date.

A considerable number of emblemata have been removed from their locations, only the borders being left *in situ*, although examples may be seen in a number of museums. Some of the craftsmen are known by name, for example Sosos, an outstanding representative of the Pergamon School. Pliny mentions two of his works which were the subjects of innumerable copies – 'Doves Drinking from a Fountain' (a theme which was incorporated in Christian mosaics) and the 'Unswept Floor' or *Asaroton*, which was a form of still-life. Included in the composition of the *Asaroton* were repre-

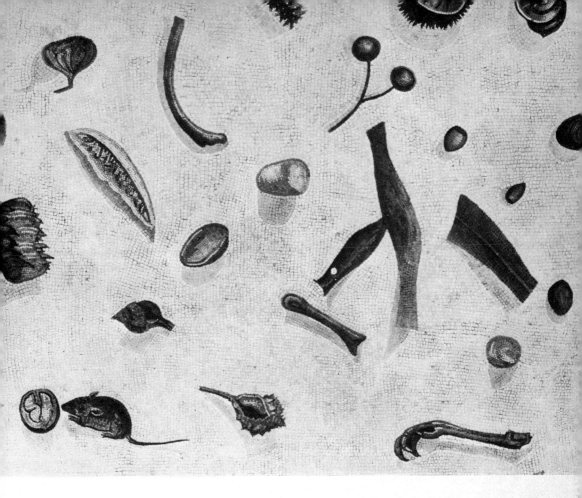

sentations of scraps left over from the meal, for instance fish-bones with the head and tail of the fish attached, lobster-claws, nut-shells, discarded fruit and peelings, chicken legs and even a small, realistically delineated mouse. These details, which were carried out in coloured tesserae, were set against a plain background, each with a delicately drawn shadow. Various imitations of these works are to be seen in Rome; an *Asaroton* dated to the second century A D was discovered on the Aventine hill, and is now in the Vatican Museum. A copy of a Sosos original, 'Doves Drinking from a Fountain', now in the Capitoline Museum, was discovered at Hadrian's Villa, and is probably of the second century A D. Another craftsman named Hephaiston was responsible for an emblema which was discovered in the palace complex of King Eumenes at Pergamon and is of great interest, as glass fragments were incorporated with natural stone in order to introduce colour of greater brilliance.

A number of pavements similar in style to those of Pergamon have been discovered on the island of Delos, and are probably contemporary. Of particular interest are some mosaics which include the names of donors, and one example bears the signature of the craftsman, Asklepiades of Arados, in Phoenicia. The houses in which these examples were

found have been given exotic names, such as the 'House of
the Dolphin', the 'House of the Masks', the 'House of the
Trident' and the 'House of Dionysos'. Apart from its importance as the central corn-market of the Aegean, Delos maintained a strong and lively theatrical tradition, with theatre
records going back to the fourth century BC. Important
actors from all over Greece performed there and, not surprisingly, a number of mosaics depicting theatrical subjects
have been found. An example from the House of the Masks
shows the young Dionysos – the god of maenads and satyrs,
of initiation and immortality, riding on a leopard. He is
beardless, and his youthful, rather flaccid face is set in a dis-
agreeable expression. As the god of tragedy, he wears the
costume of a tragic actor, and he carries a *thyrsos* in his right
hand and a *tympanon* in his left. The *thyrsos*, a fennel stalk with
a head of ivy leaves, is an attribution of Dionysos, and the
leopard is an allusion to his Indian journey. Apart from the
refined technique and the inclusion of carefully cut material,
this mosaic is remarkable for the great variety of coloured
tesserae, which include marbles, agate, onyx and glass.

During the second century BC Alexandria, an important
cultural centre in which all manner of crafts flourished, saw
the extension of the role of landscape in mosaic. The great
'Nilotic' scenes, so much admired by the Romans, were a
notable production of the Alexandrian workshops. Inevitably, with the increasing desire on the part of the Romans
to emulate the luxurious way of life of the Hellenistic princes,
the trappings of luxury were sought. With the extension of
conquests into the east, the Roman was exposed to exotic
influences which were eagerly assimilated.

ROMAN MOSAICS

Pliny alludes to the introduction of the mosaic technique
into Rome, which he attributed to the time of Sulla (138–
78 BC), although the finest Hellenistic-inspired figural
mosaics were found in Pompeii. The House of the Faun,
excavated in 1820, is an excellent example of the Roman
adaptation of Hellenistic luxury on an even more lavish
scale than that of Delos or Pergamon. After excavation most
of the emblemata were removed to the Museo Nazionale in
Naples, although their original disposition was carefully
recorded. The decorations included a cat devouring a bird,
a fish mosaic, the infant Dionysos riding a tiger, a mosaic
with doves, and a lion to ward off evil. A small Nilotic scene
was discovered on the threshold of an open *exedra* (a hall)
which contained one of the most famous mosaics of antiquity,
'The Battle of Alexander and Darius'.

The Alexander mosaic was discovered in 1831, and has
been at the centre of a considerable amount of scholarly
discussion concerning the date and place of origin. The
difficulty in dating this type of work arises from the fact that

emblemata were portable objects and they may have been reused; they are therefore not necessarily contemporary with the site. Some authorities have suggested a date as early as the third century B C; others have argued that a more realistic date would be in the region of the first century B C. The work is complex and highly sophisticated with a distinct stylistic relationship with the school of Pergamon, which suggests that, if the craftsmen were not Greek, they were at least familiar with the style and technique of Hellenistic Greece. There is a genuine sense of the dramatic, and a definite attempt to distinguish personalities and establish the tensions and relationships inherent in the subject. An able manipulation of the effects of light on form, coupled with the use of very small tesserae, engenders a considerable degree of plastic unity in the panel, although it is arguable that such an obvious interpretation of painterly values, in terms of mosaic, amounts to a misuse of the medium. It is believed that the work was actually a copy of a painting, and it is carried out in the four 'severe' colours, red, yellow, black and white, an artistic convention of the time.

An example of Roman Republican mosaic on a very grand scale can be seen in the Museo Archeologico in Palestrina, a small town on the slopes of Monte Ginestro, about twenty-five miles from Rome. This was the site of an ancient town of Latium referred to by Horace as 'cool Praeneste'. The town was destroyed by Sulla in 82 B C, although subsequently he built the Temple of Fortune, which was to become famous for its oracle. The town became a favourite retreat from the heat and disease of summer and retained its importance until the fourth century A D. During the Middle Ages the town of Città Prenestina was built over the ruins of the temple, which had occupied a site of eighty acres. The temple had been built on a series of terraces which were occupied by the medieval town. The destruction which occurred during the severe bombardment of 1944 revealed further elements of the temple, and a programme of rehousing enabled the *Amministrazione delle Belle Arti* to undertake intensive excavation on the site. The most famous mosaic – the Barberini mosaic – had been housed in a small museum in the Palazzo Colonna Barberini which occupied part of the temple site. Fortunately the mosaic had been removed to Rome before the bombing, and survived the war unharmed. It has as a subject a Nilotic scene showing the topography of the region during time of flood. The flora and fauna are included in the scene, as well as architecture, and various activities of the people of the region. The mosaic was restored by Cardinal Francesco Barberini as early as 1640, although it retains sufficient of its original character to remain an outstanding example of the medium. The high quality and technique are similar to the products of Alexandria, and it may even be of Alexandrian workmanship, probably of the time of Hadrian (A D 76–138).

The increased popularity of mosaic pavements during the early Roman Imperial period suggests a considerable reduction in the cost of production, which may have been due to the rationalization of manufacturing techniques. The production of emblemata remained in the hands of skilled craftsmen who continued to maintain the highest standards, although a form of false emblemata was produced, which were made *in situ*. It seems probable that further rationalization was encouraged in order to supply the increased demand for tessellated floors. Consequently, as decorative floors became more widely available, and moved out of the luxury class, distinct changes in technique occurred. Probably the more able workmen were called upon to assist the mastercraftsmen, and the repetitive and less skilled work was increasingly undertaken by semi-skilled, anonymous, and probably itinerant workmen. A similar method of job allocation existed in the workshops of Byzantium; indeed the practice still applies today in commercial studios in Italy. Apart from the general increase in demand, it also became necessary to devise schemes suitable for much larger areas, in accordance with the grandiose building projects which were a feature of the Imperial period. As a result, a fashion developed for stylized motifs composed in a manner suitable for this purpose. Borders consisted of typical classical motifs such as interlace, meanders and Vitruvian scrolls, which confined a central area – sometimes plain, or composed of simple grids, squares and triangles – carried out in *opus tessellatum*.

Moses before Pharaoh's Daughter: detail of a mosaic from the Old
Testament cycle in the nave, Sta Maria Maggiore, Rome (see p. 214).

During the first century B C, the mosaic of the period was characterized by a monochromatic style in which black and white tesserae – of basalt, marble or limestone – were used without colour gradation. Numerous examples of the black-and-white style can be seen in and around Rome itself, and in a number of Pompeian houses. Towards the second half of the century the emblemata style seemed to suffer an eclipse, probably due to a radical change of fashion which was motivated by the cost factor. As the century progressed, entire surface areas were occupied by decorative schemes, which included key-patterns, reticulate patterns, basket-weave and overlapping shells; the range was later extended to include circles and arrangements which combined squares and lozenges to form star shapes. Silhouettes of human and animal forms, set against a white background, made a tentative appearance about the middle of the first century A D. A typical example of this style is the *cave canem* ('Beware of the dog') panel from the house of Pansa (P. Paquius Proculus) in Pompeii. This particular house is a useful source for studying the development of the mosaic style during this period. The fully developed black-and-white figural style can be seen in a mosaic depicting symbols of the provinces and winds at Ostia Antica, which was made during the following century. A very important extension of the use of the medium occurred during the first century, when figural mosaics began to appear on walls, columns and fountain niches.

During the second century A D the fashion for black-and-white *opus tessellatum* persisted. The technique was used to decorate large areas, and simple geometric motifs were fashionable. The key-pattern was extensively used, also a rather attractive eight-pointed star which was formed from juxtaposed lozenges, and frequently employed at Hadrian's Villa (Tivoli) and Ostia Antica. An even simpler pattern was formed by the use of alternating black and white squares, again to be seen at Ostia, and also in the Markets of Trajan (Rome). During the reign of Hadrian, a significant development in the form of pattern took place. Highly stylized plant motifs were incorporated in pavimental schemes, one of which – the rosace – became very dominant, and numerous examples of this pattern occur at Hadrian's Villa. The style is important because it can be seen as the fore-runner of the arabesque, which was to persist in many forms and throughout many periods. The curvilinear tendency was further emphasized by the elaboration of the motif, and examples occur – for instance at Ostia Antica – of the inhabited arabesque in which animals and human figures occupy areas which have been formed by the fanciful inter-twining of the leaves, a road which was ultimately to lead to the splendid inhabited scrolls of S. Clemente in Rome.

The first half of the century saw a return to polychromy, in the form of the old emblemata. An example from Hadrian's Villa, now in the Staatliche Museen, Berlin, reintroduces the illusionistic technique. The emblema,

(*Opposite*) SS. Cosma e Damiano: detail of apsidal mosaic. Christ descends a stairway of clouds (see p. 216).

which measures 66 cm. × 94 cm. (about 2 ft. × 3 ft.), depicts a scene of conflict between centaurs and wild beasts. The scene is set in a rocky landscape, and is a rustic version of the Hellenistic style. Italian workshops were engaged in the production and export of emblemata during this period, and instances also occur of the use of pseudo-emblemata. The polychrome pictorial mosaic retained its popularity in many of the provinces, especially in southern France, although the severe geometric style is common in northern France, Germany and Spain. The end of the second century was a period of great activity. Mosaic workshops increased in number and tended to move inland, whereas previously they had been sited in and around the major seaports.

The third century saw the Roman school faithful to the black-and-white style, although various centres of Italy, and most of the provinces, with the exception of Syria, developed a polychrome style. The mosaics were segmental in design and included human figures, plants and geometric motifs. The continuity of the Roman school is demonstrated in a number of mosaics at Ostia Antica, although the floral style had given way to a severe geometric style. The extended decorative schemes were formed by the repetition of very simple motifs, such as squares, circles, triangles, shells and *peltae* (shield-shaped pattern forms), carried out in black against a white background, and during the second half of the century a reticular decoration, enclosing cruciform rosettes, was particularly fashionable. Human and animal silhouettes continued to be set against a white background in which there was some suggestion of landscape, although spatial relationships were not established, and anatomy – which was indicated by white lines – was crude and inaccurate. The quality of design tended to degenerate, and the so-called 'pathetic' subjects superseded the vigorous aspect of the earlier mosaics, introducing an air of mawkishness; such subjects as the abduction of Proserpina or the death of Actaeon typified the aspects of 'pathetic' mythology which gained popularity during this period. Other popular subjects included 'genre' scenes, and scenes from contemporary events, such as athletic games, which can be seen in the Caserma dei Vigili (firemen's barracks) at Ostia Antica.

In spite of being some distance from the capital, Ostia was the port and wholesale quarter of Rome. The inhabitants were largely bourgeois, and the city had a lively air of cosmopolitanism, although in general it would, no doubt, reflect the life and taste of the capital. However, the absence of the refined polychromatic mosaics and emblemata, coupled with the uniformity of technique displayed by the Ostian mosaics, suggests a school of local artisans rather than craftsmen. The foundation of the mosaics was of broken tufa, which appears to have been covered with a layer of coarse pozzolana, and with a final coat of mortar made from lime and marble dust into which the tesserae were inserted. The rubble bed, which was laid directly on to level ground,

Section of Roman floor mosaic.

was known as the *statumen* (literally, the coat of the floor); it was followed by a layer of coarse mortar known as the *rudus* (rubbish, broken stones) and finally the *nucleus* (hardest part) or setting bed. The white tesserae were usually of limestone; marble was rarely used before the fourth century.

ROMAN AFRICA

The establishment of Roman authority in Africa opened up the regions to the west of the Gulf of Sidra, and exposed them to a cultural force which appeared to be of easier assimilation than that of Hellenism. Typically, the Romans created a large class of Romano-Africans, made up from Roman and Italian immigrants, romanized Libyans and Punic people, all of whom became rich and influential, dominating local affairs and forming a select group accepting the language and customs of Rome. The primary source of wealth was agriculture, but urban centres were established, the size of which were concomitant with the productivity of the area. The only city which could be considered to be in any sense industrial was Chemtou with its marble quarries, the source of the unattractive but popular henna-red marble. Although Africa was especially rich in stone quarries (for instance, the cliff quarries of el Haouaria which supplied stone for Carthage) little profit was gained by the native Africans. The quarries were in the possession of the Emperor and were worked by slave labour. However, an enormous colour range of marble was available for use as tesserae.

The raw material used in primitive societies was usually to hand; only when a more sophisticated society emerges can the use of a particular material become a matter of artistic choice. Once the popularity of pavimental mosaic had been established, the Romans went to remarkable lengths to ensure the supply of marble to the various regions of the Empire. Evidence of quarrying by the Romans has been discovered in Italy, Greece, Asia Minor, Egypt, Sicily, Corsica, Sardinia, France and England. At Colchester in England many kinds of marble have been identified apart from the native British alabaster: cipollino from Greece (white and green), Africano from Asia Minor (black or dark green ground with white, purple or pink), Carrara from Italy (white crystalline), giallo antico from Algeria and Tunisia (yellow with red veining), Paronazzetto from Phrygia in Asia Minor (white or cream with red and purple veining), rosso antico from Greece (deep red), and green porphyry from Sparta.

We learn from Vitruvius some of the technical problems which the Romans overcame to enable them to quarry and handle enormous blocks of stone, some of them weighing as much as six hundred tons. Saws were fed by sand, which was abrasive, and blades with teeth were used for soft stone and without teeth for hard stone. Ultimately hand-operated saws gave way to saws operated by water power. Dressing tools such as axes, punches and plain or serrated claws were also used to work the marble; many of them remain in use today.

Under the influence of Hellenism, the Punic peoples had made use of cement floors encrusted with pieces of marble, referred to by Cato as *pavimenta punica*. However, in spite of these early examples, the first important figural mosaics occur under the influence of Rome during the Flavian period of the late first century. The mosaics in the villa of Dar-Buk-Ammera in Zliten (ancient Subgoli) are particularly interesting. For instance, a frieze depicting circus games employs an unusual technique: a central emblema is framed by a rectangle of *opus sectile* (see Chapter 2) which is enclosed in turn by a figural border of *opus tessellatum*. Alexandrian influence is so strong in the Zliten examples that it seems possible that, contrary to tradition, Alexandrian workmen were employed. Some authorities have suggested the possibility of the establishment of a workshop at Bizacena, which maintained the traditions of the Alexandrian school, and was responsible for examples at Acholla and the pavements of el-Alia and Sousse (ancient Hadrumetum). During the time of Hadrian a similar workshop was established at Carthage, and mosaics were produced which had certain stylistic similarities to Roman black-and-white mosaics, but retained polychromy, although examples of the two-colour style do occur.

The development of the mosaic technique during the second century AD has been established fairly accurately because of a group of buildings at Acholla of which the chronological sequence is known. The house of the Consul Asinius Rufinus (consul in AD 184) contains a mosaic with a representation of Hercules which can be compared with a similar figure on contemporary coins. The baths contain a pavimental mosaic which bears a close relationship to the Pompeian style; the entrance hall of the *frigidarium* is decorated with a Dionysiac theme with a central reference to the Indian journey of the god. The pavement has been dated to AD 115, and the non-figural areas exhibit a foliated decoration with stylistic similarities to certain pavements in Hadrian's Villa at Tivoli. A slightly earlier example, dated to the reign of Antoninus Pius (AD 86–161), forms the decoration of the villa known as the 'Villa of the Triumph of Neptune', and to the same school belongs a marine *thiasos* (a religious procession) from Lambessa (ancient Lambaesis) bearing the signature of Aspasios, which confirms the eastern origin of at least the masters of the school.

The period of Marcus Aurelius (AD 161–180) lacks a precise chronology but to the period of Septimius Severus (AD 146–211) belong a number of mosaics whose chronological evolution can be established with a fair degree of certainty. Examples include a group at Carthage, the famous agri-

cultural scenes of Caesarea (Cherchel), a fancy dress banquet at El Djem, and the 'House of Vergil' at Hadrumetum; and of the late period, the 'Baths of the Poet' at Sfax.

The third and the fourth centuries saw a new development in African society – the emergence of villa life in the manner of the Romans. Of particular interest is the villa called Domus Julius, containing mosaics in which typical villas of the period are depicted. Baths, basilicas and other public buildings continued to be decorated with mosaic, usually pavimental, although the greatest number of extant mosaics are from the extremely complex villas. Indeed, examples of African mosaics are so numerous that the technique can be considered the dominant art form of Roman Africa. The subjects were varied: geometric and botanical forms were popular, also 'genre' scenes, including scenes from country life, the circus and the amphitheatre. Unfortunately, constant repetition of certain themes, and the complexity of influences often resulted in a markedly hybrid style in which motifs were adopted on visual grounds without reference to their meaning. The advent of Christianity did not bring into being any new forms in Africa. As in Rome, traditional motifs were adapted to serve the new religion. An amazing amount of church building was undertaken but only floor mosaics have survived.

ROMAN BRITAIN

Britain was essentially a military outpost, although Roman occupation engendered a group of Romano-British who readily adapted themselves to the customs of Rome. In

Agricultural scene from Cherchel.

consequence a considerable amount of building, both military and civil, was undertaken, although little survives except earthworks, some of which reveal elements of town planning which was practised under the Romans, for instance Silchester, Wroxeter and St Albans. Villas are fairly numerous; those of Woodchester, Chedworth, Bognor, Lullingstone and Northleigh provide evidence of the development of villa life. Londinium was founded shortly after AD 45, and became a flourishing port, although its period of greatest expansion followed the redevelopment of the city after the sack by Boudicca in AD 60. The city remained important until the fourth century AD; when the Romans finally left Britain in AD 410, the city had greatly declined.

Gloucester (*Glerum*) occupied a key position on the road to South Wales: the four main streets of the Roman town actually related to the points of the compass. Chedworth Villa, near Cirencester in Gloucestershire, is in the form of a self-contained agricultural unit, and the presence of a fuller's workshop suggests that the establishment was probably a site for the marketing of prepared cloth. A large courtyard contained barns and workmen's lodgings, and a smaller court contained servants' quarters; the owner's residence combined all the luxuries of Rome, including baths and splendid mosaics of the fourth century AD. The *triclinium* (dining room) is decorated with fine pavimental mosaic representing the four seasons in the guise of four small dancing boys, one of which – Autumn – has unfortunately been destroyed. Spring, holding a bird and a flower basket, is naked except for a narrow piece of fluttering drapery. Winter, in contrast, is clothed and hooded, and holds a dead hare in his right hand. Summer, a charming winged figure, is completely naked, and is depicted with a wreath in his right hand. The pavement, which is polychrome, is divided into two sections, the figures of the seasons appearing in triangles at the corners of the northern section. The southern pavement is largely geometric, except for two horizontal bands which contain floral scrolls springing from centrally placed bowls.

Kent was a strong area of Romanization: Canterbury formed an important road junction, with roads leading to three Roman ports. The site had been inhabited before the Romans came; it was taken by the Seventh Legion in 54 BC and thereafter became a vital centre for trade with the Continental provinces. An important villa has been excavated at Lullingstone in Kent on a site which had been occupied prior to the Roman occupation. Mosaics have been revealed in the *triclinium* of the villa, and again are in two distinct parts. A figural panel to the west, which depicts the rape of Europa by Zeus in the guise of a bull, occupies an apse which is raised above the level of the remaining area. The eastern part contains a rectangular area of mosaic. The background of the apsidal mosaic is divided into two parts, the lower area representing the sea, and the upper white

Rape of Europa. Found in an apse, Lullingstone Roman villa, Kent.

area, the sky. The bull appears to have risen from the water and bears Europa on his back, centrally placed and facing the spectator. She wears jewelry and is partly draped. A small winged figure appears to be twisting the tail of the bull, and in front of the bull's forelegs a similar figure leads the group on with a beckoning gesture. The figures are linear and two-dimensional, the line being of a reddish colour. A Latin couplet from the *Aeneid* appears above the group, each line being underlined in red: 'If jealous Juno had seen the swimming of the bull, she would, with greater justice on her side, have repaired to the halls of Aeolus' – suggesting that Juno should have raised a storm to overwhelm her erring husband rather than the hapless Aeneas.

The lower rectangular floor contains a square in which is depicted Bellerophon on Pegasus, fighting the Chimera, an unusual subject in Britain. A useful comparison of design and technique can be made between the Lullingstone version and the early mosaic of the subject at Olynthos (see p. 185). The technique of this panel is similar to the apsidal panel of Europa, the form being suggested by means of outline rather than colour, although the line is black instead of red. Pegasus strains forward with remarkable buoyancy, his wings in a completely horizontal position, which conveys the feeling that the rider is boxed in by them. The Chimera, rather like a plump lion, does not seem particularly aggressive, in spite of the goat's head which protrudes from the creature's back, and the serpent's tail which parallels the line of the hind legs of Pegasus. Placed within each corner of the square, which contains the quadrilateral field upon which the story of Bellerophon is enacted, are four roundels, and contained within each is the bust of a season. Spring, Summer and Winter remain, but Autumn is missing.

Dido and Aeneas embracing: detail
of late Roman mosaic from a villa in
Low Ham, Somerset.

Another example of late Roman art in Britain from the
middle fourth century is a mosaic from the *frigidarium* of the
villa of Low Ham in Somerset, now in the Castle Museum at
Taunton. The villa was obviously the luxurious property of
a local Romanized magnate. The subject matter is again
Vergilian, derived from books I and IV of the *Aeneid*. A
large square area (approximately 19 sq. yd.) contains a
number of figural panels disposed in such a way as to guide
the spectator in a specific direction. The polychromatic
mosaic was cleared in 1946; the colours are vivid, set against
a white background, and appear to be of local origin. A
centre piece depicts a nude goddess removing her cloak –
against which she is silhouetted – flanked to left and right by
small winged amoretti. The central square is separated from
the surrounding area by a 'guilloche' border, and the figural
area which it contains is confined within a similar border
which forms an octagon. If the spectator takes a position
facing the vertical axis of the central panel, there appear to
left and right two long rectangular panels which face away
from the central scene; above and below are two rectangles
of the same width as the central panel. Both these panels face
outwards, towards the enclosing wall of the *frigidarium*; the
spectator, in this position, will see that the figures in the
lower panel are in a corresponding position to those of the
central panel, whereas the scene at the top of the pavement
appears to be upside down. Certain points of resemblance
have been observed between the Low Ham mosaic and some
of the mosaics of Ostia, although the work would seem to be
a local undertaking.

A wave of pessimism marked the end of classical antiquity, and faith in the old gods wavered, as men turned to Christianity, a doctrine which imposed a new morality in which matters spiritual became increasingly relevant to everyday life. As late as AD 305, the persecutions of Diocletian had included the destruction of the visible symbols of Christianity, such as the scriptures and the churches. Yet in the year 325 the Ecumenical Council at Nicaea saw some of the bishops who had survived the persecution of Diocletian called to the council table to discuss questions of orthodoxy in the established faith, though only twelve years had elapsed since the Edict of Toleration had been declared at Milan. An immense building programme was launched, and, significantly, a great number of foundations were of a religious nature, both in Rome and throughout the Roman world. Churches founded by Constantine included the Church of the Nativity at Bethlehem; in Rome, the Basilica of the Apostles on the Via Appia, now the church hall of S. Sebastiano; and the Basilica of the Redeemer, now S. Giovanni Laterano. This last was the prototype of the basilican churches which began to appear in the second half of the fourth century, and was known as 'the Mother and head of all churches in the cities of the world'. Also in Rome are the church of Sta Croce in Gerusalemme, founded to house relics from Jerusalem, St Peter's, and the Mausoleum of Sta Costanza fuori le Mura, which was built between 337 and 350.

The visual expression of the Christian faith was initially by means of symbols proper to paganism, which, by adaptation, expressed the mysteries of triumphant Christianity, and it is reasonable to assume that Christian art was not necessarily the product of Christian craftsmen.

As discussed earlier in this chapter, the technical development of mosaic was related to the pavimental form, the *lithostroton*, although the fact that a mural form of mosaic decoration was also developed has been established, by rather sparse evidence. Reference has already been made to the extension of mosaic as a form of decoration on fountain niches, and, although still strongly influenced by the classical pavimental style, Christ as Helios the sun god in the Mausoleum of the Julii (p. 9). Similarly, the vault decoration of Sta Costanza, also of the fourth century and again closely related to the pavimental style, offers further evidence of the use of mosaic as a wall decoration but it is impossible to establish how common or how widespread was this usage.

It is important to realize in this connection that in addition to the decorative and utilitarian purpose of pavimental mosaic, they occasionally fulfilled a secondary role on a different level, which was to do with the expression of definite functions. On a mundane level, the *cave canem*, the

Neptune and his retinue: detail of black-and-white mosaic from Ostia which aptly forms the floor of the Roman baths.

'roaring lion' (to ward off evil) and the 'skeleton at the feast' (to indicate the presence of death in life) were subjects which served such a function, and all were fairly common. The relationship between place and function was also expressed in pavimental mosaics, for example the black-and-white mosaics in the Piazzale delle Corporazioni at Ostia Antica. This square contained seventy offices of foreign representatives and workers' guilds. The mosaics occupy the floor of the brick arcade of the square, and the subjects illustrated are concerned with the various merchants, their trades and their place of origin. The incidence of the marine *thiasos* commonly used as a central decorative theme in thermae, usually depicting Neptune attended by a rout of sea creatures, is pictorially explicit of the function of the establishment.

Religious themes were similarly expressed, a typical example being the scenes of sacrifice on the floor of a chapel which forms part of the firemen's barracks at Ostia. The chapel was devoted to the worship of the Emperor, and the sacrificial scene is quite specifically religious. A number of mausolea contain floor decorations which express the theme of life after death by means of stories from mythology, such as the Rape of Proserpina, or Diana and the sleeping Endymion. The culmination of such a tradition can still be seen in the huge polychrome mosaic floors which decorated a number of foundations erected after Christianity became the state religion, although none has survived intact. The largest surviving early Christian floor is that which belonged originally to a hall church which had been established in Aquileia near Trieste, in northern Italy. The cathedral at

Aquileia was built over the foundation of the original church, but the earlier floor has been exposed. A dedicatory inscription placed within a round shield or *clipeus* records the name of the founder of the cathedral, Bishop Theodorus. The *clipeus* occupies a position in the middle of the central theme of the mosaic – a sea piece which was based on an antique formula. Theodorus was Bishop of Aquileia about 314–320, and the fact that the mosaic can be given a fairly precise date makes it especially valuable. The dedication refers to Theodorus by name:

Detail of sea piece found in Aquileia cathedral, Italy, showing the early Christian use of a pagan Nilotic scene to express the new Christian theme of baptism.

> *Theodorus, happy one,*
> *with the help of God*
> *the Almighty, and of*
> *the flock entrusted to thee*
> *from on high,*
> *thou hast made all felicitously,*
> *and hast gloriously decorated it.*

The sense of joy at the release from persecution, and delight in the work which all had undertaken, sings out so clearly in this inscription that one can understand a little of the fervent religious atmosphere of the early Christian period. The sea piece in which the inscription is incorporated includes pagan motifs and symbolizes the theme of baptism, although the scene is derived from the Nilotic tradition.

How closely the decoration of walls and vaults in Christian architecture followed an established tradition is difficult to say, although it seems fairly certain that some form of

The god Sylvanus. Detail of niche mosaic found at Ostia.

mural decoration in mosaic occurred in Hadrian's Villa, near Tivoli. A particularly interesting example of niche decoration was discovered at Ostia. The mosaic, which is believed to be of the third century A D, was discovered in the *mithraeum* of the Maritime Baths which were constructed during the reign of Antoninus Pius (A D 86–161). The mosaic depicts the god Sylvanus, delineated with the typical solidity of the period. The sense of religious solemnity is emphasized by the halo which surrounds the head of the god. The utilization of real space which involves both the spectator and the representation of the god is a principle which was to be fully exploited in later Byzantine mosaics. The colour is subtle, and the background of deep blue emphasizes the figure of the bearded god in his white tunic, which is also reminiscent of later Christian works. The Sylvanus niche suggests an astonishing relationship, both in scheme, colour and technique, between the earlier classical tradition and the Christian form.

The removal of mosaics from floor to wall is central to the subsequent development of the technique. Apart from the normal problems associated with iconography, composition and technique, a number of special problems arose which were precisely concerned with the nature of the architecture. The extensive use of dome, arch, and apse as a ground for the application of mosaic produced peculiar lighting conditions, especially when highly reflective surfaces were involved. Also, inevitably, distortions occur when figural representations are applied to curved surfaces, particularly when such surfaces are situated high above the normal eye-level. A means of counteracting distressing optical effects was evolved; figures were elongated to compensate for the distortion, and the whole composition was related to a specific point of distance from which the composition was to be viewed. Often the viewing distance was considerable, and a high degree of chromatic intensity and contrast of colour had to be introduced in order to maintain a satisfactory balance. Similarly, the actual size of the mosaic units had to be carefully calculated in relation to the location of the mosaic and the viewing distance. The rather deadening effect of a flat wall surface was overcome by the introduction of a calculated curvature of the setting bed, so that the glass smalti, which became the most commonly used material, could reflect light in different directions, introducing liveliness and sparkle. A number of problems were concerned with the relationship which existed between the spectator and the image, especially when the mosaic decoration extended continuously over wall and vault, and both image and spectator occupied the same real space of the interior.

The evolution of a style of mosaic decoration in tune with the Christian ethos can be seen in Ravenna, the refuge city on the Adriatic. The court of the Emperor was established there, and the half-sister of Honorius, Galla Placidia, governed as regent for her young son Valentinian III, between the years AD 425 and 450. She it was who began the embellishment of the city which was continued by her successors, culminating during the reign of Justinian (AD 527–65). Although a number of mosaics have been destroyed, Ravenna still retains a remarkable series of monuments which exemplify the development of the mosaic technique and its application to architecture, between the fifth and the sixth centuries AD. They provide a unique opportunity for the study of an art form which was to dominate for over a thousand years, and which in Ravenna demonstrates the fusion of Roman, barbarian and eastern influences that overflows on vaults, apses, arcades and domes.

The Byzantines were descended from an agglomeration of races, although initially the Emperor and his immediate entourage were Latins, and Latin was retained as the language of the court and the administration. Inevitably, in the course of time, the emphasis changed, and Greeks and the Greek language predominated. In Constantinople – the new city of Constantine founded on the ruins of the ancient Greek city of Byzantium in AD 330 – the major unifying factor was Christianity, and in particular Orthodox Christianity. The establishment of Constantinople as the 'new Rome' was a shrewd move as a splendid trading situation was combined with an excellent climate, good agricultural land, mineral wealth, a plentiful supply of water and a sound defensive position. The new capital was founded at a time when Christianity was elevated to a position of influence, yet the formal process by which the relationship between God and man could be expressed in visual terms had yet to be established. The reign of Justinian, however, marked the transition from the somewhat hybrid early Christian style to a fully realized Byzantine form.

The fortunes of Byzantium fluctuated during the succeeding centuries. However, a period of stability was experienced during the reign of Leo III (AD 717–40), a reign which also had a marked effect on the visual arts. His promulgation and enforcement of a policy which prohibited the representation of saintly personages was followed by a period of oppression and persecution. The iconoclast controversy was also a feature of the next reign, that of Constantine V, each side having strong adherents. The iconoclast argument was based on Exodus xx, 4: 'Thou shalt not make unto thyself an idol, nor likeness of anything. . . .' As early as AD 200, St Clement of Alexandria commented similarly, 'Makers of gods worship neither gods nor spirits, in my opinion, but the world of art.' The iconoclasts submitted that, because of the completeness of the divine nature, it could not be depicted, as the word Christ meant both God and man, '. . . and an icon of Christ would therefore have to be an image of God in the flesh of the Son of God'. They claimed that, by the attempted separation of the divine nature, the artist would fall into heresy. The iconophiles rejected such a notion completely: 'Does a man hate the teaching by means of pictures? Then how could he not have previously rejected and hated the message of the gospels?'

Although Church and State were so inextricably interwoven, and the great artistic developments of Byzantium were primarily of a religious nature, nevertheless a considerable *oeuvre* of secular art existed. Little remains from this popular tradition, and the art of Byzantium is generally evaluated solely as a religious art. Such secular art as remains exhibits to a remarkable degree elements of the Hellenistic tradition, whereas the development of religious art stems from an inspired blend of eastern and western traditions. The intervention of iconoclasm merely deferred the development of the style, although it had a distinctly chastening effect, even on the architecture. The full maturity of orthodox Christianity and the art forms which served it are to be sought after the demise of iconoclasm in the second half of the ninth century A D.

During the post-iconoclastic period, mosaic became the dominant form of decoration, and the full potential of the medium was realized in the production of a court style, which also served as a means of religious expression. During this period the canonical aspect of art was established and a hierarchy of images evolved. The maturity of this style, which post-dates the reign of Justinian, achieved perfect expression in the church of Hagia Sophia and yet presented something new. An attempt was made to produce a truly homogeneous design in which the individual picture was considered and constructed as part of a total pictorial scheme. The material structure of the church provided a setting for a system of art which was conceived as a microcosm of the real world with a heavenly and an earthly sphere, subject-matter being arranged accordingly. Christ occupied the centre of the dome, which, by virtue of its shape and position, symbolized the heavenly sphere. Thereafter, each figure and event was allocated a position in a descending pictorial hierarchy. After A D 900 the Byzantine system of images became fixed, although a certain amount of flexibility occurred in the presentation of details. The extraordinary unity of the decorative scheme and the architecture was further emphasized by the application of marble encrustations to the remainder of the wall surface. The areas of marble distinguished the pictorial zones, and because of the physical similarity between marble and mosaic these formed part of the decorative 'skin' which clothed the internal structure of the building, and became so distinctive a feature of the Byzantine style.

Links with Byzantium can be detected in the stylistic development of a number of local schools. Consider for instance the decoration of S. Marco in Venice, which was carried out at various times between the eleventh and the fourteenth centuries, and the mosaics which are to be found in the adjoining islands of Torcello and Murano. The

mosaics of S. Marco have suffered displacement during
various periods of restoration, and it is difficult to establish
the quality of the original scheme. Sicily was also strongly
influenced by the Byzantine mode, and examples may be
seen at Palermo, Cefalù and Monreale. During the twelfth
century a deliberate attempt to orientalize the interiors of a
number of foundations can be detected, although the symbols of Christianity were maintained in the decoration.

A number of ambitious schemes were undertaken; for
instance, an area of about $1\frac{1}{2}$ acres is solely occupied by
mosaic in the Cathedral of Monreale, Sta Maria la Nova,
which was built in 1172–76 by William II of Sicily, and is
one of the most impressive examples of the Norman Sicilian
style. A considerable amount of the original mosaic decoration remains. The scheme was completed in 1182, and begins
with the story of the Creation, which occupies the south side
of the nave and continues to the north side. The aisle mosaics
depict episodes from the ministry of Christ and the Passion,
and on the walls of the choir the preaching ministry of St
Peter and St Paul can be seen. The apsidal mosaic contains
an overwhelming half-length figure of Christ Pantocrator,
and below, the Virgin enthroned with angels and apostles.
A group of saints occupies the area below the Virgin,
including St Thomas à Becket, the antagonist in the struggle
between Church and State of King Henry II of England,
whose daughter was married to King William II of Sicily.

The decoration of the cathedral at Cefalù and La Martorana is roughly contemporary with the Monreale mosaics,
although in certain areas a return to the classical notion of
plasticity can be detected, with a consequent shift away from
the transcendentalism of the true Byzantine style. Cefalù is
a small picturesque fishermen's town which contains one of
the finest churches in Sicily. The cathedral was founded by

Virgin of Torcello: detail of mosaic
in the apse of the cathedral, Torcello,
near Venice.

Roger II of Sicily in 1131, and is perhaps one of the most
dramatically situated of the Sicilian group. The mosaics are
contained within the apse and at the east end of the pres-
bytery, and are dated to 1148; they are the earliest of this
particular stylistic phase, but are well preserved.

La Martorana is, in reality, Sta Maria dell'Ammiraglio,
which was founded in 1143 by George of Antioch and presented to a convent founded in 1194 by Eloisa Martorana.
The mosaic decoration was originally to be seen on the
portico, now destroyed, and the mosaics were transferred to
a position on the west wall of the interior. Those represented
are King Robert of Sicily crowned by Christ, and, at the
feet of the Virgin, the founder George of Antioch – Robert's
Admiral. The mosaics have been considerably restored,
although in view of their past history, the mere fact of their
survival is remarkable.

Apart from the predominantly religious themes of mosaic
decoration in the churches, examples remain of a secular
form of decoration in a Norman Saracenic style which was
used in the Norman palaces of Sicily. The Palazzo dei Nor-
manni, or Palazzo Reale, was originally built by the Saracens
during their occupation of the island. It was altered by
Roger II and his successors; the Cappella Palatina is one of the
most typical examples of the Norman Saracenic style. The

Two lions; mosaic from Palazzo
Reale, Palermo in Sicily.

lower area of the interior consists of a cladding of marble slabs, while the upper part is covered with splendid mosaics set on a gold ground. The triumphal arch contains angels bearing gifts, and in the cupola the figure of Christ attended by angels and archangels. The drum of the cupola contains representations of King David, Solomon and Zachariah, and figures of St John the Baptist and the Evangelists occupy the pendentives. On the second floor of the palace are the royal apartments of the Norman dynasty (the Norman Stanze), containing mosaics greatly influenced by the non-figural style of Islam, particularly in the stylized forms of animals and trees.

The reverse can be detected in the mosaic decoration of a number of Muslim sanctuaries. The non-figural style is uninfluenced by the pictorial cycles of Byzantium although motifs, technique and workmanship exhibit abundant evidence of influence. Doubt has been expressed as to the origin of the craftsmen engaged to execute the decoration of these monuments, some authorities favouring the notion that Byzantine Greeks were employed, others that the craftsmen were Byzantine-trained Syrians.

The religion of Islam was all-pervading and monotheist. Muhammad, the founder of the Muslim empire, was not only a divinely inspired prophet in the eyes of his followers but also a lawgiver, a leader and a general. After his death in AD 622 a series of victories by Arab generals gave to Islam the regions of Palestine, Iraq, Syria, Mesopotamia, Egypt, Alexandria, Persia, West Turkestan, and part of the Punjab, North Africa and Spain. Consequently Islamic art, like Roman art, is to be considered as the art of a civilization rather than of a particular country.

An important transfer of the capital of the empire from Medina to Damascus exposed Muslim culture to the influence of the late classical culture, and the art of the Umayyads is characterized by the fusion of Roman, Hellenistic and Asian elements, which may be clearly detected in the decoration of the Dome of the Rock in Jerusalem, a superb political and religious monument. This octagonal building is built over the summit of Mount Moriah, where, it is claimed, Muhammad received direct divine inspiration. The Dome, Al Qubbat as-Sakhra, was commenced by Abd al-Malik in 685 and completed in 691, and according to an early writer, Ya'qubi, 'the people took to the custom of circumambulating the rock'.

The technique of mosaic was obviously held in high regard by the Muslims and a number of references are to be found in early texts. Khalil, who died in 791, defines the actual mosaic material as being a substance made of glass and little stones, baked together, and combining much brilliance and beauty with great variety of colour, including gold and silver. A Persian traveller, Nāṣir-i-Khusra, in a text dated 1047, refers to the existence of mosaic workshops in Cairo and to the manufacture of smalti. Another writer, Baladhuri, who was active in the ninth century, makes reference to the source of supply of both workmen and materials and is of interest in that he makes no mention of Constantinople as being concerned with either. He specifies Rumi (Greeks) from Syria and Copts from Egypt.

The decoration of the Dome of the Rock is familiar to western eyes because of the classical derivation of the motifs, although with a riotous overlay of oriental luxury which lends an air of fantasy to the scheme. All images of living things have been eliminated in accordance with Muslim practice. The decoration is entirely composed of floral and conventionalized ornament, but with a marked absence of geometric motifs. These curiously hybrid mosaics are the oldest surviving Muslim examples. The decorative scheme of the Umayyad mosque at Damascus includes idyllic landscapes in which fortified cities are depicted, surrounded by lakes and vines and a wide variety of trees, a theme which would seem to be a pictorial expression of the peace of Islam.

Strong evidence of the influence of Imperial court art can be seen in three fairly isolated monastery churches in Greece. These are the church and monastery of Hosios Loukas in Phocis, of the eleventh century, the Nea Moni (new monastery), dated to about 1050, and the monastery church at Daphni, also of the eleventh century, probably the second half. The technique and composition of the mosaic schemes contained within these churches is so closely related to that of the main stylistic trend, centred on the court, that it seems impossible for them to have been produced independently, and yet the precise nature of the link has not yet been established with certainty.

The capture of Constantinople by the Crusaders in AD 1204 interrupted the development of Byzantine art, and caused the dispersal of the artists. This proved of benefit to other regions – Macedonia, Bulgaria, Serbia, Trebizond on the Black Sea, and Crete – which were established as centres of Byzantine culture under various members of the Imperial family who had escaped the invaders. What is so remarkable is the strength of Byzantine influence in the east – the Orthodox Church of Constantinople became the Church of the Slavs. As the influence of Byzantium faded in the west, its traditions were maintained in the east, to become the roots of Russian civilization and art. Many of the works produced in the lands of the Slavs were of an exceedingly high quality, and, in union with the Orthodox Church, distinct elements of Byzantine art were preserved until relatively recent times. By virtue of the preservation of the unique identity of Byzantine art, both as a court art and a religious art, the contribution of the Slavonic peoples is crucial to both the unity and the longevity of what is the most extensive period of art in the west.

10 Early Christian and medieval mosaic in Rome

Surviving examples of mosaics which can be seen in or near Rome present a fairly comprehensive picture of the development of Christian mosaics between the third and fourteenth centuries. In addition it is possible to gain a reasonably complete picture of the continuous tradition of pavimental decoration, in both mosaic and related techniques. Examples ranging from the time of the Roman Empire to the early Christian period offer a unique opportunity for a chronological survey of styles and themes.

Early Christian mosaics in Rome include a representation of Christ as Helios which can be seen (with special permission) in the cemetery under St Peter's. The vault decorations of the fourth century which are to be seen in the Mausoleum of Costanza demonstrate the continuance of the pagan tradition during the early period of Christianity, and in addition the church contains two apsidal mosaics which express the emergence of a Christian iconography. The mausoleum was built after AD 337 and was later converted into a church, although now restored to its original architectural form. The delightful small building is circular in plan, with an *atrium* and an antechamber. The central area is roofed by a cupola – despoiled of its mosaic decoration in 1620 – but the details of the scheme have been preserved in a drawing by Francesco d'Hollanda, now in the Escorial in Spain.

An outer *ambulacrum*, that is, a barrel-vaulted corridor, is separated from the central area by a double ring of columns which are beautifully distributed. The vaulted ceiling of the *ambulacrum* retains the original mosaic decoration, competently restored at the beginning of the nineteenth century. The interior lighting is strikingly theatrical: the central area is brightly lit by a series of generous openings in the central cupola. In contrast the lighting of the *ambulacrum* is diffused.

MAUSOLEUM OF COSTANZA

The porphyry Mausoleum of Costanza, who may have been the daughter or granddaughter of the Emperor Constantine, was removed to the Vatican museum, but a copy has been substituted. The sarcophagus is placed at the far end of the rotunda directly opposite the entrance and can be approached either from the left or right of the main door. The decorative scheme is substantially the same at each side,

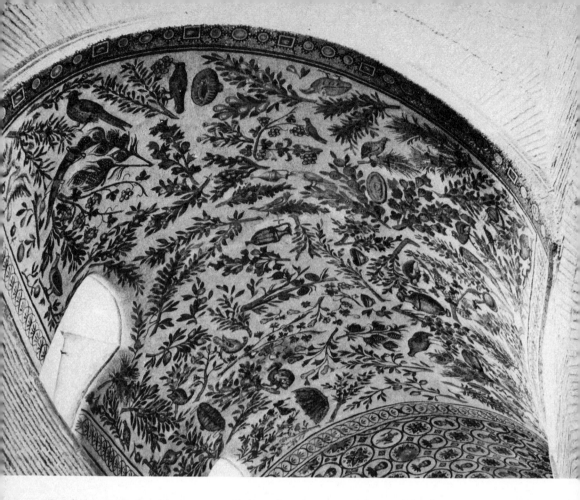

'Paradise' pattern in the vault,
Sta Costanza, Rome (see also detail
on p. 17).

and the colour becomes richer and the design more complex
as the sarcophagus is approached. The scheme is organized
in a series of panels. A simple pattern in blue and white can
be seen at the entrance, giving way to a pattern of dolphins,
which may have some significance as a Christian symbol.
This is followed by a pattern which includes figures of
Cupid and Psyche from pagan mythology, as well as sheep
and a variety of birds. The next section depicts the grape
harvest – a theme which is repeated on the sarcophagus;
this probably gave rise to the name by which the Mausoleum
was known during the Renaissance – the 'Temple of
Bacchus'. The theme is not an unusual one, although, if a
Christian meaning were intended, the reference must be
taken to mean the 'True Vine', which is Christ, a symbol of
immortality. However, it is also true that the symbol of the
vine had a similar meaning to members of the Dionysiac
cults. The panel following that of the Vine Harvest incorporates figures and busts set in roundels, and this is succeeded
by the climax of the scheme – the so-called 'Paradise'
pattern which is situated nearest the sarcophagus.

The 'Paradise' sequence erupts in splendour. The richly
coloured motifs, which include gold tesserae, are set against
a neutral background of plain marble tesserae. The plain

background is consistent with the rest of the scheme. The rich and – in comparison with the previous panels – complicated decoration includes birds, vessels, and a variety of fruits. If the symbolism is truly Christian in intention, the sequence may be read as the journey of the soul from the world of flesh to the world of the spirit. The climax of this symbolic journey would, of course, coincide with the arrival of the spectator at the sarcophagus.

The niche decorations are undoubtedly Christian, although it is now thought that they are not very much later in date than those of the vault. The true reading of the subject-matter has been a matter of controversy, although it is now generally accepted that the subjects depicted are the *Traditio Clavium* (the handing over of the keys of the Kingdom of Heaven) and the *Traditio Legis* (the handing over of the Law). Unfortunately, poor restoration makes positive identification of the subject-matter rather difficult, and appraisal of the original style impossible. The fascination of the Sta Costanza mosaics, apart from the intrinsic beauty of the scheme, lies in the fact that stylistically they represent an end and a beginning.

The apsidal mosaic of *Sta Pudenziana* dates to the fourth and the beginning of the fifth century. This church, one of the oldest of the Roman foundations, is situated near the basilica of Sta Maria Maggiore. According to legend, the original foundation was built over the house of the Senator Pudens with whom St Peter lodged when he came to Rome, although the extremely well-cared-for interior has a lightness which somewhat belies the actual age of the foundation.

The subject of the mosaic is Christ enthroned among his apostles, although the group, which is set against a porticoed

Vine Harvest: detail of vault mosaic, Sta Costanza, Rome, which understandably earned the church the name of 'Temple of Bacchus' in the Renaissance.

exedra, was severely reduced by the remodelling of the interior. In the background are groups of buildings of a markedly naturalistic character, which may represent the chief shrines of Jerusalem. The jewelled cross, which appears in the background, may be in reference to the great jewelled cross which was set up by Constantine on the hill of Golgotha. The symbols of the Evangelists appear in the sky, although they too have suffered severely by the reduction in the over-all size of the mosaic. Two female figures can be seen behind the apostles, to the right and left of the central figure of Christ. They have been identified as the Church of the Circumcision (of the Jews) and the Church of the Gentiles, although they may represent Sta Pudenziana and her sister Sta Prassede, the daughters of Pudens. The work is of particular interest as the subtlety of technique can still be appreciated in spite of the alteration. The naturalistic treatment indicates the resilience of the Roman tradition: the spatial relationship between figures and background is well established, and a number of heads – which can be considered original – are individualized and clearly within the tradition of Roman portraiture.

SANTA MARIA MAGGIORE

The fifth-century mosaics of Sta Maria Maggiore are of great importance. The church, one of the four great patriarchal basilicas of Rome, was built on the Esquiline hill during the pontificate of Sixtus III (432–40). During 1743 the interior was restored and a new façade was added by the architect Fuga. Because of the late façade the existence of the fifth-century mosaics is often unsuspected by the visitor. Twenty-five framed panels from this period survive in the nave, unfortunately rather difficult to see without the aid of binoculars. The Old Testament narrative includes the stories of Jacob, Joshua, Abraham and Isaac, and the style displays a strong classical element. The plasticity of the figures is well realized; they are proportional and solid, and are grouped in naturalistic poses. The setting technique is also markedly classical, the 'impressionist' manner being adopted throughout.

The use of gold tesserae is of great interest in these panels. The incorporation of gold as a means of highlighting and adding richness was a feature of the vault mosaic of Sta Costanza, and the apsidal decoration of Sta Pudenziana. In the nave decoration of Sta Maria Maggiore, gold is used much more exuberantly and over larger areas. The effect is striking. In certain areas the gold streaks across the panel: in others it assumes the quality of an avalanche. A further development in the use of gold can be detected in the panels of the nave, where it has been used compositionally to add emphasis to certain areas.

Sta Maria Maggiore, Rome: detail
of triumphal arch mosaic; (*above*)
top, the flight into Egypt and
underneath, the Magi before Herod;
(*below, right*) detail of festoon mosaic
from soffit of arch.

The mosaics of the triumphal arch have been dated to the
middle of the fifth century and they too retain a considerable
amount of the classical manner. The figures are solid,
individual, and three-dimensional, although transitional in
the sense that they convey suggestions of the transcendentalism which was to follow. Technically, certain areas are
extremely interesting in the almost *pointilliste* manner of
setting the individual stones. The main theme of the triumphal arch depicts the childhood of Christ, including the
Annunciation, the Adoration of the Magi, the Massacre of
the Innocents, the Presentation in the Temple, the Magi
before Herod, and an unusual scene which portrays the
welcome extended to the Holy Family during the flight into
Egypt, which is recorded in the apocryphal gospel of Jacob.
The central position on the arch is occupied by an empty
throne symbolizing the invisible presence of God, flanked
to left and right by St Peter and St Paul. Gold is used extensively, although not exclusively, on the background.

The soffit of the arch contains a very early example of a
form of decoration known as a 'festoon', which was to
remain popular. This example (*c.* 435) exhibits a remarkable
anticipation of the forms which were to follow, especially
in the degree of stylization. The festoon – a symbol of plenty
– is very full and rich, with four-petalled flowers without
foliage. The scheme is carried out largely in blue and a
pinkish-red. The volume of the form is expressed by shading
which, in contrast to the rich colour, adds to the fullness of
the festoon.

OTHER ROMAN CHURCHES

Sta Maria Maggiore, Rome: detail of triumphal arch mosaic, (*above*) top, the Annunciation and, underneath, the Adoration of the Magi; (*below*) detail of an angel from the Presentation scene.

The mosaic in the church of *SS. Cosma e Damiano* is of later date, *c.* 530. It is much closer in style to the classical work of the fourth century A D. The church occupies the site of the Forum of Peace, which was completed in A D 74 to commemorate the pacification of the East by the Emperor Vespasian. The reconstruction of the pagan foundation and its consecration as a church was undertaken by Pope Felix V (526–30), in honour of the two physician-martyrs, Cosmas and Damian. Typically, the ancient church was extensively remodelled in the seventeenth century, but fortunately retains the original mosaic decoration. Historically, the mosaics are of great importance. Stylistically, they seem to have been largely uninfluenced by the developments in Ravenna (which took place as a result of influences from the eastern Empire) and yet they were to exert a considerable influence on the composition of subsequent apsidal schemes.

The mosaic depicts Christ – very solidly modelled – descending a stairway of clouds, worked in shades of soft blue and vermilion, and set against the deep blue of the sky. The figure of Christ is nimbed and richly clothed in vestments of gold. The apostles Peter and Paul are also depicted in the act of presenting the titular saints, Cosmas and Damian, to Christ. Included in the group are Pope Felix and St Theodore – the soldier saint from Asia Minor with a martyr's crown. Below the main group is a procession of sheep flanking the Agnus Dei to left and right. The sheep, which represent the apostles, are set against a background of green and gold; the survival of classical naturalism can be seen in the variety and individuality of the sheep.

The mosaic of the triumphal arch contains a representation of the Agnus Dei reclining on a throne, two symbols of the Evangelists, angels, candelabra, and what may be taken as the remnants of a group depicting the twenty-four elders of the Apocalypse. The mosaic suffered a drastic reduction in size during the alterations to the interior of the church in the seventeenth century. The remarkable breadth of treatment, and the classical naturalism which inhabits what remains of the scheme, justify consideration of these mosaics as representative of a late phase of the classical period of Christian decoration.

Another example from the same period can be seen in the church of *Sta Sabina*, on the Aventine hill. The plan of the building has an affinity with the basilican type of Ravenna, and it seems probable that the mosaic decoration bore a similar relationship. Little remains of the original scheme save the dedicational inscription, which is flanked by two female figures representing the Churches of the Jews and the Gentiles. Both figures retain to a marked degree affinities with the classical style, exemplified by the naturalism of the draperies and the individuality of the figures. The importance of the mosaic lies in the fact that it retains that section of a typical scheme of the period which is missing from Sta Maria Maggiore.

The next phase of development, which can be traced fairly decisively in a number of Roman churches, inclines towards the influence of Byzantium to a marked degree, although the indigenous Roman tradition persisted. The emergence of a new tradition can be seen in two foundations which lie outside the walls of Rome. In the first, *S. Lorenzo fuori le Mura*, the illusion of a new stylistic direction with residual elements of the old tradition is very evident in the mosaic which commemorated the martyred St Lawrence.

S. Lorenzo fuori le Mura, Rome: triumphal arch mosaic.

The dominance of the Byzantine style can be seen in the over-all gold background, and the loss of individuality of most of the figures, although a lingering influence of the Roman portrait tradition remains in several of the heads, which retain some characterization. Apart from the prolongation of the portrait tradition, individual touches reveal the persistence of the classical form, for instance the use of glass smalti in the heads instead of natural stone which was more usual in Byzantine work (although this naturalism is itself in opposition to the linear treatment of the drapery, which again suggests the intervention of Byzantine influence).

The small round church of S. *Teodoro* at the foot of the Palatine hill was built during the last phase of the Empire over storehouses or granaries – the Horrea Agrippiana. The sixth-century mosaic occupies an apse off the main rotunda of the church. In spite of extensive restoration, it is of some importance, as it represents a period from which few examples remain. The centre of the composition is occupied by Christ seated on the globe of the firmament and flanked by St Peter and St Paul, who introduce a martyred saint. He is in the act of blessing, and holds a cross in his left hand.

The apsidal mosaic of *Sta Agnese fuori le Mura*, another church outside the walls of Rome, typifies the emergence of a style considerably influenced by that of Byzantium. The basilica was founded by Constantine in AD 324 to commemorate the young noblewoman Agnese, who was martyred under Diocletian in AD 304. The mosaic is contemporary with the structure of the church (c. AD 625–28);

(*Below, left*) Detail of St Peter, (*below, right*) St Hippolytus: triumphal arch mosaic, S. Lorenzo fuori le Mura, near Rome.

it features Sta Agnese, accompanied by Pope Honorius on
her right, offering a model of the church, and Pope
Symmachus on her left. There is little trace of composition
in the classical sense. The figures stand remote and physically
unconnected, against a background of gold smalti. The influence of the Byzantine mode is apparent in the over-all
gold background – suggestive of the atmosphere of Paradise.
The elongated, unearthly figure of Agnese is depicted with
an aura of other-worldliness which transcends reality, in
contrast to the elements of classical portraiture which have
endured in the heads of Symmachus and Honorius.

Behind the basilica of San Giovanni in Laterano, in the
south-west corner of the piazza, is the baptistery of *S.
Giovanni in Fonte*. The baptistery, founded by Constantine
in 324, was originally a domed circular structure, but was
rebuilt on an octagonal plan during the pontificate of
Sixtus III (432–40), and altered during the reign of Pope
Urban VIII in the seventeenth century. The ancient *atrium*
with side apses has been transformed into a rectangular
chapel with traces of mosaic decoration of the time of
Sixtus III. The Chapel of S. Venanzio, which was added to
the baptistery towards the middle of the seventh century,
contains an extensive mosaic decoration, which covers the
apse and the triumphal arch.

The apsidal decoration includes a bust of Christ – as the
Pantocrator – attended by angels, who are depicted as half-
figures. Immediately below stands the figure of the Virgin
Orans, somewhat dwarfed by the Pantocrator. The Virgin
is accompanied by nimbed saints and Popes John IV (640–
42) and Theodore I. The processional quality of this group –
four to the left and four to the right of the Virgin – recalls
the Justinian mosaics at Ravenna (see p. 16). The processional theme is extended to the triumphal arch, which
depicts saints and martyrs from Dalmatia, whose relics were

transferred to the chapel by Pope John IV. The Byzantine influence is apparent both in technique and detail. There is an almost total absence of depth, and the figures, in fixed poses, form a frieze from which the classical elements of composition are entirely eliminated. Yet one of the most remarkable aspects of the mosaic is the strong sense of individuality which remains in a number of details, such as the treatment of the hair and garments, which almost reject the abstraction that is so markedly Byzantine. The mosaic was extensively restored as late as 1947.

Another example of the same phase of mosaic decoration can be seen in the church of *S. Stefano Rotondo*, built during the reign of Pope Simplicius in the seventh century. The church, reputedly the largest round church in the world, is based on the plan of the church of the Holy Sepulchre in Jerusalem. The mosaic of about 650 is situated in an apsidal chapel, and depicts SS. Primus and Felicianus, who suffered martyrdom during the persecutions of Diocletian and were re-interred in the church by Pope Theodore I (642–49). The background of the mosaic is set with gold smalti, and the saints are depicted standing in a flowery field. The Byzantine practice of working faces and hands in natural stone, cut to a smaller size than the glass smalti of the rest of the work, can be seen, although the highly individualized heads which are a feature of this work are in the classical tradition.

S. Pietro in Vincoli, or the Basilica Eudoxia, which was traditionally founded by the Empress Eudoxia in AD 442, contains a curious mosaic in a chapel near the north aisle. The mosaic, of the seventh century, has as its subject St Sebastian, but not the handsome youth pierced by arrows which was so popular a subject among the painters of the Renaissance; here the saint is a bearded, elderly figure – a most unfamiliar image. The panel has been mounted as an altar-piece, and is difficult to see. Apart from the figure of Sebastian, one or two fragments from this period can be seen in the Vatican Grottoes, including an interesting portrait of Pope John VII with the square nimbus of the living and carrying a model of the Oratory which originally contained the mosaics. Byzantine influence is evident in the use of much smaller stone tesserae for the face and hands, although the classical tradition of portraiture still prevails. Another fragment very similar in technique retains part of a figure of Christ which is thought to have been a detail of the 'Entry into Jerusalem', known to have been part of the original scheme of the Oratory.

CAROLINGIAN AND PASCHALIAN MOSAICS

The mosaics from the next phase of development, that is during the late eighth and the early ninth centuries, are representative of a period during which Rome was open to

influence from two sources. In western Europe the
Carolingian Renaissance assumed importance. This period
of artistic revival was sponsored by the Emperor Charlemagne
(742–814), King of the Franks and Holy Roman Emperor,
who looked to the antique as a model. In the eastern Empire
the bitter iconoclast controversy was at its height, and
artistic development was seriously inhibited. Inevitably,
some of the consequences of the clash influenced the development of mosaic in Rome, although the elimination of the
image was never obtained there. Outside influence was
largely Carolingian, and in addition the personal taste of
Pope Paschal I, to whom we owe a number of monuments
of the period, was inclined towards the antique.

The attractive church of *SS. Nereo e Achilleo* retains a
mosaic on the triumphal arch which represents the com-
mencement of the new phase. The church – an old foundation
– was restored at the end of the eighth century, and partly
renewed in the fifteenth. The mosaic of the triumphal arch
is of the period of Pope Leo III (795–816), and portrays the
Annunciation, the Madonna and Child, and the Trans-
figuration, which is witnessed by representations of Moses,
Elias, St Peter, St John and St James. The most outstanding
feature of this mosaic lies in the heightened colour scheme,
otherwise the style and technique are not exceptional.

The apsidal mosaic of *Sta Maria Domnica* (c. 818) is one of
the group associated with Pope Paschal I (817–24). The
church, which is situated in the Via della Navicella, near to
S. Stefano Rotondo, was reputedly built on the site of the
house of Sta Cyriaca – a pious and revered Christian lady of
the third century. The word 'domnica' may be a corruption
of 'domnicum', which in early Christian usage signified a
church. The age of the building is belied by the Renaissance
doorway which forms part of the sixteenth-century
restoration. The mosaic depicts Pope Paschal as a young
man wearing a square halo. He kneels at the feet of the
seated Virgin who occupies the central position of the apse,
holding her right foot in his hands. The Virgin, enthroned

Nimbed saints on the left of the
Virgin: detail of mosaic in Baptistery
of Constantine, S. Giovanni
Laterano, Rome.

Detail of mosaic of apsidal arch, Sta Prassede, Rome: the elders offer their crowns of glory to the Agnus Dei.

with a carpet spread before her on a flowery field, holds the Infant Christ on her lap, and both she and the child are represented in a rather rigid frontal position. The attendant angels, who flank the central group to left and right, are a spectacular feature of the mosaic. The presence of a host is suggested by a number of receding light blue nimbi, the representation of individuals being confined to the foremost figures, who are nimbed with gold. The remarkable brilliance of colouring is very reminiscent of that of the triumphal arch of SS. Nereo e Achilleo.

The mosaic of the triumphal arch of Sta Maria Domnica represents Christ in a central position contained within a mandorla, and flanked by an angel to left and right. The twelve apostles are arranged alongside, six to the left of Christ headed by St Peter and six to the right headed by St Paul. Below, on the left, is a representation of St John the Baptist and on the right of St John the Evangelist. An interesting feature of this mosaic is the re-introduction of a blue background in the upper part of the apse mosaic, and in part of the background of the triumphal arch. In both instances the ground is green and sprinkled with flowers.

To the right of Sta Maria Maggiore the Via Merulana leads to the small church of *Sta Prassede*. The church is usually entered by a side door, but to gain some sense of the antiquity of the foundation one should locate the main entrance in Via S. Martino ai Monti. The main façade is substantially of the period of Paschal I, although alterations have taken place. The original paleo-Christian basilica was built towards the end of the fourth or early fifth century, on a site a little removed from the present church, which Paschal erected to house and honour the remains of Pudenziana and Prassede, the daughters of Pudens.

In spite of the alterations which were carried out during the eighteenth century, the magnificent mosaics remain intact. The theme of the apsidal mosaic (*c.* 818) derives from that of SS. Cosma e Damiano. Christ descends a stairway of clouds, with St Peter to his left and St Paul to his right presenting the sisters Prassede and Pudenziana respectively. S. Zenone makes a third in the group to Christ's left, and similarly Pope Paschal appears in the group to the right. The Pope is depicted wearing the square halo of the living, and presenting a model of the church. The main theme of the arch of the apse is apocalyptic and depicts the twenty-four elders offering their crowns of glory to the Agnus Dei. The Lamb is seen standing on the book with the seven seals, and flanked by the symbols of the evangelists. The theme of the triumphal arch is the heavenly Jerusalem within whose walls can be seen Christ, the Virgin, Sta Prassede, St John the Evangelist, Elijah, Moses and the apostles. The elect are grouped to right and left of the walls, waiting for admission, the group on the right being received by St Peter and St Paul. The work is extremely stylized, and emphasizes the transcendental nature of the scene.

Another survival from the same period is the small chapel of *S. Zenone* which is reached from the right aisle of the church. The chapel was known as the 'Garden of Paradise', which even today appears an apt description. The tiny chapel is entered through a portal with a classical architrave supported by two black marble columns. The area above the entrance contains a mosaic panel set in the form of a double arch. The inner arch is decorated with eleven roundels which contain busts of female saints, each wearing a martyr's crown, and two tonsured males, probably S. Zenone and his brother S. Valentius. The Virgin and Child occupy a roundel in the central position, set against a background of gold. The remainder of the roundels have blue backgrounds, all of which are contrasted against the shimmering gold which covers the background of the arch. The outer band contains a bust of Christ, also placed within a roundel, and flanked to the left and right by twelve roundels which contain busts of the apostles, the gold backgrounds being set against an arch of blue.

The small quadrangular interior of the chapel is completely covered with mosaics, including the vaulted ceiling which contains four angels supporting a half-figure of Christ. The figures of this group are considerably larger than those of the rest of the chapel. The angels appear to be standing on columns supporting the vault; this adds emphasis to the vertical thrust of the figures, which are set against a background of gold. The glittering background enhances the blue of their haloes and the blue background of the roundel containing the half-figure of Christ.

On the inner surface of the entrance door the Holy Presence is symbolized by a golden cross which is placed on a throne flanked by St Peter and St Paul. The haloes of Peter and Paul are differentiated from the gold background by means of a line of red tesserae. On the left is a shallow niche which contains a theme common to early Christian art – deer are shown drinking from the four rivers of paradise, which spring from a rock upon which the Agnus Dei stands. Below are represented the Virgin, Sta Prassede and another female figure, all half-length and with gold haloes outlined in red against a gold background. On the left of the group a fourth figure depicts Theodora Episcopa – Theodora the mother of Paschal – wearing a square blue halo. Representations of male and female saints flank the window openings. Above a small altar, and contained within a niche, can be seen figures of the Virgin and Child flanked by two female saints of a later date than the rest of the decoration. The saints carry crowns, no doubt the crowns of martyrdom, and may represent Prassede and Pudenziana.

Sta Cecilia in Trastevere, reached from the Via di Santa Cecilia, was probably founded by Pope St Urban I (222–30), on the site of what was believed to be the house of St Valerian and his wife Cecilia. The church was rebuilt by Pope Paschal I, but sadly altered at various periods between

Detail of apse mosaic, Sta Maria Domnica, Rome. Pope Paschal (with the square halo of the living) kneels before the Virgin (see pp. 221–2).

the sixteenth and the twentieth centuries. The glory of the church is to be sought in the apsidal mosaic which depicts Christ descending a stairway of clouds and blessing in the Greek manner. The composition is derived from the apsidal mosaic of SS. Cosma e Damiano, although not at first-hand. The figure of Christ is centrally placed, and is flanked by two groups, on his left St Peter, St Valerian and Sta Cecilia, and on his right St Paul, and St Agatha who is apparently sponsoring Pope Paschal. Christ is shown on the same level as the adjacent figures, although on a much larger scale, and the rest of the figures are extremely elongated. The group is depicted standing in a flowery field and set against a blue background. The stairway of clouds down which Christ descends is less clearly defined than either the version in Sta Prassede or the prototype in SS. Cosma e Damiano.

In the Piazza S. Marco, and almost opposite the Vittorio Emmanuele monument, is the church of *S. Marco*, reputedly founded in 336. The church, which forms part of the Palazzo Venezia, was restored in 833, rebuilt in 1468 and again

Detail of apse mosaic, Sta Cecilia in Trastevere.

restored in the seventeenth and eighteenth centuries. The remains of the mosaic decoration, which dates to the reign of Pope Gregory IV (828–44), can be seen on the triumphal arch and in the apse. The apsidal mosaic contains a figure of Christ blessing in the Greek manner, which occupies the central position, and is flanked by three figures to the left and three to the right. A curious feature of this mosaic is the manner in which each figure stands on what appears to be a carpet inscribed with their names; these carpets are reminiscent of the bases of lead soldiers. On the extreme right of Christ appears a figure of Pope Gregory with a square nimbus and carrying a model of the church. His sponsor, St Mark the Evangelist, places a reassuring hand on his shoulder. The third figure of the group is St Felicissimus, who appears on the immediate right of Christ. The figure nearest to Christ on his left is Pope Mark of Rome (336), then Pope St Agapetus (535–36) followed by Sta Agnese holding her crown of martyrdom.

All the figures, with the exception of Pope Gregory, are shown with gold nimbi; those of St Mark, St Agapetus and Sta Agnese are differentiated from the gold background by an inner line of white and an outer line of red tesserae. Those of St Felicissimus and Pope Mark are distinguished by an inner line of white and an outer line of blue, and the nimbus of Christ contains a cross which is set in blue and white. The square nimbus of Pope Gregory is set in blue tesserae and enclosed by an inner line of white and an outer line of black.

In contrast to the brilliance of colour associated with the Paschalian mosaics, the colour scheme of the work in S. Marco is extremely sombre. There is a preponderance of soft browns, yellows and whites, set against a background of gold. The triumphal arch contains a bust of Christ set in a roundel and flanked by the symbols of the Evangelists, which are also contained within roundels. The spandrels contain full-length figures of St Peter to the right and St Paul to the left. The mosaics of S. Marco represent not only the last mosaic scheme of this period but also the last example of a continuous sequence from the advent of mosaic as a form of mural decoration.

After the installation of the S. Marco mosaic in the ninth century, there followed a period of three centuries from which no major mosaic decoration has survived. The first work of any significance, from what may be regarded as a period of revival in Rome, is the apsidal mosaic decoration of *S. Clemente*, 1125, unique in its fusion of medieval and classical elements. S. Clemente, one of the most important monuments in Rome, lies to the left of the Via S. Giovanni in Laterano. This was the old Via Papale along which the papal procession accompanied the Pope on his journey to the seat of his bishopric in the basilica of S. Giovanni Laterano. S. Clemente, as it stands today, is a complex on three levels with the medieval basilica of the twelfth century at street level.

(*Above*) Head of Sta Cecilia: detail from mosaic in Sta Cecilia in Trastevere.

(*Below*) Detail of apse mosaic, S. Marco, Rome. St Mark (right) is sponsoring Pope Gregory in the traditional way by placing an arm round his shoulder.

The bowl of the apse is decorated with a huge acanthus plant at the base of which appears a stag, which is seen to be struggling with what was originally a serpent, although the motif was misunderstood by the medieval craftsmen and looks more like a decorative strap. From the centre of the foliage, directly above the stag, springs the cross with Christ crucified, witnessed by the Virgin and St John the disciple. The twelve apostles, symbolized by white doves, are contained within the arms of the cross, which is set in smalti of deep blue. Above the cross the hand of God can be seen bearing the crown of glory for His Son. The theme symbolizes the triumph of the cross and the gift of grace to mankind. Stags drinking from the rivers of Paradise can be seen directly below the base of the acanthus. The acanthus was, of course, a common motif in classical art; similar scrolls may be seen on the altar of Augustus, the 'Ara Pacis', also in Rome, and as far afield as the Dome of the Rock in Jerusalem. Further classical motifs can be detected in the inhabited scroll, as for instance the amoretti and dolphins, and within the curling fronds of the scroll are such creatures as peacocks, swans, doves and herons, and exotic plants and flowers. The Fathers of the Latin Church are also represented – Jerome, Augustine, Ambrose and Gregory – and, in contrast, a number of attractive 'genre' scenes, for instance a woman feeding hens, and a shepherd.

This impressive work is rich in colour, with a gold background set upon an uneven surface. The light plays across the gold smalti in such a way as to give the impression that the apse is lit from within. The mosaic of the triumphal arch is a work of much less refinement, although extremely decorative. St Peter can be seen on the spectator's right and St Paul on the left. St Clement is shown seated next to Peter, and the prophet Jeremiah is depicted holding a scroll and standing below the feet of SS. Peter and Clement. A similar group occurs on the other side of the arch, where St Paul is accompanied by St Lawrence and the prophet Isaiah stands below.

The church of *Sta Maria in Trastevere* is situated in the *piazza* of the same name, in the quarter 'across the Tiber' (*trans Tiberim*) which has been for many centuries the popular quarter of Rome. The inhabitants claim to be in direct line from ancient Romans, which is not true, although they preserve many of the qualities which characterized the Romans, including a strong love of liberty. Trastevere was in fact the stronghold of independence during the Risorgimento. The church is a very ancient foundation, said to have been founded by Pope Calistus (217–22). A church, listed as *Titulus Juli*, was rebuilt on the site by Pope Julius I (337–52) and restored by John VII and Adrian I in the eighth century. The church in its present form is largely the result of a rebuilding programme instituted by Pope Innocent II of Trastevere (1130–43).

The mosaic decoration is retained on the triumphal arch and in the apse, and on the façade over the main entrance.

The façade mosaic, which is in the form of a frieze, depicts the Virgin and Child occupying a central position, and flanked on either side by a small figure of a donor, and five female figures – on a slightly smaller scale than the Holy Family. These figures are contained within the border, whereas the figure of the Virgin overlaps slightly. Subject and date have both been a matter for controversy. The Virgin and Child and the two female figures on either side are almost certainly twelfth-century work, whereas the figures of the donors are in a style which suggests a thirteenth-century date. Further major differences of style can be detected in the remainder of the figures; one group may be ascribed to the early thirteenth century, and another group to a later date.

The exquisitely beautiful apsidal mosaic is devoted to the glorification of the Virgin, who is depicted enthroned. The theme is of French origin, and this version is an unusually early example of the theme in Italy. The Virgin appears, crowned and in company with her adult Son, although her appearance is one of youth and beauty. Christ is accorded the central position, and to his right are three standing figures, SS. Calistus, Lawrence and Pope Innocent II who holds a model of the church. Similarly, to his left appear the figures of SS. Peter, Cornelius, Julius and Calepodius. Here one of the weaknesses of the composition is apparent, as the uneven distribution of the figures (which is not compensated for) tends to produce an imbalance.

The superb gold background, and the elaborate vestments with which a number of the figures are clothed, give a sumptuous richness to the apse. The Virgin is a figure of great elegance; the Son is a majestic figure of power and dignity. The heads are particularly fine; they are worked very closely with small tesserae, which suggests at least the influence if not the participation of Byzantine craftsmen. The imbalance of the apsidal decoration occurs again in the mosaic of the triumphal arch. The central position is occupied by a cross bearing the symbol of Alpha and Omega, which is flanked to right and left by seven candlesticks, three to the spectator's left and four to the right. The symbols of Evangelists are also depicted, and below appear representations of the prophets Isaiah, to the left, and Jeremiah

Detail of apse mosaic, Sta Maria in Trastevere.

Head of Virgin: detail of apse mosaic, Sta Maria in Trastevere.

to the right. The obvious symmetry of these groupings fails to correct the asymmetry of the candlesticks. The caged birds which accompany the figures of Isaiah are symbolic of the suffering of Christ – *Christus dominus captus est in peccatis nostris* ('In our sins Christ the Lord is imprisoned').

The church of *Sta Francesca Romana*, or more properly Sta Maria Nova, was erected in the podium of the Temple of Venus and Rome on the summit of the Velia near the Colosseum. Originally the church was an oratory of the eighth century, but in the ninth century the diaconate of the church of Sta Maria Antiqua was transferred to the Oratory which became Sta Maria Nova. The popular name of Sta Francesca Romana was given in honour of Francesca Buzzi, who founded a Congregation of Oblates in 1425. She herself joined the congregation after the death of her husband and was canonized in 1608; she is the patron saint of motorists. The church was converted to the Baroque style at the beginning of the seventeenth century, but happily the mosaic of the apse has been retained. Again the main theme is that of the Virgin and Child. The Virgin is enthroned and holds the Child on her left arm. St James and St John appear on her right and St Peter and St Andrew on her left. A very interesting feature is the representation of an arcade, strongly reminiscent of a type commonly encountered on classical sarcophagi in which each figure occupies a separate arch. In contrast to the exquisite ethereal Virgin of Sta Maria in Trastevere, this example has a somewhat plebeian appearance.

BYZANTINE MOSAICS

The beginning of the thirteenth century heralded an apparent increase in Byzantine influence, although little remains in Rome from this period. The fire of 1823 destroyed the thirteenth-century mosaics in S. Paolo fuori le Mura, and the replacements display little of what one imagines to be the spirit of the originals. The Cappella Sancta Sanctorum is not open to the public, although descriptions of the mosaics suggest that they are strongly influenced by the Byzantine mode. The church of S. Tommaso in Formis is represented by a single entrance door, all that remains of the Trinitarian Hospice. The doorway is Cosmatesque and retains a mosaic roundel of 1218, and an inscription which records the names of the craftsmen who were responsible for the work – Magister Jacobus and his son Cosma. One of the functions of the Trinitarians was the ransom of Christian slaves, which explains the unusual subject-matter. The mosaic depicts the figure of Christ between two slaves, one white and one black. The gold background, the use of small tesserae for faces and hands – and, in this case, other areas which required greater detail – and the strongly marked eastern features of Christ, suggest a definite Byzantine influence.

FROM MEDIEVAL TO RENAISSANCE

The next period which marks a transition from the medieval to the Renaissance style is represented by the apsidal mosaic in Sta Maria Maggiore. The apse was reconstructed at the end of the thirteenth century by Pope Nicholas IV, who employed a Franciscan, Jacopo Toriti, to carry out the decoration. It seems fairly certain that the mosaic of Toriti follows the general lines of the older work; indeed there is a possibility that details from the original work were incorporated in the new. Again the central theme was the French-inspired 'Coronation of the Virgin', although the original scheme probably contained a figure of the Virgin and Child. The central group includes the figures of the Virgin and her adult Son, seated side by side on a throne. In contrast to the similar group in Sta Maria in Trastevere, the figures are symmetrically composed to left and right of the centre. The group is contained within a roundel with a deep-blue background upon which are scattered stars of gold, and at the edge a band of light blue scattered with stars of silver. This representation of the firmament is completed by the presence of the sun and the moon which appear at the base of the throne.

The roundel is flanked to left and right by groups of angels, which are considerably smaller than the main group. The remaining space is decorated with an elegant inhabited scroll set against a gold background. The scroll is derived from the classical model, and the lively arabesques are inhabited by an assortment of creatures such as birds, a rabbit, a snake and splendid peacocks. To the right of the central roundel are the kneeling figure of Cardinal Colonna, who helped to finance the work, St John the Baptist, St John the Evangelist and St Anthony. On the right a similar group contains the figures of Pope Nicholas IV (1288–94), who is kneeling, and St Peter, St Paul and St Francis. The two kneeling figures are similar in scale to the angels, whereas the saints are represented on a larger scale, although quite small in comparison with the figures of the central group.

A frieze which runs along the lower edge of the main decoration is certainly of classical derivation, and may contain genuine classical fragments. The colours of this superb

Detail of apse mosaic, Sta Maria Maggiore, Rome.

mosaic are rich and beautiful, and the figures are composed with great elegance. The Byzantine manner can be detected in a number of details, especially the hands and faces, where much smaller tesserae have been used. The decoration of the apse honoured the Virgin as the Mother of God and a continuation of the Marian theme can be seen in the series of panels directly below the main apsidal mosaic. These panels were designed by Toriti between 1294 and 1305, and contain scenes from the life of the Virgin. The panel which illustrates the death of the Virgin is placed directly below the Coronation scene in the apse. Interesting comparisons can be made with a similar scene by the Roman painter Cavallini, *c.* 1295, which decorates the apse of Sta Maria in Trastevere. Although of similar date, the work of Cavallini achieves greater naturalism, and seems further withdrawn from the influence of Byzantium than the work of Toriti. The degree to which Cavallini's work anticipates the illusionistic intention of the Renaissance places it in a transitional category. Several of the panels exhibit greater naturalism in the pose of the figures, increased spatial depth and the expression of mood and feeling. Similar changes can be detected, however, in Toriti's 'Dormition of the Virgin', which suggests the impact of new influences sufficiently strong to cause a change of style in the last panel of the series.

The constant factors which distinguish medieval mosaic from that of classical antiquity, and which formed the basis of the change in style and technique, can be summarized as ideology, location and material. The propagation of a Christian ethos increasingly demanded a degree of stylization which differed from the representational intention of classical art. It also demanded greater scale and a different format for the presentation of narrative. Unlike modern mosaic, medieval work retained an internal position in architectural schemes, but the shift from floor to wall surface was crucial. The craftsman was obliged to overcome the distorting effects of an extended viewing range, especially when combined with the decoration of curved surfaces. This led to a simplification of detail and, with the almost exclusive use of glass tesserae, to a technique which constantly adjusted the angles of setting to achieve maximum luminosity in the prevailing light.

The presence of these constants over such a long period would suggest that the mature medieval style was an overwhelmingly conservative art with a tendency to consolidate rather than experiment. Hence the need to redress the balance by closely searching for changing factors which will help us to recognize the characteristics of individuals within the medieval period as a whole. Such an activity may prove telling in the modern craftsman's search for artistic identity during the transition from an inherited tradition to a form in keeping with the artistic demands of the age.

Further reading

Anthony, E. W., *A History of Mosaics*. Boston, 1935; repr. New York, 1968.

Bovini, G., *Ravenna Mosaics*. New York, 1956; London, 1957.

Caputo, Giacomo, and Abdelaziz Driss, *Tunisia, Ancient Mosaics*. London and New York, 1962 (in Unesco World Art series).

Carmichael, Elizabeth, *Turquoise Mosaics from Mexico*. London, 1970.

Demus, Otto, *Byzantine Mosaic Decoration*. London, 1947.
The Mosaics of Norman Sicily. London, 1949.
The Church of S. Marco in Venice. Washington, 1960 (Dumbarton Oaks Studies, No. 6).

De Rossi, G. B., *Musaici cristiani e saggi di pavimenti delle chiese di Roma anteriori al secolo XV*. Rome, 1873–99. (Particularly the sections entitled 'Abside della basilica di S. Clemente' and 'Abside dei SS. Cosma e Damiano'.)

Grabar, Andrei N., *Byzantine Painting*. Geneva, 1953.
Greece, Byzantine Mosaics. London and New York, 1954 (in Unesco World Art series).

Hinks, R. P., *Catalogue of the Greek, Etruscan and Roman Paintings and Mosaics in the British Museum*. London, 1933.

Kitzinger, E., *Israeli Mosaics of the Byzantine Period*. Milan, 1965.
The Mosaics of Monreale. Palermo, 1960.

Lazarev, V. N., *Old Russian Murals and Mosaics*. London, 1966.

L'Orange, H. P., and P. J. Nordhagen, *Mosaics from Antiquity to the Early Middle Ages*. London, 1966.

Matthiae, G., *Le chiese di Roma dal IV al X secolo*. Rome, 1962.

Oakeshott, Walter, *The Mosaics of Rome from the Third to the Fourteenth Centuries*. London, 1967.

Povstenko, Oleksa, *The Cathedral of St Sophia in Kiev*. New York, 1954.

Schapiro, M., and Michael Avi-Yonah, *Israel, Ancient Mosaics*. London and New York, 1960 (in Unesco World Art series).

Severini, G., 'Mosaico e arte murale nell' antiquità e nei tempi moderni' in *Felix Ravenna* LX (1952), 21–37.

Swift, E. Howland, *Hagia Sophia*. New York, 1940.

Toynbee, J. M. C., and J. B. Ward Perkins, *The Shrine of St Peter and the Vatican Excavations*. London, 1956.

MOSAICS,
HISTORICAL

MOSAICS,
PRACTICAL

Argiro, L., *Mosaic Art Today.* Scranton, N.J., 1968.

Berry, J., *Making Mosaics.* London, 1966.

Hendrickson, E., *Mosaics: Hobby and Art.* New York, 1957; London, 1962.

Hetherington, P. B., *Mosaics.* New York, 1967.

Hutton, H., *Mosaic Making.* New York, 1966.

Jenkins, Louisa, and Barbara Mills, *The Art of Making Mosaics.* Princeton, N.J., 1957.

Seidelman, J. E., and Grace Mintonye, *Creating Mosaics.* New York, 1967.

Stribling, M. L., *Mosaic Techniques: New Aspects of Fragmented Design.* London and New York, 1966.

Unger, H., *Practical Mosaics.* London and New York, 1965.

Williamson, R., *Mosaics: design, construction and assembly.* London, 1963.

Young, J. L., *Mosaics: principles and practise.* New York, 1963.

Glossary

ACANTHUS   A prickly-leaved plant; the conventional representation of its leaves in architecture.

ALUMINA   One of the earths, the only oxide of aluminium.

AMBULACRUM   A covered walk or arcade.

AMORETTI   Infant gods of love.

ANNEALING   Toughening by gradually diminishing heat.

APATITE   A crystallized phosphate of lime, varying in colour from green to blue, violet or brown, transparent, translucent or opaque.

APSIDAL   Of the form of an apse, a semicircular or polygonal recess.

AZULEJOS   From the Arabic *zuleija*, 'burnt stone'; ceramic tiles varying between 12 cm. and 14·5 cm. on a side, with a surface entirely covered with decoration.

BASILICA   An oblong hall with double colonnade and apse. In Rome. one of the seven churches founded by Constantine.

A slab of plaster of Paris upon which pottery can be formed and dried; it can also be used to remove excess moisture from clay.	BAT
Unglazed low-fired ware; a bisque firing involves a much lower temperature than does a glaze firing.	BISQUE (or biscuit)
A knob of glass.	BULLION
Channelled strips of lead used to bind together sections of stained glass.	CALME (or came)
Drawing on strong paper, usually full-size, as a design for a painting, mosaic, stained glass, etc.	CARTOON
An ornament in the form of a scroll, or an oval ornament derived from Egyptian hieroglyphics.	CARTOUCHE
Roman shield or medallion.	CLIPEUS
A type of sectional mosaic executed in marble or stone; from the Latin committere, 'join together'.	COMMESSO
A typical product of a school of early medieval marble workers active in and around Rome. Squares and disks of white or richly coloured marble are surrounded by geometrical designs in decorative and sometimes precious stones.	COSMATI WORK
Tiles with a decoration similar in effect to that of cloisonné enamel; ridges of clay delimit the different colours of the glazed surface.	CUENCA
Supplication: Christ in majesty blessing the Virgin and St John the Baptist.	DEESIS
A literary exercise designed to bring about seeing through hearing, and to ensure that the expression fits the subject.	EKPHRASIS
A pictorial mosaic insert (pl. emblemata).	EMBLEMA
Prepared slip, halfway between a glaze and a clay, used to give an all-over coat to clay.	ENGOBE
A portico, for instance of a gymnasium, or the vestibule of a private house.	EXEDRA
Earthenware covered with a lead tin glaze. The name is derived, via the French, from Faenza in Italy which was the centre of production of such ware during the Renaissance.	FAIENCE
A chain or garland of flowers, leaves, etc., hanging in a curve between two points.	FESTOON

FILATI	Sometimes referred to as 'spun smalti'; a dense substance, including crystal glass, melted and drawn into threads.
FLOREATE	Decorated with floral ornaments.
FRIT	Calcinated mixture of sand and fluxes used as a material for glass-making.
GEL	A semi-solid (jelly-like) state formed by coagulation.
GESSO	Gypsum prepared for use in painting and sculpture.
GOUACHE	Opaque colour ground in water and gum.
GREEN CLAY	Unfired clay.
GROG	Ground bisque which is added to moist clay for texture, or to decrease shrinkage.
GROUT	A mixture of cement and fine sand (or marble dust) used to fill crevices between mosaic tesserae.
GUILLOCHE	Architectural ornament imitating braided ribbon.
HYPOCAUST	Hollow space under a floor in which heat from a furnace was accumulated and used to heat a house or a bathing establishment.
HYPOSTYLE	Hall with roof supported on pillars.
ICONOSTASIS	Screen separating the sanctuary from the main body of a church, and upon which the icons were placed.
INHABITED	Occupied by forms human or animal.
INTAGLIO	Incised work.
INTARSIA	An inlay, executed in various materials, which may be embedded in the surface and subsequently planed to give a uniform surface.
INTERLACES	Intricately crossed forms.
LEHR	Glass-annealing kiln, sometimes spelt 'lear' or 'leer'.
LITHOSTROTON	A floor made of stones.
LUNETTE	A semicircular space decorated with painting, sculpture, etc.
LUSTRE	Type of metallic decoration developed in Persia during the ninth and fourteenth centuries, the ware being fired at a reduced temperature.

Crude, pastry-like mixture of mineral or organic matter. MAGMA

A fine kind of pottery coated with an opaque white enamel ornamented with metallic colours. MAIOLICA

A bright golden disk surrounding the head, especially of a saint, and representing heavenly light. MANDORLA

Gum or resin; also used for certain kinds of cement. MASTIC

Images on a huge scale. MEGALOGRAPHY

Literally, 'a thousand flowers'; the term for glass made from coloured glass rods fused together. MILLEFIORI

Place of worship for the cult of Mithras, the Persian sun god. MITHRAEUM

An early type of mosaic, similar to Cosmati work, used as floor decoration, in which small glass tesserae and precious marbles were arranged in patterns and meandering bands. OPUS ROMANUM

Coloured stone and marble cut to shape and dovetailed so as to fit closely together to form a pattern or a figurative design. OPUS SECTILE

Mosaic formed of tesserae (hence the name) which were of roughly equal rectangular shape although of variable thickness and fairly coarse size. They were sometimes tightly packed so as to render the background invisible. OPUS TESSELLATUM

Small tesserae, not necessarily rectangular, set in worm-like (Latin *vermis*, 'worm') courses following the form. OPUS VERMICULATUM

In an attitude of prayer. ORANS

'Ruler of all': the depiction of Christ, usually bust or half-length, blessing with his right hand and holding a book of the Gospels in his left. PANTOCRATOR

Ornament worn on the breast. PECTORAL

A small, light shield, or shield-shaped ornament. PELTA

Placing in acid solution for cleansing purposes. PICKLING

Glass, coloured in melting so that the colour pervades the whole. POT METAL

Arranged in small squares or with intersecting lines. RETICULATE

A Greek drinking vessel. RHYTON

Scroll ornaments or pattern. RINCEAUX

ROSACE	Rose-shaped ornament or design.
SGRAFFITO	A method of decoration by scratching through a superficial layer.
SINOPIA	An underpainting as a preparatory drawing for a fresco. The name is derived from Sinope in Asia Minor, a city famous for the red pigment often used for the purpose.
SMALTI	Opaque coloured glass which is melted in a furnace and then broken into cubes.
SPRIG MOULDS	Small blocks of plaster with depressions shaped like an ornament in reverse. Damp clay may be worked into the depression and carefully lifted out to form a decorative unit.
SQUINCH	Small arch built across a corner of a rectangular structure. Squinches convert the upper part into a circle or an octagon.
STORIATED	Decorated with designs representing historical, legendary or emblematic subjects.
STUCCO	Plaster or cement prepared for coating wall surfaces or mouldings in architectural decoration.
STUCCO DURO	Hard stucco, the hardened product of a mixture of slaked lime, marble dust, sometimes fine sand and hair, and burnt gypsum, well beaten with a stick.
TESSERA	A cubical fragment of stone, marble, glass or terracotta, used to make mosaics. From the Latin; pl. tesserae.
THAUMATURGICAL	With the power of working miracles or marvels, wonder-working.
THEANDRICAL	Tending to embody divine and human form.
THERMAE	Greek or Roman baths, especially public baths.
THIASOS	Bacchic dance.
THYRSOS	A staff tipped with an ornament like a pine-cone or ivy-tipped fennel stalk; an attribute of Bacchus.
TRAGACANTH	White or reddish gum from certain herbs, often used in pharmacy.
WEDGING	The pounding and kneading of moist clay to remove air bubbles, and also to distribute additives, e.g. grog, evenly.
ZIGGURAT	A staged tower, in which each storey is smaller than the one below it.

Appendix: some suppliers in Britain and the USA

The mosaicist makes use of materials and equipment proper to so many other arts that a comprehensive list of suppliers would be unwieldy. This short list names only a few specialist firms.

Design Craft Mosaics, Christchurch Road, Ilford, Essex.
  Vitreous glass mosaics
Elder Reed & Co. Ltd, 105 Battersea High Street, London
  SW11.
  Vitreous glass mosaics, marble
Michel & Polgar Ltd, 41 Blandford Street, London W1.
  Vitreous glass mosaics, tools, spring-type cutters and
  Japanese mosaic nippers, perspex, metal table frames
Proctor & Lavender Mosaics Ltd, Solihull, Warwickshire.
  Swedish, Portuguese and Turkish vitreous glass, small
  ceramic mosaics
Edgar Udny & Co. Ltd, 83 Bondway, Vauxhall, London
  SW8.
  Smalti, vitreous glass mosaics, small ceramic mosaics,
  marble, tools, adhesives (Fixite, Unibond), spring-type
  cutters and Japanese mosaic nippers

F. E. Beigert Co. Inc., 4801 Lemmon Avenue, Dallas, Texas.
  Glass and glazed porcelain mosaic, small ceramic mosaic,
  tools, grouts, mastics
Dillon Tile Supply Co., 252-12th Street, San Francisco 3,
  Calif.
  Glass and glazed porcelain mosaics, small ceramic mosaic,
  tools, grouts, mastics
Latco Products, 3371 Glendale Boulevard, Los Angeles 39,
  Calif.
  Smalti, glass and glazed porcelain mosaic, small ceramic
  mosaic, tools, grouts, mastics
The Mosaic Shop, 3522 Boulevard of the Allies, Pittsburgh
  13, Pa.
  Stained glass
Leo Popper & Sons Inc., 143–147 Franklin Street, New York,
  N.Y. 10013.
  Smalti, stained glass

Index

Sta Pudenziana, 213–14; Sta Sabina, 217; S. Stefano Rotondo, 220; S. Teodoro, 218; S. Tommaso in Formis, 46, 228; S. Zenone, 223; Tribune of Benedict XIV, 32–3
Rudstone, 38

SALONICA, 8, 9
sand-casting, 150
sandstone, 111–12, 115
Schlein, Charles, 176
Schulze, Eberhard, 169
sedimentary rocks, 111–12
semi-precious stones, 10–11
setting, agents, 154; beds, 150–3; tesserae, 145–58
Severini, Gino, 160–5
sgraffito, 95, 127–8
Siena, 44
silver, 12, 116, 119–20
sinopia, 8, 9
sketches, 139–40
slate, 178
slip, 93–5, 103
smalti, 71–3
sprig moulds, 106

squaring up, 140
Stocker, Hans, 168
stones, 111–13
storage, 84, 89, 138–9
stucco, 58–60
studio, 53, 137–9
support materials, 53–61, 147–9; cement, 54–8, 147–9, 150–3; concrete, 56–8; gesso, 59–60; for glass, 85; plaster of Paris, 58–9, 99–101; stucco, 58–60; wood, 60–1

TACCA, Pietro, 48
tarsia, 39–48
Tebaldo, 46
tesserae, cutting, 50–2; production, 107–8; setting, 145–58
texture, design, 145; on tiles, 105–6
tiles, 101–10; ancient techniques of manufacture, 101–3; cutting, 52–3; decorative finishes, 102–7; rolling and cutting, 107–8; texture, 105–6; vitreous glazes, 75–6
tilting tesserae, 9–10, 12, 150

tin, 122
tonal effects, 10
tools, 48–9, 53, 138; cutting, 51–2, 78, 177
Toriti, 22
traditional methods, 158–9
transparent panels, 180

UNDERGLAZE, 96, 102
underpainting, 8, 9
undulating surfaces, 9–10
Unger, Hans, 169

VENICE, 157, 206–7
vertical surfaces, 147–8
vitreous glass mosaic, 75–6
vitreous pastes, 41
vitrification of clay, 97–8

WARKA, 181
wedging clay, 89–90
Westminster Abbey, 47
Wildenhain, Frans, 176
wood, as support material, 60–1
workshops, 53, 137–9

YOUNG, Joseph, 172–5

ZLITEN, 196

240